SOCIAL CHANGE IN W

THE RETURN TO INCOMES POLICY

SOCIAL CHANGE IN WESTERN EUROPE

IN THE SAME SERIES

Industrial Privatization in Western Europe
edited by VINCENT WRIGHT

Long Term Unemployment
edited by ODILE BENOIT-GUILBOT & DUNCAN GALLIE

Muslims in Europe
edited by DOMINIQUE SCHNAPPER & BERNARD LEWIS

The ethics of Medical Choice
edited by JON ELSTER & NICOLAS HERPIN

The *Social Change in Western Europe* series developed from the need to provide a summary of current thinking from leading academic thinkers on major social and economic issues concerning the evolving policies of Western Europe in the post-Maastricht era. To create an effective European Union governments and politicians throughout the region must work to provide satisfactory social, economic and political conditions for the populations of Europe, and each volume affords an opportunity to look at specific issues and their impact on individual countries.

The series is directed by an academic committee composed of Arnaldo Bagnasco (Turin University), Henri Mendras (CNRS, Paris) and Vincent Wright (Nuffield, Oxford), assisted by Patrick Le Galès (CNRS, Rennes), Anand Menon (University of Oxford) with the support of Michel Roger and Olivier Cazenave (Futuroscope in Poitiers).

SOCIAL CHANGE IN WESTERN EUROPE

THE RETURN TO INCOMES POLICY

edited by
RONALD DORE
ROBERT BOYER
and
ZOE MARS

PINTER
PUBLISHERS
LONDON, NEW YORK

DISTRIBUTED IN THE USA AND CANADA BY ST MARTIN'S PRESS INC

Pinter Publishers
25 Floral Street, Covent Garden, London, WC2E 9DS, United Kingdom

First published in Great Britain 1994

© Actes Sud 1994

Apart from any fair dealing and for the purposes of research or private study, or criticism or review, as permitted under the Copyright, Designs and Patents Act 1988, this publication may not be reproduced, stored or transmitted, in any form or by any means or process, without the prior permission in writing of the copyright holders or their agents. Except for reproduction in accordance with the terms of licences issued by the Copyright Licensing Agency, photocopying of whole or part of this publication without the prior written permission of the copyright holders or their agents in single or multiple copies whether for gain or not is illegal and expressly forbidden. Please direct all enquiries concerning copyright to the Publishers at the address above.

Distributed Exclusively in the USA and Canada by St Martin's Press, Inc., Room 400, 175 Fifth Avenue, New York, NY10010, USA

British Library Cataloguing in Publication Data

A CIP catalogue record for this book is available from the British Library

ISBN 1 85567 247 2 (hbk)
1 85567 225 1 (pbk)

Library of Congress Cataloging-in-Publication Data

A CIP catalog record for this book is available from the Library of Congress

Typeset by Florencetype Limited, Kewstoke, Avon
Printed and bound in Great Britain by SRP Ltd, Exeter

CONTENTS

List of contributors   vii

1 **Introduction: incomes policy: why now?**   1
   Ronald Dore
2 **Incomes policy in Britain: lessons from experience**   31
   William Brown
3 **Wage reforms imposed by the state: some paradoxes in French incomes policies**   47
   Robert Boyer
4 **Wage control and cost-push inflation in Sweden since 1960**   71
   Rune Åberg
5 **Wage formation and incomes policy in Denmark in the 1980s**   94
   Thomas P. Boje and Per Kongshøj Madsen
6 **Pay restraint without incomes policy: institutionalized monetarism and industrial unionism in Germany**   118
   Wolfgang Streeck
7 **Corporatism and incomes policy in Austria: experiences and perspectives**   141
   Alois Guger and Wolfgang Polt
8 **Procedures and institutions of incomes policy in Italy**   161
   Tiziano Treu
9 **Incomes policies, institutions and markets: an overview of recent developments**   175
   Colin Crouch

Appendix: Sources and methods for country statistics   197

LIST OF CONTRIBUTORS

Rune Åberg is Professor of the Department of Sociology, University of Umea, Sweden.

Thomas P. Boje is Associate Professor in Social Sciences at Roskilde University and in 1992-93 was Jean Monnet Fellow at the European University Institute, Florence.

Robert Boyer is Senior Researcher at Centre National de la Recherche Scientifique (CNRS) and Professor (Directeur d'Etudes) at Ecole des Hautes Etudes en Science Sociales (EHESS).

William Brown is Montague Burton Professor of Industrial Relations at the University of Cambridge and is the Chairman of the Faculty of Economics and Politics.

Colin Crouch, Professor at Trinity College, Oxford University.

Ronald Dore is senior Research Fellow at the Centre for Economic Performance at the London School of Economics and Adjunct Professor of Political Science at Massachusetts Institute of Technology (MIT).

Alois Guger, University of Vienna.

Per Kongshoj Madsen is Associate Professor at the Institute of Political Science, University of Copenhagen and Scientific Secretary to the Ministry of Labour.

Wolfgang Polt is Researcher at the Department of Technology Research, Research Center Seibersdorf and Lecturer for Macroeconomics and Industrial Economics at the University Linz and the University of Economics in Vienna.

Woflgang Streeck is Professor of Sociology and Industrial Relations at the University of Wisconsin-Madison.

Tiziano Treu, Professor at the University of Milan.

CHAPTER 1

INTRODUCTION: INCOMES POLICY: WHY NOW?

Ronald Dore

'The return to incomes policy?' may seem to need some justification as the title of a book which surveys the history of wage determination and wage level movements during the decade of the 1980s in Austria, Britain, Denmark, France, Germany, Italy and Sweden. Surely, it will be objected, with neo-liberalism/radical liberalism/marketism/monetarism not only dominating the Anglo-Saxon economies well after the disappearance of its original charismatic prophets, Reagan and Thatcher, but reaching out, even, to such bastions of corporatism as Sweden and Denmark, we have *found* the solution to the endemic inflation to which the incomes policies of the 1970s were the misbegotten non-solution. Inflation rates have been coming down steadily. In all the major economies they are now well within manageable limits; wage-cost push is no longer the big problem.

Can one be so sure? *The Financial Times*[1] commenting on the departure of its Minister of Finance from the New Zealand government wonders if this is a straw in the wind. The minister, it says,

was a key member of the so-called razor gang, a group of members committed to reducing the welfare state (in a country which) has been the most extreme of the developed countries that participated in the renaissance of liberal economic policy since the early 1980s.

But it goes on to say that this radicalism has been slow to produce the growth it promised. It obviously takes more time than expected. Meanwhile there are more and more losers as unemployment rises and 'huge shifts in the geographical location of jobs and industries make the need for social security all the more pressing' — and at a time when the ideological programme calls for ever deeper cuts in public expenditure.

In the longer run the question is whether the combination of weak governments and structural budget deficits will produce a retreat from the policies which brought inflation down.

And, next time round, inflationary pressures will be harder to contain because of the weakening of the traditional instruments of monetary and fiscal policy, as deregulation and the continuing cheapening of communications internationalize financial markets. The leader just quoted speaks of the problem of the 'narrowing of national tax bases, as increased capital mobility forces governments into open fiscal competition' – a phenomenon which the chapter in this volume on Sweden's recent experience clearly illustrates. Nor is a steady controlled depreciation of the exchange rate (or a devaluation jump) any longer a relatively painless option for countries which run inflation rates higher than those of their trading partners. Instant electronic transacting means that the amount of money prowling around the world on the look-out for speculative gains from exchange-rate shifts is so much greater than the intervention reserves even of a combination of the most powerful central banks that no country can expect to have control over its exchange rate.

'A first-world fiscal crisis before the end of the decade cannot be ruled out', concludes the *Financial Times*. In Italy, that crisis has already arrived, and as Treu's chapter in this volume shows, an incomes policy was found to be an essential element in the package of countermeasures.

Policies and institutions

And if there are good reasons for thinking again about incomes policies, there are good reasons also for looking again at the fate of such policies in the recent past. And as several of the chapters in this volume emphasize, this involves getting away from simple dichotomies of state versus market and looking closely at the institutional arrangements which affect the determination of wages: the patterns of collective organisation; the mixture of political and economic agendas which organisations of workers and employers and state mediators have (their declared agendas, the agendas of their bargaining representatives and – not always the same – the agendas of their members); the various elements – ideas of fairness and perceptions of their effect on work motivation, perceptions of product market competition, an awareness of the effects of local action on national macroeconomic trends, a sense of responsibility for those trends – all those elements which inform the 'logic', the bargaining attitudes, of those who sell and those who buy labour.

There is a growing literature on these institutional aspects to which we hope this volume will usefully add. It remains true, however, that the dominant body of writing on wages (represented here mostly clearly by Boje and Madsen writing on Denmark) is that of labour economists concerned primarily with the interrelation of movements in aggregate wage levels with trends in other macroeconomic variables, notably employment, unemployment and inflation. Underlying most of this writing is an implicit model which goes something like this.

The market model

Imagine a reasonably well-functioning market economy. Employers, who are all price-takers needing to keep their product prices as low as possible, hire labour (in fact, could only make the profits they are in business to make *if* they hire labour) at the 'going rate' in the market – for most skills, a quite local market. Wages, in short, are closely determined by the supply of particular skills and the demand for their use. To be sure, convention creates a certain stickiness in wages' response to changes in supply and demand, but this at most means a few months' lag. In depressions, when the demand for labour falls off and unemployment increases, wages will fall (though whether they fall faster than prices depends on your model; see Michie, 1987)

That model could reasonably be taken as a stylized description of the nineteenth-century British economy in which modern economics has its home – at least of the small-firm sector outside the much more convention-bound sphere of domestic service. Nominal wage rates are estimated, for example, to have dropped about 9 per cent between 1873 and 1879 (Michie, 1987, p. 170). And still, in the Western economies, the depressions of the interwar years almost universally saw declines in nominal wage rates

But, in post-war industrial economies, three things intervened to change this; to 'spoil' the functioning of the system by making markets less perfect. On the one hand, the growth of large-firm oligopoly meant that over large areas of the economy employers were not exactly price-takers, they had greater freedom to raise their prices without too great a loss of sales volume. Second, the growth of trade unions and the legal reinforcement of their collective bargaining rights, made the conventional stickiness of wages far, far greater than it had ever been, blunting the impact of an over-supply of labour – unemployment – in holding down, much less *lowering*, wages. Third, governments were committed to using fiscal and monetary policies to stimulate demand and so reduce unemployment whenever it threatened to occur – to holding it down to the 'necessary frictional' level of 2–3 per cent which counted as 'full employment'.

The result was endemic inflation. Government deficits from employment-maintaining expansionary policies, shifts in the terms of trade, wage gains in high-productivity growth industries – various forces could give an initial kick-start to inflation, but once the *expectation* of continuous inflation set in, behaviour began to change in such a way as to make that expectation self-fulfilling. Unions' wage demands took compensation for past and/or expected inflation as the starting-point minimum. Firms responded with regular cost-plus price mark-ups, catching up with, but generally overshooting and consequently accelerating, inflation. A sudden worsening of the terms of trade, like the 1973–4 oil crisis, can add great acceleration to the spiral in a way which also cuts into profits and hence investment. (Wage claims seeking to compensate for imported as well as domestically generated inflation push ahead and shunt the effects of the terms-of-trade loss, and the production loss during adjustment to new relative prices, on to profits.)

But do not despair, said the economists. The world may have changed, but the eternal verities of our market models still hold. The old forces of supply and demand, however blunted, are still at work and still tending to restore equilibrium. What Boyer calls in chapter 3 'something like an iron law existing since the emergence of capitalism' still ensures that unemployment weakens the bargaining power of workers. Real economists' economics is still possible. Depress demand, increase unemployment, and, to be sure, wages and prices don't actually come down any more, but at least the rate of price inflation comes down. The great discovery of the 1950s, the Phillips curve, told one just how much extra inflation one would get by moving one per cent closer to full employment, and conversely, how much abatement of inflation one would get by putting how many people out of work.

For a brief period it was thought that this was a law of modern capitalism finally pinned down in numerical terms, but it soon became obvious that the curve was shifting. Once upon a time, an increase in unemployment to 4 or 5 per cent of the labour force had the inflation problem more or less beaten. But, like the addict who needs an ever bigger fix to get the same high, economies seemed to need an ever bigger dose of unemployment to keep inflation under control. Prodigious ingenuity was displayed in econometric studies designed to track the shifting equilibrium point, the so-called 'natural rate' or the 'non-accelerating-inflation rate of unemployment' (the NAIRU) – the rate at which inflation could be expected to remain stable and low. In the only example of such analysis in this volume – Boje and Madsen's chapter – the contention is that Denmark's Phillips' curve made a sudden leap in 1973; most studies elsewhere seem to suggest a more gradual and continuing process. In Britain, for instance, the NAIRU is reckoned to have doubled between 1978–9 and 1984–6.

As to *why* the NAIRU seemed to be constantly shifting – upwards – some variant of 'insider/outsider theory' spreading from Scandinavia has gradually gained ground (see especially the Swedish and Danish chapters): the view that a growing number of the unemployed are structurally outside the mainstream labour market and have little effect on the wage-bargaining behaviour of those who are in it. This has led to a certain amount of illuminating econometric work on the changing (age, skill-level, duration, etc.) parameters of unemployment, but still the data used are almost entirely confined to official statistics, with very limited supplementation by surveys or case studies. Much less has there been any detailed study of the micro-mechanisms by which the employment level – the state of the labour market – affects the perceptions and calculations of people involved in wage-setting to reach decisions which when aggregated produce either inflation-accelerating or inflation-dampening effects. Surveys of where bargaining takes place and over what issues, yes; but case studies of wage bargaining of the 'who used what threat, what argument to whom' type, almost never.

There was even an authoritative Nobel-prize winner's dictum which confirmed that macroeconomists were not obliged to worry about micro-mechanisms. The name of the game in macroeconomics, said Milton Friedman in a famous paper, is prediction. Provided your model can accurately forecast the effect of changing one variable on all the other variables, your model is a good one. As an economist you've done your job. If you can chart the correlations among changes in unemployment, changes in wages and changes in prices – and between changes in the rate of those changes – you don't have to worry about exactly *what* micro-economic causal mechanisms might underlie those correlations.

Policy intervention; the largely dismal record

Fortunately, there are other Nobel-prize winners whose stance is somewhat different. Franco Modigliani has recently recorded his conviction that the incomes policy agreement was crucial to the beginning of Italy's turn-round; at a critical stage in the June 1993 negotiations he appeared in Rome to give a widely reported speech intended to contribute to an 'expectations consensus' on which a settlement might be based (*Financial Times*, 5 May 1993, *La Repubblica*, 1 July 1993).

By and large, however, academic economists have been slow to do the economic microanalysis which underlies, and is required to explain, the intercorrelations of macro-economic variables. Policy-makers have by and large had to do their own analysis by casual empiricism. In the sixties and seventies in Britain, and, as these papers show, still, today, in Austria, Sweden, and Italy, officials and politicians, still addicted to Keynesian notions that their job is to make economies *grow*, thought that it might be possible once again, as in the 1950s, to have growth and low unemployment without too much inflation by working on the micro-mechanisms of inflation itself – the discrete decisions of individual managers and union wage bargainers responsible for the wage 'spin' in the upward spiral of wages and prices – and to do so *not just* (1) through the blunt instruments of fiscal or monetary policy – by altering the price signals and the demand-level expectations offered by the market to economic actors assumed to have, sometimes rational, sometimes learned, expectations – and *not just*, (2) by legal and other measures to change the structures and the union–management power-balance within which free-market bargaining over wages takes place, but also and especially, (3) by direct prescription or by working on bargainers' hearts and minds.

(A note about definitions. In most of our chapters, including this introduction, the words 'incomes policy' are used to mean policies of the third type, designed primarily to control inflation, though sometimes with secondary distributional objectives too. Robert Boyer, in his chapter uses it to cover the gamut of all three types of measures listed above. In his introduction to the French edition of this book he includes a tabular matrix of the ends and means of policy which is reproduced here (Table 1.1).)

The reasoning behind these attempts was as follows. The root cause of inflation was the tendency of sectional groups which enjoyed a strong market position to raise their prices (which in the case of workers are called wages). This (a) pushed other less well-placed groups into demanding similar rises in order to protect their standard of living against those initial price rises, and (b) gave them a moral justification for doing so on grounds of equity and comparability. As a result, all-round inflation erodes the income gains of the sectional groups that started the 'round' in the first place. Since the gains they make from

Table 1.1 Policies affecting incomes and their effects on various objectives

Ends Means	Reducing inequality	Moderate demand inflation	Enhance competitiveness	Response to supply shocks	Increase employment
Minimum wage	Significant impact 1960–7	Possible	Depends on price and quality competition	Unsuited	Doubtful for period 1980–93
Progressive taxation	Powerful	Little effect	Uncertain effects	No effect	Indirect effect
Wage and price freeze	Stabilizes inequalities	Impact usually transitory	Effect if competition is price competition	Impedes adjustment of relative prices	Uncertain effect
Wage increase norm	Modifiable for the purpose	Moderate effect if precedes inflation	Frequent objective	Possible if intended as such	Possible but rare
Inflation tax	Favourable	Too complex to be tried	No example	No example	Hard to imagine effect
Subsidy for profit-sharing	Can well increase inequalities	Indirectly	Indirectly	Conceived for this purpose	Clear effect in theory but in practice less so

their aggressive profit-seeking behaviour are thus obviously bound to be temporary, surely, surely, there ought to be some way of persuading them to exercise restraint.

But how? 'If you demand a 6 per cent increase instead of 4 per cent in February, you will only exacerbate inflation so that you will have lost all benefit of that extra 2 per cent by October' is obviously no argument. Let October take care of itself; if we can get that extra 2 per cent now let's do so and enjoy it as long as we can.

The argument from self-interest clearly has to be more complex. 'If you cooperate in restraint, it is easier to persuade others to do so too. If everybody cooperates, we ease inflationary pressure. If we ease inflationary pressure (a) we keep down our costs and improve our position in foreign markets, and (b) we can afford to have a more expansionary fiscal and monetary policy, both of which will induce growth which will (i) accelerate productivity increases and hence increase in your real wage, and (ii) reduce unemployment and your risk of being threatened with it. So you see, your February to October sacrifice will be rewarded by much greater gains next year or the year after.'

To that argument from self-interest can be conjoined two other arguments – depending on the role of (a) avowed patriotism and (b) avowed altruism in particular societies at particular times. The patriotism argument is; 'Look! Our beloved Ruritania is getting the reputation of being the sick man of Europe. We've got to pull our economy round and improve our competitiveness or nobody will respect us any more. And beating inflation is a precondition for that.' As for altruism, the 'fraternity' or 'social solidarity' argument goes something like this: 'Look, you're all right Jack. You've got a good job and the sort of skills that will always get you one. [Version for managers: 'You're in an expanding market and you've got a good product and you're not in danger of going bankrupt.'] But your pushing for the highest wage (price) you can get is causing the inflationary spiral which will simply have to be countered by deflationary economic policies. And that means that some of your fellow-Ruritanians are going to become unemployed [bankrupt].' To paraphrase a British wartime poster (when both patriotism and altruism were in vogue, if only because the upper classes knew they could not win their war without the lower classes), 'YOUR understanding, YOUR unselfishness, YOUR restraint will bring US victory in the war against inflation.'

The history of incomes policies is in part (the other part – the tough self-interested corporatist bargaining part – will be tackled later) the history of attempts (a) to deploy these three arguments – the self-interest argument, the patriotism argument and the altruism argument – (b) to generate levels of mutual trust which assured those who were swayed by those arguments that others would not take advantage of them, and/or, where trust was weak, to back them up with statutory instruments and legal sanctions.

The legal sanctions could work both ways: to enhance trust by protecting a public-spirited majority against a minority of antisocial free riders – the Danish case, perhaps – or weaken it by seeming authoritarian or class-biased and hence encouraging cheating. They often did, indeed, reflect the conviction that state officials knew best and that the spokesmen for capital and labour were either – see Boyer on France – too set in warring contention to agree on anything, or – more the British case – too unintelligent to understand the reasoning behind policy anyway. One thing the cases in this book demonstrate is that the countries which have been most successful in institutionalising income restraint have not used statutory instruments, which Crouch defines in his chapter as a sign of weakness in the institutional fabric. Which is not necessarily to say that statute is unimportant even in consensual systems – see, for example, German legal controls on strikes or compulsory membership in Chambers of Commerce, which provide statutory support for the wage determination mechanism.

Where voluntary norms or legal controls have been used, they have sometimes been imposed on product prices as well as on wage increases, but the general assumption has usually been that it is wage increases which are the prime movers, because they are the prices which are most obviously haggled over rather than set impersonally by publication of price schedules in the market. Producers, it has generally been thought, do not greedily cash in on rising product markets since competition still exercises discipline and rules out price increases except as a mark-up on the sort of increased costs which, like wage increases, all competitors are likely to share. (Which, may underestimate the extent of oligopoy with quasi-institutionalized price leadership, but in the British textile industry in the 1970s, the standard form of sales contract provided by the industry association allowed for the automatic pass-through of cost increases consequent on the annual industry wage agreement.)

And, if wage increases were the key it was further assumed that the major determining factor in wage increases was the stance of union leaders, and their power, their ability to deploy strike action to support their claims. Persuasion, then, meant primarily persuasion of union leaders and of their members on whose willingness to take 'industrial action' those leaders' power depends. There is already a considerable body of writing by a mixture of political scientists, sociologists and institutional economists, which illuminates the question of why some countries have been more successful in this than others. (For example, Flanagan, Soskice and Ulman, 1983; Bruno and Sachs, 1985; Pekkarinen, Pohjola and Rowthorn, 1992) The work in this volume adds significantly to the story. As to which countries did better in the 1980s, let readers draw their own conclusions from the raw material of Table 1.2 according to their own scale of values, though the 'misery indexes' to the right provide some ready-made scales. More interesting, perhaps, are the conclusions the chapters suggest about the mechanisms involved in producing these different outcomes.

1. Small countries, where (a) the sense of vulnerability to international markets is stronger, and (b) there is greater cultural cohesion – in our

Table 1.2 Comparative country performance 1980–1991

Country	(1) GDP growth	(2) GDP growth % p.a. per capita	(3) Inflation % p.a.	(4) Growth employ-ment %	(5) Unemp. (monthly av.)	(6) Terms of trade	(7) Misery index	(8) Poor workers' RMI
Austria	28	2.0	3.5	3	3	107	3.7	13
Belgium	24	1.8	4.4	2	10	103	11.9	(90)–10
Denmark	24	1.9	5.6	5	9	109	11.5	(90) 8
France	26	1.7	6.0	2	9	117	11.7	(88) 7
Germany	28	1.9	2.7	7	6	112	5.1	(88)–15
Italy	29	2.0	9.5	5	10	125	15.0	(87)–2
Japan	58	3.8	2.2	14	2	155	–4.9	n.a.
Netherlands	23	1.4	2.7	5	9	104	9.3	n.a.
Sweden	21	1.3	7.7	5	2	112	7.0	–7
UK	28	2.0	6.5	3	10	98	14.5	9
US	35	1.3	4.7	17	7	114	7.8	(89)23

Notes and sources:
(1) Real GDP at market prices, % 1980–91. World Bank, *World Tables 1993*.
(2) Previous column minus percentage population growth, 1980–91, annualized. (Source as (1).)
(3) CPI, p.a. (Source as (1).)
(4) (percentage increase over the 11 years) and (5) (average of annual monthly or quarterly averages, standardized for national definitional variations) OECD, *Labour Force Statistics, 1970–90*, and *OECD Economic Outlook*, Dec. 1992.
(6) Terms of trade from IMF, *International Financial Statistics Yearbook*, 1992.
(7) Variant of the 'enriched misery index' developed from Okun's original. (3) + (5) – (2) – (4) (recalculated to % p.a.) – annual percentage improvement of terms of trade calculated from Col (6).
(8) Relative Misery Index. Percentage increase or decrease since 1980 in the real income of the first decile wage-earner up to 1991 or the year indicated, minus the total percentage growth in per capita income over the same period of years and multiplied by –1. Where figures are not provided for both sexes, an average of the male and female figures has been used. OECD, *Employment Outlook*, July 1993, pp.143–63.

sample, Sweden, Denmark and Austria – are better able to deploy the patriotism argument.

2. The strength of the patriotism, and to some extent the social solidarity argument, depends also on the degree to which a sense of economic crisis grips the country – as exemplified in the 1992 Italian agreement, when a union leader, having signed in anguish, immediately resigned his union position because he perceived that in doing what he saw

as necessary for his country (and maybe his members' long-term interests) – he would be seen as betraying both their immediate short-term interests and their lingering addiction to the heroics of class struggle.
3. Countries with a strong social democratic tradition, and governments dominated by social democratic parties, are better able to deploy the social solidarity argument – *vide* Sweden and Denmark where the wage policy which it was sought to maintain was explicitly described as 'solidaristic'.
4. In other countries, too, the ability to deploy the patriotic and social solidarity arguments depends on the extent to which what is seen as a sacrifice by wage-earners is matched by sacrifices by other segments of the community – *vide* the promised crackdown on taxation of self-employed workers which was part of the Italian agreement just mentioned, and also Boyer's remarks about the failure of the 1960s Centre d'Etudes des Coûts et des Revenus to tackle profits.
5. The Olson point about the 'encompassingness' of union and employers' associations as a condition for their ability to internalize a 'public interest' (see Crouch's chapter in particular) is illuminated in these chapters by illustration of the diversity of divisions that have to be encompassed: white collar workers and manual workers (Sweden's problem in particular); tradeables sector and non-tradeables sector; public and private; sectors with high- and sectors with low-productivity growth. They also show how wide is the range of the encompassingness dimension within Europe. In descending order on the employee side there are: central union organisations crucially empowered by their control over strike funds – as in Austria and Sweden; sectoral federations dominated by a major pace-setting leader like Germany's IGMetall; a congress of politically divided central federations with their attendant sectoral satellites (sometimes rogue satellites), increasingly cooperatively coordinated in Italy, increasingly divided in France; a not-very-solidary council of industrial union barons in Britain's TUC. On the employers' side the centralisation and comprehensiveness of national organisations tends to mirror that of unions.
6. But, not the least of the merits of these studies is their documentation of what seems to be a universal trend of the 1980s – for the national organisations, encompassing or not, to lose their importance in wage matters as centralized bargaining breaks down, and wage-setting effectively takes place increasingly at the enterprise or establishment (less often regional or sectoral) level. This is a trend of remarkable

universality, strong throughout the 1980s in Britain (with concentration, as Brown notes, at the enterprise rather than the establishment level) accelerating in the late 1980s in Italy, Sweden and Denmark where it is endorsed as state policy, and so far resisted only in Germany. There, if anything, wage drift figures in the 1980s suggest that there has even been a strengthening of the role of central wage-setting. But even in Germany, as Streeck shows, the incorporation of Eastern Germany has firmly put what in Germany is known as the 'opening clause issue' firmly on the agenda and subjected the system to great strain.

All the evidence suggests that the otherwise universal shift to enterprise-level bargaining is primarily driven by employers' wishes. National union leaders have obvious reasons for resisting the erosion of their power which this shift implies, but there is reason to suppose that local union leaders are ambivalent – welcoming the enhanced importance of their role, but somewhat fearful of the increased exposure – in proportions which differ depending on how well their members are engaged in favourable product and labour markets. As to what structural changes underlie and accompany this shift, this is a question to which we shall return.

7. Institutionalization counts. As patterns of wage bargaining restrained by the three arguments are repeated from year to year, they acquire a certain robustness; they have a better chance to come to be seen as 'part of the way things are'. If they evolve (as in Austria) within organisations which have a long history of performing other functions, so much greater their legitimacy. Lengthy institutionalisation did not save the long-established Swedish system of bilateral bargaining or the tripartite arrangements in Denmark, but it surely accounts in part for the stability of the Austrian system and for the strength of wage-leadership in Germany by a wage leader responsibility-conscious IGMetall. The contrast with Britain is clear. The fact that Britain has been, with France, of all our countries the least able to bring the three arguments to bear on wage settlements must be partly ascribed to the failure to institutionalize anything. In the 1960s and 1970s, one after another, alternating party governments destroyed the institutions built by their predecessors, only, a year or two later, to start over again.

8. Of the 'three arguments', the first two, appealing to patriotism and to social solidarity, are relatively simple; their strength depends on emotions and values other than self-interest, plus, perhaps, at the margin, leader charisma. But how important can they be compared with the third argument, from self-interest? Adherents of the 'rational

choice' school of political science would have no doubts; zero importance. That seems unlikely to be true. Nevertheless, the history of the Scandinavian countries where patriotism and social solidarity seem to be strongest, confirms the view that, in the end, it is the self-interest argument which is the key to achieving any kind of inflation-controlling wage restraint.

9. That self-interest argument, as it was set out on an earlier page, is extremely complex. To be swayed by it, a union leader, or a union member deciding to support his leader's wage restraint policy, has:

   (a) *either* to understand, at least in outline, the relationships among the major macro-economic variables; wage increases, inflation, money supply, profits, interest rates, aggregate demand and employment – some of which relationships are in any case controversial, *or* to take the argument on trust because it is propounded by someone whose judgement he respects, and

   (b) to care more about long-term than short-term gains – to be willing to sacrifice more cash in the pocket from tomorrow for a larger supply of even more cash with better purchasing power in the more distant future.

10. The variation, among our countries, in these respects seems very wide. One factor which affects the level of understanding seems to be (a) the intellectual calibre and economic sophistication of union leaders, and (b) the extent to which they are accepted as full members of what it is still convenient to call 'the establishment'. Since none of our countries are countries where left-wing revolutions are immediately in prospect, and all are countries which have arrived in the last two generations at highly institutionalized systems of career recruitment via the educational system, the two dimensions tend to be highly correlated.

Hence, in countries such as Sweden, Denmark, Germany, Austria and Italy where unions have been accepted as 'social partners', they have had substantial resources of money and prestige. They have been able to recruit for their national administrations considerable numbers of elite university graduates, some of whom who have subsequently gained leadership positions in their unions. Their origins and talents make them the intellectual equals of, and help them to have easy relations with, their opposite numbers in business and government, as do the organisational positions which tripartite corporatist institutions or, as in Germany, the supervisory boards of companies, afford them. (So much a part of the establishment in Germany that the head of IGMetall could apparently make large sums from insider trading.)

Neither in Britain nor in France have unions been to this degree embedded in the establishment. In Britain, earlier generations of union leaders contained many men and women, intellectually fully the equals and often the superiors of their governmental and employer counterparts, who became union leaders because their family's poverty and the inequality of educational opportunity forced them down the mine or on to the shop floor at an early age. Greater equality of educational opportunity in later generations has siphoned off such exceptionally able people into other careers. Less-effective and less-commanding leaders have contributed to the decline in the social prestige of unions and thus diminished their chance of offering rewarding careers to the able.

In future, declining union densities could set off the same downward spiral, even in countries where the unions are relatively establishment-entrenched. Much will depend on the possibilities of deliberate 'social promotion' à la Suisse which Crouch discusses in his paper.

11. Such recruitment/mobility questions apart, of greater importance for the 'understanding' variable seem to be three other things. First, whether or not, before each annual round begins, there is some authoritative and widely publicized forecast of how the economy will develop over the next year under certain alternative assumptions about wage increases. Examples described in these chapters are the pronouncements of the newly established Swedish Rehnberg Commission, the reports of the Economic and Social Advisory Board of the Austrian Parity Commission, the Bundesbank's annual review which as Streeck shows is the pivot of the German system, the 'annual economic assessment' on which, as Brown records, the British TUC and CBI once reached tentative agreement in 1979, and which the British Labour Party promised to introduce if it won the 1992 election. In the same category, to go outside our sample countries, is the sort of 'emergent consensual forecast' produced by the intense discussions which take place in Japan from December to March before the annual (and these days increasingly tame) 'spring struggle' begins.

Second, such a forecast is more likely to affect outcomes if the crucial wage bargains take place soon after it is issued. There is a sharp contrast here between Germany where the single IGMetall negotiation is a crucial pace-setter and Britain where the annual round is spread throughout the year – the source of the famous leap-frogging. That is why, in 1991, when it seemed that the Labour Party might form the next government, some of those who supported the

Labour Party's notion of an annual economic assessment as a means of influencing wage bargainers also considered the need for 'synchropay' – i.e., engineering a bunching of wage negotiations in the months immediately following the assessment – an idea about which Brown expresses considerable scepticism in his chapter, as part of his generally sceptical view of the usefulness of trying to establish 'norms' or 'going rates'.

The third factor is the following, highlighted by Streeck's account of the effectiveness of the Bundesbank's annual statement in influencing the unions. The chain of events presupposed by the self-interest argument, as set out above, involves action by governments and central banks. The credibility of those authorities' threats and promises – to deflate if inflation reaches such-and-such a level, for instance, or to eschew devaluation, or to go for growth if inflation comes down to a certain level – is crucial. And what determines that credibility is primarily the record of past performance. Again, the contrast between the Bundesbank's unflinching adherence to its policy (be it said, its threats rather than its promises), and the stop–go *ad hoc*ery of successive British governments' records could not be more marked.

12. In fact – and apologies for only now getting to what is a central feature of much of the stories our papers tell – the extent to which governments have sought to achieve wage restraint by getting across these long-term self-interest arguments – indeed, through appeal to *any* of 'the three arguments' – has been limited. They have played a part, a significant part, in Sweden, Denmark and Austria, (as they do also in Japan). Streeck suggests that to some extent 'internalizing unemployment' unions are affected by them in Germany. In these countries employers' and workers' representatives are expected to behave 'responsibly'. Such considerations have played a far smaller role in the attempts to control incomes in Britain or, until recently, Italy. Instead, governments have sought cooperation from unions, not so much by offering the longer term benefits promised by the self-interest argument, as by offering more immediate short-term benefits, not to put too fine a point on it, bribes – better pensions, improved social security, more expenditure on health, the improvement of unions' legal status. These deals have been the very stuff of corporatist bargaining, the pattern set informally in Britain in earlier rounds of incomes policy but made explicit in the 1975 'Social Contract', the process begun in Italy after the 'hot autumn' of 1969 and the entry of the Socialist Party into the coalition, and continued after the *compromesso storico* ten years later. In Sweden and

Denmark, too, the 'solidaristic' element in incomes policies was in part a means of securing union consent to measures seen to be necessary for growth without inflation.

Our studies seem to suggest that corporatist bargaining of that sort is bound to reach a dead end. Governments have only so many shots in their locker. If they encourage union short-termism and use the enhancement of union legal powers as bargaining counter they are liable to end up, as the British Labour government did in the winter of discontent of 1978-9, feeling that they had unleashed a sorcerer's apprentice they could no longer control. If they offer social welfare benefits as the main bargaining counters, they end up either with the manifest fiscal crisis of today's Italy (a public debt well over a year's GNP and the well-founded fear of ending up in the European Community's second tier), or as in Sweden they reach levels of taxation and pressures from groups chafing under the compression of wage differentials which even a Social Democrat government found no longer viable in a country as exposed to international competition as Sweden.

The nineties: a new era?

But all this is old hat, the reader may say. The history of the 1980s turns out to have been, throughout the industrial world, an era of declining inflation. The trend, in the second half of the decade especially, has been steadily downward, an effect which may largely be attributed to Bundesbank discipline transmitted through the Exchange Rate Mechanism, and continued, even in those countries which left the ERM and devalued after the 1992 turmoil, by the depth of the 1991–3 recession.

Suddenly the international organisations discovered in the summer of 1993 that it was no longer inflation, but employment which was now the crucial issue. The European Community held a special ministerial meeting on the employment problem; at the G7 summit in Tokyo President Clinton announced a special Camp David meeting for the autumn. The OECD's *Employment Outlook* concentrated on unemployment, and genuinely illuminated its nature by including a detailed analysis of the trends in income distribution which have accompanied rising levels of 'structural' unemployment.

The first point to make is that there is no evidence at all that inflation is permanently beaten. As these papers show, it was only with the use of incomes policy that Italy and Sweden have recently held their inflation rates down, even in a recessionary period. As Boyer argues in the introduction to the French edition of this book, making wages more subject to competitive forces is no obvious cure for inflation, when in the most dynamic sectors which expand in an upturn technological change is constantly increasing the need for skills in scarce supply. Wages could soon be driven up – even with a high level of long-term unemployment among unskilled workers.

The second point is this. The present consensus, reflected in the 1993 *Employment Outlook* quoted above, has taken aboard an elaborated version of the 'insider/outsider' thesis. The steady increase in numbers unemployed at the peak of each economic boom, the increased proportion of the unemployed who have been unemployed for over a year at a stretch and of those others who never managed to hold on to a permanent job, is a sign that the labour market has become – segmented is the word usually used, but 'attenuated spectrumisation', though even uglier, would be a more accurate description of what is a *continuing* process. A growing number of people have skills the market clearing rate for which – given our present technology and pattern of demand – is below the minimum wage or the social security minimum, even when the economy is working at full capacity. Hence the apparent correlation between the level of the minimum wage or the social security welfare guarantee on the one hand, and the level of unemployment on the other. Both are higher in Europe than in the United States, the main deviants from this correlation being Sweden until recently, thanks to an 'active labour market policy' involving workfare, and Japan where the stigma effect of taking social security payments is still strong.

It is astonishing how many well-fed people are latching on to the conclusion that the obvious solution to the evil of unemployment is to lower the level of the social guarantee – to make the poor poorer in order that they can hold up their heads as fully participating citizens again – and get those dreadful unemployment figures down. Thus Samuel Brittan, in the *Financial Times*, reviewing the evidence about the increase in wage dispersion collected by the OECD notes, 'if pay differentials had to widen so much, even with an ever-growing departure from full employment, how much more would they have to widen to price all workers into jobs?' He adds that, of the three ways in which the changes in the labour market make themselves felt, 'unemployment, less stable employment and greater differentials . . . the third may be the least bad of the three choices' (22 July 93). The compromise solution – wage subsidies for low-paid jobs – would allow the employer to pay the market-clearing rate but provide an acceptable wage to the worker. The practical difficulty of avoiding deadweight subsidy in such schemes is, however, well known.

The third conclusion concerns a change in the relation of wage increases – the increase in *some* people's wages – and inflation. The OECD's *Employment Outlook*, in its special chapter on pre-tax income distributions, showed how widespread was the enlargement of wage dispersion (measured, usually, as the distance from the median wage of the first and ninth decile wages). One aspect of these shifts is reflected in the last column of Table 1.1. Only five of 17 countries (Denmark, Finland, Germany, Italy and Norway) showed no increase in the distance from the first to the ninth decile, and only Germany showed any actual compression of differentials. The greatest increases were in those countries (the USA, especially) characterized by what OECD *Employment Outlooks*, vintage mid-1980s, consistently applauded as highly 'flexible' and mobile labour markets, least bound by institutional and conventional 'rigidities'.

In most countries the top has pulled away from the median more than the bottom, and this would seem to offer an explanation for a seeming British paradox. Throughout the mid-1980s there was continuous concern that the rate of wage increase embodied in collectively bargained settlements and regularly reported by the CBI and the Department of Employment was consistently ahead of consumer price inflation by a margin which well exceeded gains in productivity. So much for employment grades whose collectively bargained wages are publicly known. At the same time, the rise of chief executives' salaries was notorious, and what one knew about managerial salaries in general suggested that greed at the top was translating into a certain shamefaced magnanimity towards the salary increase claims of immediate subordinates, of them to their own immediate subordinates and so on down the line. *And*, of course, there were real market factors at work too. The talent required to run British Steel may not really be quite as rare as to justify the many millions that Mrs Thatcher arranged to pay for Ian MacGregor, but the changes in technology really have, in most countries – even in Japan, managers will tell you – outrun the capacity of educational institutions to produce the skills the new technologies – and even more the creation of ever newer technologies – needs. There clearly are skill bottlenecks.

These trends (more the bargained settlement trend than the executive salary trend) were viewed with alarm as causing inflation. There was indeed inflation, higher than in Britain's trading partners, and these wage-cost shifts are a strong candidate for the role of prime mover in maintaining that inflation. And yet, in spite of these movements of wages ahead of inflation plus productivity growth, the wage share – the proportion of employee compensation in total national income – did not grow. It is apparent that these gains in real income were partly the result of a redistribution from the bottom to the top. But that does not mean that they were not a mainspring of inflation.

That growth of social inequality is in itself a problem, and will undoubtedly become political issue number one of the industrial democracies over the next decade. Alternatives to the Brittan solution (and the reliance on a steady increase in policing, security-fencing and prison custodial expenditure which it probably entails), are legion. Among them are: wage subsidies, 'active labour market policies' – the limited effects of which have recently been well documented; vastly improved basic education; an expansion of 'inefficient' service and distribution industries; the engineering of a long-run transition to a society in which all citizens receive a basic citizen income from the state and in which – over and above a certain range of community duties shared by all, 'work' is perceived no longer as a duty, but as a privilege for the lucky.

The fact that Austria and Germany, have avoided the extreme widening of wage dispersion found in the USA and the UK (and Australia) may suggest that incomes policies can serve to hold back divisive trends when either stability or compression of differentials is an explicitly acknowledged goal. But for how long? And for how long in particular in an increasingly internationalized world, and increasingly integrating Europe? The wage dispersion figures began to widen in both Sweden and Denmark in the second half of the decade, as soon as their solidaristic wage policies were declared unviable.

Incomes policies are unlikely to have much of a role to play in dealing with the social inequality problem. This is not necessarily to accept Crouch's point (chapter 9) that incomes policies have to be market-conforming – what is the outcome pure market forces would bring; American levels of wage dispersion or a German-type compression? It means only that other types of policy than those designed for inflation control are more likely to be suited to influencing the primary distribution of incomes, and the other equalization instruments – redistribution through taxes – are still bound to be overwhelmingly important.

The micro-mechanisms of wage determination

Which is not to say that – the other way round – widening social inequality has no implications for anti-inflation incomes policies. It is important to recognize the intimate links among:

1. growing wage dispersion;
2. the decentralization of wage bargaining to the enterprise level;
3. a second, pronounced 1980s trend (see the chapters on Sweden, Denmark, France), a shift from rate-for-the-job-category wages to rate-for-the-person wages;
4. wage-cost-push inflation.

No amount of macroeconomic studies charting shifts in the equilibrium level of unemployment will tell one much about these interrelations. Indeed, it can be argued that such studies are doing society a disservice by aiding and abetting policy-makers' fixation on deflation and unemployment as the only cure for inflation. (What is left out in Boje and Madsen's 'incomes policies are irrelevant' demonstration of a near-perfect fit between wage-increase levels and those predicted by their inflation/unemployment equation are the questions: *What* caused the turns in the curve? and *What* was prime mover?)

To answer that sort of question, one needs to know more about the micro-mechanisms – at the individual wage-bargainer level – which provide the links between the macroeconomic aggregates. There is a certain amount of scholarly industrial sociology which helps in this. The following picture derives from this plus the casual evidence of hints and hearsay.

What explains the generally observed inverse correlation between unemployment rates and inflation? Several quite different strands of causation.

1. The straight 'market supply–demand relationship'. If unemployment increases, employers take on new workers, now competing more intensely for jobs, at lower wages. They may even sack existing workers to do so. They are more likely to answer a worker's request for more wages: 'Well, if you don't like your wage you can lump it. There's plenty more out there who'd be glad of a job for half what you're getting.'
2. In the mid-nineteenth century, a high enough proportion of the population was involved in that kind of employment relation for economists to be justified in assuming that that was how 'the labour economy' works. But even then, John Stuart Mill (who looked at the world about him while a subsequently more influential person was filtering his knowledge of the world through the Blue Books in the British Museum) noted that there were a large number of employment relations which were governed more by convention than by the market. The employee had job security and wages were

insulated from the pressures of external supply. Public service and domestic service were the chief examples. Equally sticky, though not in an employment relationship, were professional fees. There was, in short, a market-dominated sector and a market-insulated sector.
3. Towards the end of the century some of the emerging large firms joined the market-insulated sector, revitalizing in a more bureaucratic form the personal paternalism of some of the small manufacturing firms of the early part of the century. A high proportion were public utility firms with a local monopoly whose owners could afford the luxury of a contented and loyal workforce. One can still find 'gas company villages' (now gentrified for the middle classes) from Manchester to Budapest.
4. What has happened since then is a steady expansion of the market-insulated at the expense of the market-dominated sector. To start with, there has been an enormous increase in the size of the public sector where wage scales and hiring practices are far more bureaucratically regulated, transparent, conventional and sticky than they were in John Stuart Mill's day. But the market-insulated sector has expanded in the private half of the economy too, for at least three reasons.

First, growing oligopoly has made it possible for more and more managers to 'afford the luxury of a contented and loyal workforce' – or at least did increasingly in the 1950s and 1960s; arguably the intensification of international competition in recent decades has altered this. 'I remember,' said a former Philips manager, 'when Philips was like a Japanese firm, lifetime employment and all – until we had to face up to Japanese competition.'

Second, with the growth of trade unions, the alternative has increasingly threatened to become a stroppy and organized obstructive workforce. We referred above to the tendency noted in many of our chapters for central collective bargaining to disintegrate and for effective bargaining to take place at the local level. A major reason is the attempt on the part of managers to conduct their negotiations in-house, with representatives of their own employees, and to focus those negotiations on their own particular wage structures with all their complex incentive elements. Domesticated unions are also one way of keeping in touch with 'grass-roots sentiment' in their organisation.

And – the third and perhaps the strongest factor – this keeping in touch is seen as necessary not only in unionized firms, but also in firms which have rigorously excluded unions but which increasingly have some sort of employee council instead. It is seen as necessary (and this is a factor of continuously *growing* importance because technology-derived) because 'shop-floor sentiment' becomes more important with the *change in the nature of work*. Once, when most production workers were doing simple routine tasks, it was enough to ensure that 'first-line' supervisors were firmly 'on the side of' management, and that they were given enough carrots and sticks to deploy. That gave efficient production despite what was defined as a wholly adversarial relation. Now, a far higher proportion of the jobs in large firms, and even in small ones, require the responsible exercise of discretion which is in essence unsupervisable. They require, in other words, some sort of inner commitment – either to professional self-respect or to the employing organization. As such they are incompatible with an employment relationship defined as too deeply adversarial for there ever to be much coincidence of interest or mutual trust. Even more, as international competition becomes increasingly focused on product novelty or improvements in quality or performance, an increasing proportion of jobs require, not just responsibility in the exercise of discretion, but also the taking of initiatives, the offering of suggestions.

5. What all this amounts to is a subtle shift, not so much in the legal definition of the firm as in its social definition, though legal definitions certainly count – the enactment of co-determination laws in Germany, or the election of worker directors in Sweden and Denmark, for example. Equally important as a significant legal shift seems to be the succession of French laws since 1969 which have promoted *intéressement*, greater 'involvement' through profit-sharing within firms. But even in Britain, where employers' opposition to the European Commission's draft Fifth Directive and to the Maastricht social chapter has been unyielding and where the legal innovations have been marginal (a few words about 'responsibility to employees' in the 1981 revision of the Company Act plus a succession of tax concessions for profit-sharing on French lines), something of the same shift in social perceptions has taken place. It is a shift along a dimension which stretches from, at one end, the 'full-blooded capitalist firm' to, at the other, what one might call the 'Japanese community firm'.

In the full-blooded capitalist firm the managers are the trusted agents of shareholder owners, dedicated (and by various sanctions disciplined) to rendering the maximum returns on the shareholders' capital. They hire labour as they buy their steel sheet: they get the best quality at the lowest possible price. At the other end of the spectrum, the firm is seen as a (usually, and in Japan certainly, hierarchical) community made up of all the people – managers, technicians, white collar and blue collar workers – who have become its members and hitched their fate to its success. Shareholders are just one outside group, like the banks and the raw material suppliers, whom the community has to keep happy if it is to survive.

An incident in Britain in the mid-1980s illustrated the fact that even such thoroughgoing adherents of market capitalism as Mrs Thatcher no longer endorse the full-blooded capitalist notion of the firm. She was very cross when the chief executive of British Airways awarded himself a massive salary increase at a time when she was urging every effort to hold wages down. Now, in a full-blooded capitalist firm a chief executive who screws down wages is doing an admirable job in increasing the shareholders' profits, and could justly claim his reward. Only in firms where at least *some* rudimentary notion of community holds would such a difference in rewards be seen as 'unfair'.

6. The significant increase in the size of the market-insulated sector of companies with at least some 'community firm' characteristics means that the effect of increased unemployment on wages is complex. The market-dominated sector still exists – a great deal of construction work, cleaning services, temporary secretaries, shop assistants. Even in that market-dominated sector, markets are still stickier and more imperfect than they were 50 years ago, thanks to a higher level of unionization, wage councils, etc., but still, unemployment does halt wage increases and even bring wages of new appointments down. In the market-insulated sector, however, the effect is quite different. Employers just do not say: 'Look! If you're going to insist on higher wages you can take your cards and go; there are plenty of people out there who'll do your job for much less than you're getting.' What they do say is indicated by Brown's table quoting the annual surveys by the CBI. It has a lot to do with using, *not so much unemployment itself*, as unemployment as a symptom of recession, to build persuasive arguments revolving around notions of 'fairness', viz:

– Of course we recognise that we have to keep up with inflation; you have a right to maintain the real value of your earnings. But inflation is coming down because of the recession.

– Profits last year were down and they're going to be down this year. We're having to cut the shareholders' dividends and managers' bonuses. You read in the paper about all these Company Chairmen taking fabulous pay rises. Well, our Chairman's getting less this year than last. It's only fair that we should share the misery around and ask you to make do with a tiny increase this year.

– You can see what the recession is doing to our sales. The only way we can keep up our sales volume is by keeping prices down and expanding exports, and that means containing costs. If we don't then we'll be forced to cut back. And that will mean that we'll have to make people redundant.

Note that it is only the last of these arguments which is directly affected by labour market considerations. (It derives extra force from the fear that, because of high unemployment, those made redundant will have greater difficulty finding another job.)

7. It is because of these changes that movements in wages correlate just as well with other indicators of recession such as company profits as they do with movements in unemployment. (Aberg, 1990) It is only addiction to market paradigms that explains why we hear a great deal about NAIRU but never about the other factors that enter into quasi-community firms' wage negotiations. Why not NAIRIE, for instance, 'the non-accelerating inflation rate of inflation expectations', or NAIRMSI (managerial self-indulgence), acknowledging the fact that union bargainers' knowledge of managers' salary increases (which have in fact, in the 1980s been much greater than those of blue collar workers in Britain) do indeed exert an upward pressure on wages?

8. So if it is the effect of *recessions* rather than unemployment itself which moderates wage increases, that could explain why the start of an upswing intensifies pressures for wage increases well before there has been much fall in unemployment. But why should those pressures in the market-insulated private sector be such, in some countries – Britain and Sweden, for instance – as to have a marked inflationary effect? (The range of variation in inflation rates shown in Table 1.1, cannot all be attributed to shifts in terms of trade or credit expansion.)

– The militancy or determination of union bargainers? Probably a factor of diminishing importance, though, if one compares Britain and France, for example, British enterprise-level union bargainers were experienced and backed by relatively strong firm-level organizations, whereas the more sudden, state-enforced decentralization of bargaining after the 1982 Delors law found unions ill-prepared and badly organized.

– Fairness arguments? Managers who have used the low-profits argument to hold down wages find it harder to resist demands for high wage increases when profits are good. Managers who concede the justice of compensation for expected inflation can overshoot. Most important of all is the expectation that a wage increase which is not considered 'fair' will lead to a loss of morale and productivity.

– Coercive comparisons? These do, indeed, determine what 'fair' means – above all 'not below the going rate'. (A fact acknowledged in the CBI survey Brown quotes by the question concerning *whose* going rate counted most – other firms in the same industry, other local firms or nationally known firms.) It only needs a few generous settlements widely publicized to have a widespread effect on subsequent increases throughout the economy.

– Skill bottlenecks? There is also, clearly, a real market element at work. The market-insulated sector contains most of the economy's high-tech high-skilled jobs, for which there can be shortages even when unemployment levels are high. In a firm with integrated internal wage structures where arguments about fairness count in wage negotiations (and in the effect of wage settlements on morale and productivity) it is difficult to raise wages to compete for particular skills in short supply without some knock-on effects on the wage structure as a whole.

9. One further element in these wage rises needs singling out for special attention. In both Britain and France, and in the new Italian agreement which ties enterprise-level bargaining to 'productivity', there exists considerable confusion as to what should be *the principle* for determining an acceptable wage rise. (And nowhere more so than among politicians resorting to exhortation as a means of restraining wage increases.) Should it be the increase in productivity in the particular firm? Or should it be the increase in productivity of the economy as a whole? Many statements by British leaders have explicitly asserted the former – in line with the shift towards the community firm, greater involvement, profit-sharing, etc. The abortive French inflation tax of 1975, described by Boyer, explicitly made the 'allowable' wage rise dependent on the increase in total factor productivity of the individual firm. Several studies show increases in the inter-industry dispersion of wages in many countries during the 1980s which may be linked to the shift towards the community firm, simultaneously with the general devolution of bargaining to the enterprise level.

But consider its consequences. Imagine an economy which consists of two sectors, car production and hairdressing. In the former, technical advances raise productivity by 4 per cent a year. Hairdressers who try to cut hair faster are likely to lose their customers; their productivity stays constant. But are they to be penalised because they happen to be hairdressers and not car workers? They consider themselves to have the right to the same standard of living and their only way of achieving this is to raise their prices. At the next round the car workers claim an increase of 4 per cent for productivity, plus an inflation compensation for their dearer haircuts. Thus the inflationary spiral commences.

So what should be done? Insist that car workers, too, should take a wage increase equal only to the rise in productivity of the whole economy and expect the car makers to lower their prices so that cheaper cars compensate for dearer haircuts, thus keeping the overall price level constant? Or somehow prevent inflation from spiralling and accept a steady 'distributional inflation' as part of the economic mechanism? It is a problem – largely a problem of political practicalities – which any incomes policy has to confront. It does mean that any minister who insists on wage increases geared to individual firms' productivity gains and at the same time sets a target of zero inflation, is talking through his hat.

Internationalisation

The second 'discovery' of the eighties is the effect on the inflation problem of the increasing internationalisation of our economies, in part a world-wide process measured by the rate at which world trade increases faster than the increase in world GNP, in part an equally diffused tendency to dismantle the regulatory barriers to the free flow of goods, services and money, especially marked in a Europe moving towards economic integration.

One long-since apparent effect is the increasing ineffectiveness of demand management through fiscal policy. Increases in demand lead increasingly – and the more so in less competitive economies – to increases in imports rather than in domestic production. The 'fiscal multiplier' steadily diminishes.

The more recently noticed effect is on the availability of devaluation as a means whereby countries which are unable to keep their inflation rates at the same low level as their major competitors can adjust their production costs in order to remain competitive in world markets. The mobility of capital is such that countries with currencies marked out by their inflation rates as bound to decline in value are doomed to low investment rates; the nominal interest rates necessary to keep real interest rates high enough to retain or attract capital form a psychological deterrent to investment, as does the greater margin of uncertainty in predicting what real returns on capital will be. Sweden's decision to forswear devaluation and keep the kroner tracking the Germany mark – after decades in which periodic devaluation had been accepted as a probably inevitable safety valve for a fully employed economy – is one dramatic indication of the change. So was the decision of Italy at the beginning of the decade, and Britain at the end of it, to go into the European Exchange Rate Mechanism. In all three countries the declared policy of maintaining the exchange rate required such a restrictive policy of high interest rates – both to prevent capital flight and to get inflation down – that growth was seriously impaired. And in all three, between the summer and autumn of 1992, the failure to keep inflation rates down to a level which made the declared policy credible contributed to speculative movements of hot money which eventually forced resort to the very devaluation which had been forsworn.

Conclusions?

Most of the participants at the conference at which these papers were first presented would agree that putting side by side the experience of several European countries helped us to understand the mechanisms at work, to sort out what were the problems shared by all modern industrial societies and what were the local problems unique to particular countries. But did that understanding help to provide prescriptions, solutions? None that would be agreed, even by that more-or-less like-minded group of authors. Perhaps the following five points are worth emphasis.

First, a macroeconomics that can deal only with the conjunctural and ignores the secular trend, the structural change, is doomed to failure. The secular changes our book records – greater technical complexity, greater international vulnerability, the change in the nature of the firm, the decentralisation of bargaining structures – have changed both the problems and the solutions. 'Combining growth with low inflation' is no longer an adequate definition of policy goals if, with a growing hardcore of long-term unemployed, one can no longer assume that growth means to approach full employment. And the traditional deflation–unemployment remedy for inflation comes to look less and less politically acceptable as it becomes less and less effective a remedy.

Second, the experience of the eighties does suggest that 'leave everything to the market' is not only no solution to the inflation problem; it has side-effects on growth and employment which are only now coming to be recognized.

Third, some form of restraint or self-restraint by powerful groups in the exercise of the market power available to them, remains an essential feature of attempts at incomes policies. But restraint exercised by persuasive appeal to what we called the 'three arguments' needs to be distinguished from restraint achieved through corporatist bargaining in exchange for compensating short-term material benefits. The latter sooner or later reaches a dead end. Only the former has any chance of long-term institutionalization.

About that possibility, about the realism of that prospect, it will be apparent that our authors' opinions are divided – ranging from extreme scepticism to moderately sanguine optimism. All the way, as a Confucianist might say, from the Original Virtue to the Original Sin position. There is also disagreement as to which of the 'three arguments' might potentially be appealed to: long-run self interest alone, or (that plus) some altruistic appeal to patriotism or social solidarity – concern for the national well-being. That disagreement extends also to interpretations of the past. Compare, for instance, the interpretation of the German scene given by Streeck in this volume with that offered in a recent book by Michel Albert (1992). Streeck sees the behaviour of German unions as sufficiently explained by their rationality and their pursuit of the collective self-interests of union members – or sometimes of their leaders, but not of the nation as a whole. Albert says by contrast: 'the authorities exert informal pressure on employers and unions alike, urging them to observe certain limits and avoid upsetting the collective apple-cart', the unions 'show a greater sense of economic responsibility towards the nation as a whole than many of their counterparts abroad'. He cites unions' behaviour in the 1981–2 recession as an example, and explains the mechanisms of cooperation as a sort of 'administrative guidance' facilitated by the unions' integration into the establishment (a large number of ex-leaders being Christian Democrat MPs). There are some who would interpret even the very explicit 'solidarity' emphasis of earlier Swedish policies, as purely the outcome of balanced compromise between sectional interests. This is clearly a debate which will continue.

Fourth, some form of national economic assessment based on wide-ranging public discussion and producing credible forecasts about the likely consequences of different overall levels of wage increase seems to be a precondition for any such persuasive appeal. Austria, Sweden and Denmark still have, and Italy has recently reactivated, tripartite forums which have as part of their task to hammer out an 'expectations consensus' – a consensus about the 'if . . . then . . .' predictive elements (as prelude to an agreement on the normative elements) of such an assessment. Germany has the diktat of the Bundesbank, backed up by its independent control over interest rates and a conventional pattern of wage leadership. To take an example outside Europe, in Japan it is the national simultaneity of the contract-revision date which has institutionalised an annual public media debate from which comes an emergent 'expectations consensus' with marked effects on wage bargaining (even formerly when unions really did have the power to strike). France and Britain, by contrast, have to make do with *ad hoc* statements by their governments of the rationale of their public sector wage policies – which usually are so opportunistically *ad hoc* that they fail to persuade anyone as reasoned justifications of a 'norm'.

Fifth, the constriction of available policy options by the internationalization of our economies, in particular by the deregulation of capital flows, can only be dealt with, either by the reimposition of national controls or by the creation of some kind of international controls. Even if Europe reaches the nirvana of a single currency and a single monetary policy, some framework for international agreement over interest rates which involves NAFTA and Japan will still be on the agenda.

Note

1. 1 Dec. 1993. Second leading article.

References

Aberg, Rune (1990), 'Internal Labour Markets and the Inflation/Unemployment Tradeoff', paper presented at World Congress of Sociology, July.
Albert, Michel (1993), *Capitalism Against Capitalism*, Whurr, London.
Bruno, Michael and Sachs, Jeffrey (1993), *The Economics of Worldwide Stagflation*, Harvard University Press, Cambridge, MA.
Financial Times, London.
Flanagan, Robert J., Soskice, David W. and Ulman, Lloyd (1983), *Unionism, Economic Stabilization and Incomes Policies: European Experience*, Studies in Wage-Price Policy, The Brookings Institution, Washington DC.
La Repubblica, Rome.
Michie, Jonathan (1987), *Wages in the Business Cycle: An Empirical and Methodological Analysis*, Pinter, London.

Okun, A. M. (1983), cited in D. Soskice, 'Collective Bargaining and Economic Policies, Manpower and Social Affairs Committee, OECD, MAS (83) 23, Paris.

Pekkarinen, Jukka, Pohjola, Matti and Rowthorn, Bob (eds.) (1992), *Social Corporatism - A Superior Economic System?*, Clarendon Press, Oxford.

Rostow, W. W., (1948), *The British Economy of the Nineteenth Century*, Oxford University Press, London

CHAPTER 2

INCOMES POLICY IN BRITAIN: LESSONS FROM EXPERIENCE

William Brown

Country statistics

Union members as a proportion of total dependent employees
 1980 56.4% 1991 43.1%

Public sector employees as a proportion of total employees
 1980 21.1% 1990 19.2%

Participation rates of working age population (ages 15–64).
 Men 1980 91.5% Men 1991 88.4%
 Women 1980 61.7% Women 1991 68.2%

Per capita GDP in US dollars (1993 exchange rates)
 1980 $9,340 1991 $17,689

Per capita GDP (PPP)
 1980 $8,250 1990 $15,882

Main collective bargaining institutions above the enterprise level

1980

Collective bargaining covered about 75 per cent of private sector employees and almost 100 per cent of public sector employees. Of those covered in the private sector, approximately one-third were covered for pay bargaining purposes by some form of national, industrywide (multi-employer) agreement and the remainder by enterprise (single-employer) agreements, many of which were specific to individual establishments. There were no supra-industry pay fixing arrangements.

The state played no direct role in private sector pay determination, but statutory minimum wage fixing arrangements existed for about one employee in eight in a limited number of weakly organized industries such as hotels and catering. Public sector bargaining was all at the national and industrywide level with little allowance for regional variations.

1990 (or 1991)

Collective bargaining had contracted to cover about 47 per cent of private sector employees and perhaps 80 per cent of public sector employees. Of those covered in the private sector, only one-fifth were now covered for pay bargaining purposes by some form of national, industrywide (multi-employer) agreement and the remainder by enterprise (single-employer) agreements, an increasing proportion of which were multi-establishment and subject to centralized enterprise control. There were no supra-industry pay fixing arrangements. The state engaged in limited exhortation for pay restraint and had weakened, and was soon to abolish, statutory minimum wage fixing in certain industries. Public sector bargaining was increasingly fragmented according to different functions, separate units and by region.

Britain's departure from the Exchange Rate Mechanism in September 1992 has forced the question of incomes policy back on to the political agenda. Throughout the 1960s and 1970s it had occupied the centre of the political stage. Successive governments had felt themselves reluctantly obliged by economic events to try to slow the rate of increase of pay settlements. Their successes were generally short-term and the political costs high. The governments of Wilson, Heath and Callaghan had all suffered severe electoral damage when their incomes policies spawned industrial conflicts.

When Thatcher took office in 1979 she was spared from this curse. The commencement of the extraction of North Sea oil in substantial quantities removed the pressure on the balance of payments which had made domestic inflation a major source of economic instability for her predecessors. In addition she discovered that it was possible to restrain inflation by running the economy with far higher levels of unemployment than had hitherto been thought electorally acceptable.

In the 1990s, declining oil revenues and falling manufacturing exports have made the balance of payments once again a critical issue for the Major government. It was believed, however, that entry into the Exchange Rate Mechanism would provide both the stimulus and the stability of an external source of discipline, and that this would be tolerable even if it would entail continued high levels of unemployment. In practice the level of unemployment implied by the chosen sterling exchange rate proved to be politically unacceptable. But Britain's departure from the Mechanism in 1992 threw political responsibility for counter-inflation policy back on the shoulders of the Major government. At the time of writing it appears to have decided that further rises in unemployment might deliver lasting damage to both the economy and its own electoral prospects. The unspoken question is whether the government can avoid returning to the past hazards of incomes policy as the only means of controlling inflation.

What form might an incomes policy for the 1990s take? This chapter will address the problem in three stages. The first will summarize British postwar experience of different forms of incomes policies. The second stage will be to provide an account of how the context of pay determination has changed since 1980. Many of these changes in the conduct of bargaining will have direct relevance to other countries. The final stage will be a discussion of the incomes policy options for the 1990s.

Postwar British experience of incomes policies

The most effective postwar British incomes policy was the first. Over the period 1948–50 the Labour government of Attlee negotiated a voluntary policy of pay restraint with the Trades Union Congress (TUC). This was, however, at a time when both private and public sector pay bargaining was characterized by relatively few, national, industrywide (i.e. multi-employer) agreements. The domination of pay bargaining by a few dozen national trade union leaders, so convenient for pay policy coordination, was to diminish dramatically in the following years.

Anxieties about inflation in the late 1950s led the Conservative government to appoint a supposedly independent panel of three experts with the intention of educating public debate. Its early diagnoses diagnosed the inflation as largely demand led. But economic analysis is inherently controversial. This was reflected in the fact that a change in the panel's membership in 1959 was accompanied by a rapid conversion to cost-push explanations.

This purely didactic approach was not enough. In 1961 public sector wage increases were frozen with a plea from the government for the private sector to follow suit. Deepening anxiety prompted the Conservative government of Macmillan in 1962 to announce a 'norm' for incomes increases, accompanied by a substantial list of circumstances in which it might legitimately be breached. A National Incomes

Commission (NIC) was established to comment retrospectively on pay settlements referred to it by government. Chaired by a lawyer, and devoid of either employers or trade unionists, it undertook no research and accepted the evidence presented to it with breathtaking credulity.

The Commission's ineffectiveness was overshadowed by another Macmillan creation of earlier in 1962, the tripartite National Economic Development Council (NEDC). In marked contrast, the NEDC contained senior industrialists, ministers, and members of the TUC and had a substantial staff of experts. Although the NEDC was to limp on in existence for 30 years until Major abolished it, its first two years were its finest. Its analysis of economic growth prompted the government to announce a 'guiding light' percentage rate for permissible annual pay increases. The NEDC provided grounds for optimism about tripartite approaches to the inflationary problem.

Wilson's Labour government acted on this when it took office in 1964. A tripartite 'Declaration of Intent' placed on record a diffuse commitment of trade union and employers' leaders to wage and price restraint. The NEDC was to provide the broad overview, while a new tripartite body, the National Board for Prices and Incomes (NBPI) was to investigate not only specific pay settlements but also any price rises referred to it.

The NBPI was to prove itself a far more effective body than the NIC it replaced. It had considerable powers of inquiry, and did not require the consent of those under investigation to use them. Its chairman, an ex-journalist and ex-cabinet minister, assembled a powerful board and an outstanding team of advisers and researchers. Frustrated by the inadequacy of official pay data, it instituted ambitious earnings surveys which were to lead, by 1970, to the establishment of the incomparable and continuing annual New Earnings Survey. Frustrated by the apparent ignorance of most managements as to what went on in their firms, the Board pioneered fieldworking techniques which were to transform the academic study of industrial relations. Its reports were produced rapidly and in unusually accessible English. They extended beyond specific wage and price references to examine broader issues, such as payment by results, overtime working, productivity agreements and job evaluation. In retrospect their most impressive feature was the emphasis they placed, not on pay restraint, but on understanding the sources of productivity growth.

The NBPI's function might have remained wholly educational had it not been that the government introduced an 'early warning' system of pay rise notification for the Board to police. Within a year, in 1966, a sterling crisis and a seamen's strike forced Wilson to declare a total pay freeze. The Board was given the additional task of assessing and clarifying the criteria for exceptional treatment in the ensuing periods of 'severe restraint'. It did this on the basis of a unique body of empirical expertise. But the Board's independent zeal was to become a source of embarrassment for a government increasingly anxious to give way to illegitimate pay demands without a politically costly struggle. By the time Labour lost office in 1970, the Board was being ignored and over-ruled; it had effectively been neutralized by the government which had created it.

The Conservative disdain for incomes policies when it took office lasted only two years. In 1972, unable to win the support of an alienated TUC in combating inflation, Heath embarked on an intricate statutory incomes policy, threatening sanctions against employers who allowed the cost of pay settlements to exceed precisely specified limits. The space left by the now defunct NBPI was filled by a new Pay Board and a new Price Commission. They lacked both the tripartite commitment and the investigative resources of their predecessor. In an eloquent act of political linguistics, the government removed the word 'productivity' from the name of the relevent ministry and from all policy documents. The lawyers and accountants had taken over.

Their insensitivity to the processes and politics of pay determination quickly contributed to their policy's downfall. Early in 1974 Heath lost the election he had called to challenge a coal-miners' pay strike. He bequeathed to the Wilson government that took over an expensive commitment whereby, for a period of several months, additional monthly pay rises could be index-linked to the consumer price index. It was a poorly thought-out expedient which has probably (and unfairly) discredited for a generation the idea of compensating unions for cost-of-living increases as a *quid pro quo* for pay restraint.

Attempts to run incomes policies had by now been a source of political torment for a decade. Wilson returned to power in 1974 determined to avoid this by having a non-statutory understanding on wage restraint with the trade unions. At a time of world-wide inflation they could deliver nothing. In 1975, as domestic price inflation rose to an annual rate of 25 per cent, the government was forced to seek support from the IMF in its efforts to protect the sterling exchange rate. As surety it offered a statutory incomes policy which was supported by, and largely designed by, the TUC. Boldly named the 'Social Contract', the policy's pay rise ceilings embodied a substantial redistributive element, and it was, in part, a *quid pro quo* for a package of industrial relations legislation intended to improve trade union security, strengthen employee rights, and increase industrial democracy.

The government delivered much of this legislation (which in retrospect can be seen to have had relatively little practical impact) and the TUC made strenuous efforts to deliver wage restraint. A substantial economic down-turn provided unwelcome but powerful support. But the Social Contract had no equivalent to the NBPI to monitor its progress dispassionately; the Pay Board had been an early casualty of Wilson's return. As a result the Labour politicians who designed successive stages of the Social Contract were blind to the cracks appearing in its foundations, and slow to understand the basis of the rank-and-file trade union discontent which boiled up from 1977 into politically catastrophic strikes in the winter of 1978/79.

The largest of these cracks resulted from the fact that the policy was strictly adhered to in the large public services (health, local government, education, etc.), but increasingly violated in private manufacturing, and in many public corporations. Callaghan (who had taken over from Wilson in 1976) was thus poorly informed and had lost TUC support when he announced a further stage of pay restraint in 1978. It was public service strikes which were to cause him (and subsequently the trade unions) so much political damage in the election he lost to Thatcher in 1979. The TUC and the employers' body, the CBI, made more than a gesture of help by indicating their interest in a procedure whereby a non-statutory, bipartite incomes policy could develop out of a centralized, annual 'agreed economic assessment'. But it was too late. Callaghan's last, hasty incomes policy action, early in 1979, was to establish a Pay Comparability Commission, instructed to restore the relative pay of public service workers, so damaged by the later stages of the Social Contract. Thatcher followed tradition by abolishing the Commission in 1980.

That is the end of the story of explicit incomes policies in Britain. Greatly assisted by oil revenues and high unemployment, Thatcher's successive governments directed their efforts at reducing the power of organized labour and at exposing some of the more sheltered product markets to competition. A continuing succession of new laws since 1980 has made both strike action and trade union organization more difficult. Probably more important was the active part played by Thatcher's government in the defeat of unions in a series of major strikes in both public and private sectors during the 1980s. More important still was the extensive programme of privatizing publicly-owned corporations and of forcing public services to surrender many of their functions to private sub-contractors. As a result, many long-established collective institutions of the British labour market have been reduced to rubble. When Major took over in 1990 it was hoped that the external market discipline of the Exchange Rate Mechanism would encourage more responsive institutions of pay determination to grow out of the rubble. Withdrawal from the ERM extinguished that hope.

The changing policy context of the 1980s and 1990s

Military men are warned against making the mistake of planning for their next war with too great an assumption that it will be like the previous one. Any thoughts about incomes policies for the 1990s must take account of the remarkable change in the context of British pay bargaining since conventional incomes policies were abandoned in 1979. This account starts with economic developments and moves on to changes in the institutions of pay fixing.

There was a sharp rise in unemployment in the early 1980s to high levels that were sustained until a partial recovery at the end of the decade. This was short-lived, with unemployment rising beyond 10 per cent again during 1992. Despite the recession, skill shortages became a severe problem throughout the late 1980s. Labour productivity rose rapidly during the period of rising unemployment, but has slowed to stagnation more recently. Price inflation was slowed in the mid-1980s but increased subsequently, slowing down again in the 1990s. Despite the high levels of unemployment during much of the period, earnings rose steadily, with those in employment achieving, on average, steady increases in real earnings. Indeed, increases in real earnings that are substantially greater than those of Britain's major competitors over the period have negated the unit cost benefits of the productivity growth of the early 1980s. Over the decade as a whole Britain's international competitive position deteriorated.

These sustained increases in average real earnings – in part the result of increased availability of consumer credit augmented by a temporary surge in property prices – conceal a very substantial increase in the inequality of income distribution among the employed. Between 1980 and 1992 the ratios of the lower decile and lower quartile points to the median of weekly earnings fell by between 6 and 10 percentage points for both men and women, while those of the upper quartile and upper decile points rose by between 11 and 23 percentage points. The earnings distribution has thus both widened substantially and become more stretched on the higher income side. The substantial increase in the inequality of income distribution over the 1980s was amplified by taxation policy. The top 20 per cent of households saw their share of total pre-tax income rise from 70 per cent to 75 per cent between 1979 and 1989; over the same period, post-tax, their share rose from 60 per cent to 66 per cent.

What has happened to pay bargaining arrangements? As a preliminary we should note that trade union membership has undergone a sharp decline in recent years. Having covered around 45 per cent of the employed workforce from the 1940s until the early 1970s, it rose to a high point of 55 per cent in 1979, then falling sharply to 40 per cent or even lower at present. Much of this decline has been the result of structural change and, in particular, the decline of traditionally highly organized industries. Recent legislation has made union recruitment and retention more difficult. But much of the decline appears to have reflected a withering of enthusiasm at the grass roots, with an increasing number of workplaces where unions are not recognized by management as a result not of anti-union policy, but of lack of employee interest (Millward *et al.*, 1992). Despite the recent contraction of the public sector, the majority of trade union members are now public sector employees and are relatively poorly paid. The groups who gained the larger pay increases in the 1980s tended to be in sectors such as finance which were not highly unionized.

There are two points to be made here for incomes policy formulators of the 1990s. The first is that the trade union movement has been massively weakened. The second is that the employees whose pay now sets the pace in the British economy are much less likely to be unionized than was the case in the 1970s. The same point is evident when we look at the coverage of collective bargaining. Table 2.1 is based upon a series of estimates of the coverage of different sorts of pay-fixing arrangements for private sector employees in Britain. The

Table 2.1 Private Sector Bargaining Structure 1950–90

Extent and nature of collective bargaining (c.b)	Percentage of private sector employees covered (manufacturing and services)					
	1950	1960	1970	1980	1984	1990
Pay not fixed by c.b.	20	25	30	30	40	50
Pay fixed by c.b.	80	75	70	70	60	50
c.b. is multi-employer (industry, regional etc.)	60	45	35	30	20	10
c.b. is single-employer (company, factory etc.)	20	30	35	40	40	40
Source on which estimate is based	varied	varied	varied	WIRS 1	WIRS 2	WIRS 3

public sector has been fairly comprehensively covered by collective bargaining over the whole period. From 1980 onwards the figures are based upon the results of successive official Workplace Industrial Relations Surveys (Daniel and Millward, 1983; Millward and Stevens, 1986; Millward *et al.*, 1992). It is evident from the first row that the proportion of the private sector workforce not following collective agreements has grown from being under a third until the early 1980s to now being at least half.

The table also shows how the structure of bargaining has changed. In 1950 the dominant form of agreement was multi-employer and industry based. Single-employer pay bargaining at the level of the individual company or below was relatively unusual. Since then, and with accelerating pace, multi-employer bargaining has declined as the main determinant of pay so as to cover, by 1990, only one private sector employee in ten. Its industrywide agreements generally cover employees in industries which are not at the cutting edge of wage bargaining, such as construction sub-contractors, road haulage, and parts of retailing. From the point of view of incomes policy, the bargains that matter are those conducted by enterprises acting on their own.

The number of distinct bargaining units with which an incomes policy might have to concern itself has become even greater than is implied by this accelerating shift to single-employer bargaining. Large corporations have tended to establish separate internal pay bargaining units around divisional profit centres. Divisional managers in multi-divisional companies have been given responsibility for pay and productivity, as well as profit. In the very different context of the public sector, similar developments are taking place, with the once monolithic pay structures of, for example, the Civil Service, or British Rail being fissured by semi-independent agencies and divisions with increased discretion over their internal pay structures (Brown and Walsh, 1991).

Several important implications for the control of pay arise from the spread of the divisional single-employer bargaining unit. Some flow from the fact that these divisions within enterprises are almost invariably shaped around the products and services being provided rather than the labour markets wherein employees work. An employee's pay, as a result, owes less than in the past to the skill being used and the part of the country where it is being used, and more to the nature of the firm in which the employee works and which part of the business he or she works in. There has thus been an acceleration of a trend that has long been evident for primary workers in industrialized societies: the increasing tendency for pay to depend more on product market factors than labour market factors.

Since product markets are spatially more extensive (and international) than labour markets, this development implies greater variation in pressures behind wage levels in a given locality. One consequence is to increase the potential for inflationary pressure as a result of coercive wage comparisons. Because a higher level of unemployment is likely to be required to achieve a given reduction in inflation, this also implies that, as a means of controlling inflation, conventional deflationary macro-economic policies are increasingly expensive as alternatives to incomes policies.

Another consequence of the rise of the product-based bargaining unit within the enterprise is that, in order to go with the grain of contemporary employer practice, the successful management of incomes policies requires greater responsiveness to product market variation than in the past. Employee acceptance, however, is probably inherently more difficult for policy-makers to achieve in these circumstances than in those requiring greater responsiveness to labour market variation because its outcomes are less likely to accord with labour's notions of comparative fairness in pay. The wages of people with similar occupations in the same local labour market are a more obvious point of aspiration than are those of people who may be in the same product market but geographically remote.

A second important feature of these developments in bargaining structure concerns the extent of fragmentation, not of pay bargaining as such, but of the managerial control of pay bargaining. The decentralization of pay bargaining within an enterprise, whether to divisional or establishment level, is often closely monitored and constrained by higher management at head office. A survey in 1985 reported that in two-thirds of cases where the establishment was ostensibly the most important level of pay bargaining, the local manager was subject to higher level guidelines (Marginson *et al.*, 1988). A survey in 1990 reported that three-fifths of apparently independent local managers in multi-establishment firms consulted with their corporate superiors during pay negotiations (Millward *et al.*, 1992).

The result is that the apparent fragmentation of bargaining structure in both private and public sectors over the past 20 years has not been matched by comparable fragmentation of control over pay. Effective control over pay may, paradoxically, thus be substantially more concentrated in 1992 through the efforts of independent employers than was the case in, say, 1962, when the bargaining structure relied upon weak employers' associations struggling to uphold relatively few, but increasingly ineffective, industrywide agreements.

A further important policy implication arising from the tendency for the locus of pay bargaining to be product-specific and single-employer is that it permits greater scope in the management of labour productivity. Indeed, this is a principal reason for the rise of single-employer bargaining, not only in Britain, but throughout most industrialized market economies. Employers are better able to elicit productivity improvements from their workforces if they can shape and reshape their jobs and skills to changing technologies, and if they can offer employees a predictable trajectory of pay expectations. This requires employers to have close control over internal pay structures, and as far as possible to insulate their internal labour market from the external labour market. The more freedom they have to use pay as part of a broader strategy of career, capability, and compliance management, the better employers are able to control unit costs, not so much by restraining wages, but by raising productivity.

Any consideration of incomes policy must be sensitive to the dynamics not just of institutions and markets, but also of employees' conceptions of fairness. The most intensely felt sources of wage comparison for most employees are proximal; the closer the group with which comparison is being made, both socially and spatially, the more distress is caused by an adverse disruption of relative pay. Because of this, the growth of single-employer bargaining has been accompanied by the spread of job evaluation techniques to permit the orderly management of internal wage structures. When carefully linked to a programme of skill- and responsibility-acquisition, pay can be a powerful device for productivity growth. When mismanaged it can become a devastatingly potent demotivator.

However much an employer tries to isolate an organization's pay structure, external influences cannot be avoided. Table 2.2 gives the results of regular CBI surveys of the factors which employers report to be of importance of their current (almost exclusively single-employer) pay bargains. It is notable how the relative importance of these different factors varies over the years, with the significance of the 'cost of living' fluctuating with price inflation, and the salience of 'recruitment and retention' rising and falling with the level of unemployment. External comparability appears to be a fairly consistent, if diffusely focused, influence. It is also notable that the most important downward pressures on wage aspirations appear to be the essentially product market related factors of price constraints, profit levels, redundancy risk, and orders. It underlines the primacy of product market mechanisms in pay determination. All in all, Table 2.2 implies that any incomes policy would have to be responsive, at different times to different degrees, to a variety of both parochial and national influences, if it is to be other than a brief, crisis measure.

Table 2.2 Pressures on Pay Settlements Reported by Employers in Manufacturing, 1980–91

	1980	1981	1982	1983	1984	1985	1986	1987	1988	1989	1990	1991
'Very important' upward pressures												
Cost of living	47	45	36	40	45	38	26	23	59	67	52	31
Recruit/retain	7	6	5	9	12	14	14	22	30	29	15	9
Profits	11	16	19	21	23	17	20	25	20	12	9	8
Productivity	n.a.	n.a.	n.a.	n.a.	n.a.	17	15	19	17	14	12	15
Order levels	n.a.	n.a.	n.a.	n.a.	n.a.	11	11	15	11	7	6	6
'Very important' downward pressures												
Price constraints	56	52	52	51	43	43	42	36	38	40	48	56
Profit levels	62	60	53	45	40	32	27	20	19	28	47	54
Cost of living	n.a.	n.a.	n.a.	n.a.	n.a.	10	18	11	4	5	13	26
Risk of redundancy	43	35	27	21	17	16	16	10	10	12	30	31
Order levels	n.a.	n.a.	n.a.	n.a.	n.a.	15	13	9	9	17	37	40
External comparability												
Same locality	17	15	14	18	19	22	20	25	35	30	22	17
Same firm	23	23	24	21	23	18	19	19	18	19	12	15
Same industry	12	13	15	17	18	18	18	19	22	22	16	14
Pay rises nationally	16	16	18	19	20	16	19	16	24	26	21	13

Source: CBI Pay Data-bank

Incomes policy options for the 1990s

Debate on incomes policy in Britain was virtually silent throughout the 1980s. It revived in the 1990s when it became apparent that the Conservative government had no effective counter-inflationary policy beyond raising the level of unemployment, and when the prospect of entry into the Exchange Rate Mechanism threatened to deny the government what little influence over interest rates it still possessed. It became apparent that, if and when there is a substantial upturn in the level of economic activity, renewed inflationary pressures will once again push incomes policy high up the political agenda.

The debate on incomes policy has been conducted by rather different people than 20 years earlier. This time very few politicians have entered into what they remembered as high-risk electoral territory. Among academics, the industrial relations specialists of earlier debates have been largely silent, their hopes for collective bargaining solutions dampened by a decade of trade union defeats. It has tended to be the more empirically minded macroeconomists who have made the running, impressed by the evidence from other countries that centralized, or coordinated pay bargaining has been a means to achieving above average growth and below average inflation.

The starting point of the new debate has been roughly where the old debate was stopped so abruptly by the arrival of the Thatcher government in 1979. At risk of over-simplification it has been as follows. Public and private sectors must be dealt with differently. The public sector – much reduced in complexity since the privatizations and subcontracting of the 1980s – is probably best managed through routine, periodic pay comparability exercises. The experience of the Clegg Pay Comparability Commission would suggest that external comparability should not be rigidly applied, that integrity of internal pay structures should be respected, and that labour productivity is best sustained by some sort of independent audit arrangement, of both costs and quality. At the time of writing, the Conservative government has taken the extraordinary step of imposing a 1.5 per cent pay freeze for the public sector, but in the longer run it is likely that the sort of procedure outlined will command fairly wide support.

For the private sector the main debate has been over how pay bargaining might be coordinated. The tentative proposals of the TUC and CBI in 1979 for an annual 'agreed economic assessment' are not forgotten. The Labour Party included them in its 1992 election proposals. Furthermore, in 1993 the Conservative government has set up a consultative panel of the country's leading economic forecasters. It has been suggested that an annual Parliamentary Select Committee procedure might provide a very satisfactory forum for the informed debate of pay increase norms, and criteria for variations from them (Marsh, 1991). After the industrial confrontations of the 1980s, an inflationary crisis in the 1990s is likely to find a heightened appetite for consensus-forming.

It is, however, unclear what collective representation might be appropriate for consensus-forming. Few would now argue that controlled trade union pressure is playing the lead in driving up pay. Consequently few would argue that the Trades Union Congress could play a pivotal role in sustaining a policy of pay restraint. Even if the Labour Party were not currently trying to loosen its partnership with the trade unions, their increasingly marginal position in private sector pay determination denies any plausible prospect of another 1970s-style Social Contract.

An argument that carries conviction is that a *sine qua non* of coordination is some sort of unity of employer action, either overtly or covertly (Brown, 1986; Soskice, 1990). How this might be achieved in a country which has never had strong traditions of employer solidarity is far from clear. But the rise of better controlled single-employer bargaining is of considerable assistance, and hopes are likely to be pinned on some sort of orchestrated discussion among the hundred or so leading private sector employers. Some in the CBI have suggested that this might be done through informal meetings of broad industry groupings, thus reflecting better the varied pressures along the product market dimension. Such meetings would need to build up a collective discipline among employers sufficiently strong to rein back any employers tempted (or pressured) to make unjustifiably large pay concessions.

Much discussion has been devoted to the value, and feasibility, of synchronized annual pay settlements, concluded in the wake of an agreed economic assessment. It is argued that an extended bargaining 'season', with settlements spread over most of the year, encourages successive settlements to escalate upwards, whereas if all bargainers were obliged to settle on the same date, they would be forced to be cooperative rather than competitive. There are, however, strong practical objections. Perhaps the most cogent is that the synchronization of pay settlements would reinforce a corrosive emphasis upon pay alone, and in particular on the notion of a 'going rate' of pay settlements, to the neglect of the need for individual employers to manage pay in close harness with productivity.

It is unlikely that any influential voices will call for substantial government involvement in managing a private sector incomes policy. Quite apart from the political risks involved, such action would be seen as both hard to implement and possibly counter-productive. It would be hard to implement because the private sector is ever more open to the forces of international competition than before, and private sector capital is more internationally footloose. Intervention is liable to be counter-productive partly because if government once again undertook responsibility for controlling private sector costs, it would provide excuses with which private sector employers might further postpone collective action of their own. A return to the government imposed pay 'norms' and 'ceilings' of the past would also threaten the delicate internal pay structures so important for motivating workforces.

A more important reason relates back to the importance of productivity improvements in inducing international competitiveness. With the honourable exception of the efforts of the NBPI in the mid-1960s, subsequent British incomes policies have been obsessed with the issue of short-term pay restraint at the expense of long-term productivity growth. It has been pointed out that if the secret of the success of the 'social corporatist' Nordic economies had simply been pay restraint, they would have become low-wage economies relying on labour intensive techniques (Landesmann, 1990). On this argument it has been investment policy, not pay policy, and investment policy in labour skills as much as in capital, which is the key to keeping real wage growth sufficiently in step with productivity growth that inflation is controlled. Coordinated bargaining aimed at pay restraint alone can never achieve sustained economic growth.

The implication is that British governments in the 1990s would be wise to avoid being directly involved in private sector incomes policies. Instead they should stick to three objectives: managing public service pay bargaining efficiently; facilitating debate by collective representatives on pay-related issues; and providing the statutory underpinning for education and training. Perhaps the most a British government can be expected to do is to assist the private sector to adopt more productive technologies under the protection of whatever pay coordination strategies might be devised by employers themselves.

References

Brown, W. A. (1986), 'Facing up to Incomes Policy', in P. Nolan and S. Paine (eds.), *Rethinking Socialist Economics*, Polity, Cambridge.

Brown, W. A. and Walsh, J. (1991), 'Pay Determination in Britain in the 1980s: the Anatomy of Decentralization', *Oxford Review of Economic Policy*, 7(1).

Daniel, W. W. and Millward, N. (1983), *Workplace Industrial Relations in Britain*, Heinemann, London (WIRS1).

Landesmann, M. (1990), 'Industrial Policies and Social Corporatism', Department of Applied Economics Working Paper 9009, University of Cambridge.

Layard, R. (1990), 'How to End Pay Leapfrogging' *Employment Institute Economic Report* 5v, Employment Institute, London.

Marginson, P., Edwards, P. K., Martin, R., Purcell, J. and Sisson, K. (1988), *Beyond the Workplace:* Managing Industrial Relations in the Multi-Establishment Enterprise, Blackwell, Oxford.

Marsh, I. (1991), 'Mobilizing Consent for Income Norms in the UK: the Promise of a Parliamentary Framework', mimeo, Australian Graduate School of Management, Sydney.

Millward, N. and Stevens, M. (1986), *British Workplace Industrial Relations 1980-84*, Gower, Aldershot (WIRS2).

Millward, N., Stevens, M., Smart, D., and Hawes, W. R. (1992), *Workplace Industrial Relations in Transition*, (WIRS3) Aldershot, Dartmouth.

Soskice, D. (1990), 'Wage Determination: the Changing Role of Institutions in Advanced Industrial Economies', *Oxford Review of Economic Policy*, 6(4)

CHAPTER 3

WAGE REFORM IMPOSED BY THE STATE: SOME PARADOXES IN FRENCH INCOMES POLICIES

Robert Boyer

Country statistics

Union members as a proportion of total dependent employees
    1980   18.7%   1985   16.5%

Public sector employees as a proportion of total employees
    1980   20.0%   1990   22.6%

Participation rates of working age population (ages 15–64)
    Men 1980   83.4%   Men 1991   75.7%
    Women 1980 55.6%   Women 1991 58.1%

Per capita GDP in US dollars (1993 exchange rates).
    1980 $12,140   1991 $21,192

Per capita GDP (PPP)
    1980 $9,780   1990 $17,376

Main collective bargaining institutions above the enterprise level

1980

Five main workers' unions (CGT, CFDT, FO, CFTC, CGC) have been recognized by the state as representative and are entitled to be part of bi- or tripartite negotiations at the sectoral or national level. The results of these agreements are extended to the rest of the firms, whatever their degree of unionization.

Union density is the lowest among OECD countries and has been declining since 1974, with the exception of the public sector.

The state intervenes frequently and can impose by law what business associations and unions have been unable to agree upon. Most of the time, sectoral or national bargaining is complemented by lower-level negotiations.

1990

Loi Auroux (1984) has made compulsory an annual negotiation on wage and related issues at the firm level. French unions are poorly organized at the plant level, with some minor exceptions. The importance of national and sectoral wage bargaining has been declining.

The state has used the public sector and nationalized firms to promote guidelines for nominal wage increases and these norms have been used by the private sector to engineer wage moderation. Laws promoting a new wave of profit sharing, easier employment adjustment and welfare tax exemptions have been implemented in order to promote flexibility and job creation.

Minimum wage policy has been used more cautiously than during the seventies, to avoid increasing unemployment amongst the unskilled and semi-skilled.

1. Incomes policies in retrospect: varying objectives and tools

How to explain the general concern for an incomes policy at the end of the fifties and the early sixties, for the first time after nearly two centuries of capitalist development? A brief retrospect of income distribution mechanisms might be helpful in order to disentangle what is general among contemporary OECD countries and what is, on the contrary, quite specific to France.

The story begins with the long struggle of workers to strengthen their bargaining power through union organization (Webb and Webb, 1894, Phelps Brown, 1987), which nevertheless had limited effects on the processes of wage formation. For instance, in France before World War I, the workers could only resist drastic contraction in the nominal wage, but not change the effect of labour market competition on wages (Boyer, 1979). Phillips (1958) showed that in England nominal wage variations were associated with fluctuations in the unemployment rate. Paradoxically enough, the interwar period exhibits some strengthening of unions' demands that wages should be indexed to prices, but the fluctuations in activity still play a major role in disciplining nominal wage formation, at least in France.

But the Great Depression changed perceptions. In spite of a significant nominal wage flexibility, labour markets turned out to be unable to restore full employment. This was rather surprising, given the declining union density and bargaining power, along with the absence of any significant unemployment benefit systems. Keynes argued that the nominal wage was not set by pure market mechanisms but according to parity arguments and bargaining between a series of unions and firms. There was, he said in his *General Theory*, no typical market for labour: not only was nominal wage rigidity not the culprit for unemployment, but any attempt to make it more flexible would probably increase macroeconomic disequilibria. Meanwhile, the United States and France tried to reinforce trade union organization and bargaining power by legislation during the late 1930s, though without any clear success. After World War II, however, such legal changes seem to have had a significant and lasting impact upon nominal income formation.

The sixties: a method for curbing inflation

The three decades after 1945 exhibited an unprecedented institutionalization of wage formation, either via minimum wage policies, or by unemployment benefits or more generally the institutionalization of a welfare system. It can be argued that this change, along with a new monetary regime and the consequence of Pax Americana upon the stability of the international regime, brought transition from a competitive mode of 'regulation' towards a monopolist or administered one (for France see Benassy *et al.*, 1979, and for the United States, Aglietta, 1982; Boyer 1989). Growth became faster and steadier, but with almost continuous inflation, with few or no declines in consumer prices during the mild recessions, which were the closest economies came to the cumulative depression of 1929.

Enter incomes policies. In the early 1960s, many OECD countries experienced long and active strikes, leading to significant wage increases. Governments fear a fuelling of inflation, which is seen as increasingly dangerous with the growth of international trade competition. The first phase of incomes policies clearly concerns a moderation of inflation via the direct or indirect control of the nominal wage. In most cases, in the United States and France for example, this strategy failed due to the high level of employment and thus the significant bargaining power of unions. But, even with quite accommodating monetary policies, it was possible to devalue the national currency when needed. The tools of this variant of incomes policies span from a minimum wage to a price and wages freeze, and to government guidelines for wage settlements (Pennant-Rea, 1987).

The eighties: the search for competitiveness

A second episode took place after the first and second oil shocks, i.e., during the 1970s. For the first time, since the institution of administered regulation modes, a significant and negative evolution of the terms of trade generated a large supply shock. This was no simple demand perturbation (Shapiro 1987). Unfortunately, most of the wage mechanisms were adapted to Keynesian demand management. Thus, a significant profit squeeze was the logical outcome of the indexing of wages with respect to consumer price, when producers' prices rose more slowly in the context of a recession of a magnitude unprecedented since the 1950s. In France, reforming wage formation became the main objective of the governments (OECD 1989). Not past inflation but expected inflation, export or product prices were supposed to be the only legitimate references in wage bargaining. This second brand of incomes policies aimed at flexibility, competitiveness and growth, and sought to promote a shift in income distribution which would benefit profits, investment and hopefully production and employment. At the same time, high unemployment and union weakness reduced wage-earners' bargaining power. Statutory norms and direct interventions into the public sector wage formation then replaced exhortatory guidelines and temporary wage freezes.

During the eighties, the same strategy was prolonged but complemented by a series of proposals to completely redefine the pattern of price and wage formation. On the one hand, external competition became more and more acute, and world disinflation exerted strong pressure for a significant redesign of wage formation (Artis and Omerod 1991). On the other hand, major uncertainties about macroeconomic prospects as well as sectoral demands led to proposals for profit- (and risk-) sharing as a major alternative to a wage economy (Weitzman 1986). Finally, in Europe, and especially in France, the new surge of unemployment focused attention on the possible adverse effects of prevailing wage mechanisms: consequently, any incomes policy should address the issue of employment (Worswick, 1987).

Thus, this third variant of incomes policies is of broader scope since the objectives during the 1990s have changed: to design wage principles which would promote adaptability, worker commitment, productivity and quality. State interventions are less straightforward since the situation is more complex and uncertain than it used to be in the 1960s. Subsidies to provide incentives for the adoption of profit-sharing and programmatic laws organizing collective bargaining at a decentralized level seem to be replacing wage norms or temporary and discretionary measures enforced by the state.

France: a complete repertoire for incomes policies

These new issues call for an assessment of the French experience: what can be learnt from nearly four decades of trial and error in the field of incomes policies? There is a long French tradition of conflictual capital–labour relations, with few explicit compromises, still less consensus. Thus, the state has been a central actor in price and wage formation, often imposing norms and rules of the game on weak business associations and reluctant unions (Section 2).

In retrospect, it is quite surprising that the governments could keep under control such conflict-ridden industrial relations. Basically, the underlying reason is now clear: social conflicts used to focus upon wage increases, whatever their real origin, and this configuration fitted quite well into the Fordist growth model. Why did such a nicely organized configuration enter into crisis during the 1970s? The inflationary bias associated with this quite lax stance could not be tolerated after 1973 and 1979, since income formation came to appear as the blocking factor, preventing the perpetuation of the prevailing 'regulation' mode. An adverse evolution of profits, and so of investment and ultimately production capacity and innovation, as well as a higher French inflation rate, challenged the current institutional setting (Section 3).

Consequently, wage bargaining has been in institutional flux and most empirical studies seem to show some transformation, significant if not overwhelming: the whole institutional legacy inherited from the golden age has only marginally been transformed but not totally destroyed (Section 4). Finally, a lot can be learnt from the successive tools which have been conceived and used to try to solve nearly a century of macroeconomic imbalance (Section 5).

2. Income policies are embedded into rather specific industrial relations

Any theoretical discussion about the merits and difficulties of any incomes policy has to take into account the idiosyncrasies of the national context within which it is supposed to be implemented. Thus, the French configuration is quite specific by comparison, for example, with those of Denmark as described in other chapters of this volume. In Crouch's terminology, France is evolving from a long legacy of state-imposed incomes policy towards a difficult involvement of social partners, at a rather decentralized level (see chapter 9).

A highly conflictual society

The French economy was transformed after World War II. A modernist bourgeoisie undertook to rebuild France's industrial base, but intense political and labour struggles led to an implicit and new compromise. In practice, even the more leftist unions and parties accepted the logic of modernization, while leaving the initiative almost completely in the hands of management. But the *quid pro quo* for this acceptance was wage increases embodied in the Parodi-Croizat wage schedule (Boyer, 1984). Thus, most labour disputes used to end in wage demands, even if initially the strike had arisen from labour discipline, work organization, or questions of union rights. In this highly conflictual system, wages were the general expression of worker protest and aspiration (Erbes-Seguin, 1980).

The heterogeneity of union goals, strategies and ideologies reinforced these tendencies. Even if union density was quite low by international standards, the leadership fell to the more leftist unions, at least as far as the rhetoric was concerned. Overbidding in wage bargaining was the name of this quite conventional game. Symmetrically, the main business association (CNPF) was composed of a large spectrum of heterogeneous firms, with sometimes diverging economic objectives and ideological visions. Sectoral or local business associations were even less efficient in expressing the will of their members, and consequently many negotiations had to take place at the national level.

Therefore, any compromise was perceived by both social partners as a transitory armistice, in a sequence of conflicts. There was alternation between periods of domination by employers and conservative policies, followed by social unrest and major advances in laws promoting benefits to wage earners and unions. Both managers and workers designed their organizations in order to lobby the state efficiently and seek its intervention in labour and industrial issues. Consequently, French industrial relations are very different from German ones: state interference is not only tolerated, but seen as welcome and necessary by both social partners.

Strong and recurrent state interventions

The inability of unions and managers to reach easy and regular bilateral compromises calls for systematic and sometimes overwhelming third party arbitration. Back in the fifties, the state played this role and has developed a complete set of tools in order to control price formation (the Direction des Prix, Ministère des Finances, was only abandoned in 1986) and wages via a series of mechanisms and incentives (Table 3.1).

Table 3.1 Number of firm-level agreements

	1983	1984	1985	1986	1987	1988	1989	1990	1991
Number of agreements	1,955	3,849	4,889	4,890	5,966	4,891	5,346	6,233	6,600

Even if a quite limited number of firms and unions had concluded a collective agreement, a law of 1950 made compulsory the implementation of this agreement to the rest of the sector, without any further bargaining. Thus, in France the state has been instrumental in connective bargaining, whereas in the United States for example, the market and union strategies have been the main mechanisms for such a diffusion of key bargaining compromises.

Simultaneously, the state has an active minimum wage policy. According to the pressure of social conflict and the current macroeconomic performance, the government will push the minimum wage faster than the aggregate wage, or keep it in line with other incomes, or in some circumstances keep it constant in real terms (Rotbart, 1990). Some econometric studies tend to suggest that this policy might have had a significant impact on average wage formation, at least during periods of fast and unexpected increases. This is one of the rare incomes policies tools which has been in constant use from 1946 until 1992, whereas most other instruments have been abandoned (for example, price controls).

The implementation of a complete welfare system, co-managed by business associations and unions under the active control and supervision of the state, significantly changes private incomes formation, especially wages. For example, unemployment benefits do mitigate the disciplinary impact of unemployment spells and thus reinforce the maintenance of nominal and even real wages (Bowles and Boyer, 1992).

This feature explains the smoothing out of business cycles, and also the inflationary bias of private bargaining (Benassy, *et al.*, 1979).

These interventions concerning incomes policies are not exceptional emergency measures but on the contrary conventional policies of the French state. Traditionally, political elites and public opinion have been generally sceptical about the efficiency and fairness of pure laissez-faire strategies based upon market mechanisms. Incomes policies belong to a long legacy and are not emergency measures to control inflation, for example. The permanence and the variety of incomes policy tools are quite impressive.

A large degree of centralization of bargaining and institutionalization of incomes formation

This state activism (Delorme and André, 1983) and its concern with income distribution has meant that, contrary to social democratic countries, most of the innovations have been proposed and tentatively implemented by the state. The state has been the leading social partner in most tripartite agreements, at least until the mid-1980s, seeking to circumvent the strong antagonisms between industrialists and unions. The number of laws and decrees elaborated by the Ministry of Labour is large and they have had a definite impact upon the mood in industrial relations.

Given the strong centralization of the French state – at least until the 1982 decentralization law – collective bargaining used to take place at the national or sectoral levels and only rarely within firms or plants. The exceptions were large public firms, such as Renault which plays a major role in wage-setting in the engineering industry, and by extension for the rest of the manufacturing sector.

To avoid the repeated strikes and social conflict in the public sector, the state has tried to design sophisticated wage formulae which would preserve the long-run viability of nationalized firms, take into account the macroeconomic context and sometimes, also, eventually parity arguments aimed at reducing wage differentials (CERC, 1969, 1970, 1971). Thus, even if explicit indexing on general macroeconomic indexes was forbidden by law, *de facto* many collective agreements used to institutionalize such revision mechanisms according to past inflation. It was the generalization of such formulae which finally brought a significant nominal wage explosion from 1968 until 1973 (Figure 3.1). When the first oil shock took place, these underlying mechanisms delivered a significant real wage rigidity.

WAGE REFORM IN FRANCE

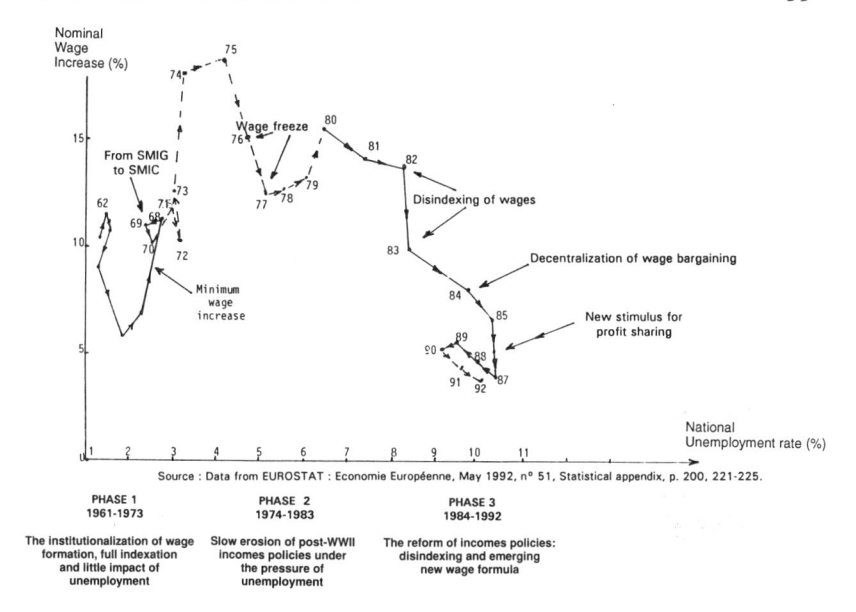

Figure 3.1 The three phases of wage formation

Simultaneously, the parity argument was frequently used in order to link wage increases from one job to another – taking as given the previously negotiated wage hierarchy – and from one sector to another, generally from the Parisian motor industries to the rest of the French manufacturing sector. Thus, many wage-to-wage, price-to-wage and price-to-price spirals took place throughout this period. Very tight cross indexations therefore propagated any initial inflationary impulse, to the vast majority of wage earners. The inflation rate could only be stabilized via a small fraction of unindexed incomes (Boyer and Mistral, 1982). The monetary policy had to be quite accommodating and included repeated devaluations of the franc.

Thus, France exhibits a quite genuine configuration for incomes formation: highly institutionalized and centralized under the auspices of the state, in contrast both with the fragmented and market-oriented USA or UK and with social democratic countries (Sweden, Austria and in some respects Germany). This might explain why civil servants and governments have spent so much time and effort inventing a whole spectrum of incomes policy tools in response to changing internal crises and external pressures.

3. Three contrasted phases

Both institutional and statistical analyses of wage and income formation suggest that there has been a succession of quite different configurations and economic dynamics (Figure 3.1).

1947–1973: a wide compatibility of wage formation with the regulation mode

Until 1973, state intervention promoted a wave of institutionalization of income distribution. Both large productivity increases, quasi-full employment and the political pressures exerted by workers' unions allowed and/or induced definite advances in minimum wage policy, welfare state measures and complex wage formulae for the public sector. This was part of the structural reforms, undertaken under the aegis of Commissariat Général du Plan, which turned out to be rather successful until the mid-1960s. The French economy was then growing at a fast rate between 5 and 6 per cent and was experiencing quasi-full employment. Precisely for these reasons, the bargaining power of wage earners allowed them to go on strike and get significant wage increases (the 1963 miners' strike). Consequently, the government tried to convince the social partners to be more aware of the inflationary consequences of excessive wage increases (Masse and Bernard, 1969).

From 1967 to 1973, the state created a series of bodies or tools in order to promote an incomes policy. For instance, a special centre (Centre d'Etude des Coûts et des Revenus) was created in order to promote income transparency and facilitate tripartite bargaining about income formation. Unfortunately, workers' unions argued convincingly that this was mainly a means for holding down wages excluding profit or interest payments from the analysis and the bargaining process. Similarly, the nationalized firms such as EDF and SNCF have been used as laboratories for the implementation of sophisticated pay formulae linking wage increases to a complete series of factors, including the evolution of total factor productivity. The basic idea was simple enough: in order to maintain price stability, wages should not grow faster than productivity. All over the period, civil servant salaries and the public sector wage have been used as guidelines for income formation in the private sector. Nevertheless, the objective of tripartite and centralized annual bargaining over incomes has been progressively decaying since the famous 'Accords de Grenelle' which put an end to the May 1968 social and political upheaval.

During the boom of 1968–73, the same policies were pursued, even if inflation speeded up (Figure 3.1). It is not surprising to observe that unemployment no longer had any clear disciplinary effect on nominal or real wage increases. This was the direct outcome of a substantial embeddedness of incomes into a largely institutionalized compromise and the strong bargaining position of wage earners, associated with significant job creation.

How to explain that from 1947 to 1973, the impact of large wage increases was not detrimental to growth and employment? The answer seems to be as follows. French firms benefited from the related increases in consumer expenditures; there was no decline in their profit rate and consequently their investment continued to grow. Competition was essentially oligopolistic and mainly concerned national firms; thus almost any wage hike could be passed on into final prices so that the firms had few reasons to block wage increases, given a rather accommodating monetary and budgetary policy. Second, during this period, the diffusion and maturation of mass consumption stimulated the dynamism of consumers' expenditures, which turned out to be the major determinant of investment decisions by firms. Third, given the rather low degree of internationalization, the national firms derived most of the benefit from the related demand increases, a situation quite distinct from the interwar period as well as the present decade.

Therefore, as long as the French economy was rather insulated from external competition and moderately open, provided that Fordist organizations could deliver significant productivity increases, the focus on wage demands by the wage earners might have played a positive role in the growth regime (Bowles and Boyer, 1992). The inability of the state to engineer a fully fledged incomes policy was not so detrimental.

1974–1983: rising imbalances and the progressive erosion of wage compromise

The first oil shock triggered a series of disequilibria, first hidden but progressively perceived as quite detrimental, which led to a complete revision of the objectives of French income policies. The stagflationary property of the administered regulation mode became apparent: the deterioration of the terms of trade was passed onto prices, thence to wages, and provoked the coexistence of an accelerating inflation along with a large increase in unemployment (Figure 3.1). But contrary to past experience, the 1974–5 recession did not end with reversion to full employment and fast growth. Since 1973, the growth rate has been far lower in comparison with the previous decade.

First of all, an increase in internal demand no longer evokes equivalent production capacity increases, since productive investment suffered from declining profits and major uncertainties both national and international. At a deeper level, R&D expenditures were reduced too, while the lower investment rate inhibited the diffusion of new products, processes, equipment and organizational methods. Thus, the productivity slowdown, first interpreted as transitory and merely related to energy shortages, persisted through the seventies and early eighties: real wages could no longer increase at the previous rate and this brought some revisions in income formation.

Post-World War II income policy orientation was first altered around 1976, when a severe wage freeze was intended to suggest that the period of laxity was over and that disinflation and external competitiveness had to be given priority. Given the deflationary context, and especially after the reversal of monetary policy in the United States after 1982, all subsequent French governments have directed their incomes policies towards price stability, profit restoration and external balance. The tools have changed and holding down wages is the main objective: temporary price and wage controls, the imposition of wage norms, the call for decentralization of bargaining, or risk-sharing by the workers: i.e., a kind of mild but effective social deregulation. Thus, for the first time since the 1930s (Boyer 1979), the nominal wage is highly sensitive to unemployment (Figure 3.1). Contrary to the new classical hypothesis, the real wage is itself sensitive to unemployment; nominal wages do not automatically catch up with inflation. Incomes policy might have some impact on real incomes and not only on their nominal components.

These major changes were confirmed and strengthened after the failure of the Keynesian reflation launched by the new government run by socialists and communists after the 1981 election. The minimum was drastically increased, along with public expenditures in the hope of fighting against unemployment. But 1981–83 was not at all the repetition of the 1968–73 boom. Most of the extra demand went to foreign competitors, such as Germany, since the French economy was more exposed to foreign competition than during the sixties. Difficulties were compounded by financial liberalization, which spread world-wide the real interest increases initiated in the United States. Similarly, the insertion of France into the European Monetary System tended to remove the degree of freedom previously given by periodic exchange rate adjustments. Finally, a rising public deficit and chronic external disequilibria prevented governments from compensating through subsidies or tax reduction the erosion of direct wages. Thus, an extra pressure in favour of more drastic reform of income formation resulted.

The last decade: the backlash of profit restoration and competitive disinflation

The priorities of the government were clearly reversed and have been maintained until 1993. On one side, the slowing-down of inflation became the key objective in order to keep a stable exchange rate between the French franc and the German mark. Nominal wage increases show a significant reduction from 1982 to 1987 (Figure 3.1). Competitive disinflation aims at enhancing competitiveness, thereby triggering an export-led recovery. At the same time, higher profits are perceived as a requisite for a return to faster growth and ultimately more job creation – the famous Schmidt theorem: today's profits feed tomorrow's investment and hence productive capacity of the day after tomorrow which will ultimately bring new employment opportunities.

This is a rupture with respect to the Fordist wage-led growth in favour of a more classical vision according to which profit restoration and the search for competitiveness are the two ingredients for economic performance and fast growth. During the mid-1980s, France tried to implement some components of the strategy proposed in OECD reports urging the 'flexibilization of labour markets'. Wages were not to be indexed to past inflation. Minimum wage increases were slowed. Severe wage guidelines were set for the public sector and nationalized firms in order to initiate wage moderation to be diffused to the whole private sector. Job security legislation was relaxed. Welfare payments, including unemployment benefits, were slimmed.

In retrospect, surprisingly enough, a decade later this policy is still maintained and has delivered an impressive reduction in wage settlement increases. For instance, German wages have increased more than French ones since 1991 and the inflation rate has become lower in France than in Germany. The first objective of the French government is finally fulfilled . . . but this has not delivered the expected surge in growth and employment creation. This mixed achievement may be interpreted quite differently.

One view is that the adverse macroeconomic environment has induced or constrained unions and wage earners temporarily to accept such a pattern, but not to accept that the rules of the game have permanently changed. Unemployment has reached unprecedented levels since the interwar period, and union density has declined to such a level that among OECD countries France is located at the bottom of the unionization spectrum; not surprisingly strike activity has almost disappeared, at least in the private sector, and workers now prefer to defend employment instead of asking for more wages which could price them out of their jobs. But, on Kaleckian lines, one could contemplate that a return to higher growth, if not full employment, would shift the bargaining power from firms back to wage-earners and might bring back a configuration similar to that observed during the 1960s.

The other view is that structural and institutional changes have taken place which have altered income formation mechanisms. Due to financial deregulation and the surge of cross-border investment, capital has become more mobile and thus multinational firms have gained an extra bargaining power with respect to labour, far less mobile than capital. Similarly, the Single Market is progressively reorganizing competition at the European level, thus inducing significant shifts in the previous division of labour among countries: the previous complementarity between strong unions and oligopolistic power at the national level is challenged, and divided national unions are generally unable to impose European collective agreements which could re-establish at a continental level the various national configurations now eroded.

Further, labour legislation, firms' human resources management and pay systems have been significantly altered, even during the 1984–90 boom which gave the illusion that structural problems would progressively be solved by a return to high growth. The 1992–3 recession has challenged this optimism and suggests a deeper analysis of the current state of incomes policies.

4. New principles, but still uncertain outcomes

By comparison with the 1960s, the landscape of the 1990s exhibits many features which might delineate possible alternatives to state-guided centralized and highly institutionalized incomes-formation mechanisms.

Decentralization, individualization and profit-sharing

According to a trend observed in almost every other European economy, but with some lags, French governments and firms have adopted new principles, seemingly in partial contrast with those of the Fordist era of wage formation.

Firms increasingly seek to utilize competition within all their departments, by organizing competition between internal production and sub-contracting, among various plants within the same holding. They also seek to adjust hours worked and wages to sales volume and financial results (Aoki, 1988). Wages come to be more determined by product than by labour markets.

From a macroeconomic standpoint, the failure of wage-led Keynesian reflations has convinced many experts and governments that the profit share should be increased in order to enhance investment, innovation and thus growth. This objective is reinforced by the continuous trend towards internationalization of production (Bowles and Boyer, 1992): if wages are too high, the production costs will price the firm out of the market and/or induce the transnational firms to delocalize their production facilities towards low-wages (but high-skills) regions, within Europe or outside (e.g., South Asia). Consequently, the wage bill should be minimized, quite a novelty by comparison with the ideal of income shares stabilization under the Fordist regime.

A third conceptual change concerns what wage income should pay for. Previously, the industrial pay systems were based upon the ability to perform carefully delineated tasks and this ideal permeated even the services sector. Wages were linked to jobs in quite stable job hierarchies. Nowadays, blue collar work increasingly resembles white collar work with the evolution of modern technologies and the need to respond more quickly to large variations in the volume and composition of demand. Hence, individual differences in skill, ability and commitment may play a key role in economic performance. Thus, wages should remunerate individual competences and no longer standardize jobs (Reynaud and Najman, 1992).

These forces have triggered three major structural changes in French incomes policies. Wage bargaining has been decentralized, largely to the firm level. Both economic and institutional forces are responsible. In the last two decades differences in performance among firms and among sectors have increased due to the erosion of the post World War II growth regime and the unequal impact of stiffer international competition. Thus, if employment is to be maintained, wage settlements have had to take account of ability to pay. Second, the Loi Auroux (1982) made collective negotiation compulsory at the firm level. The law was supposed to provide extra bargaining power to the weak and divided French unions, but ironically it has made it easier for managers and human resources departments to design new pay systems, quite different from those preferred by unions. Table 3.2 shows the rapid increase in firm-level agreements.

Table 3.2 The distribution of wage increases according to their individual or collective nature

Proportion of firm-level agreement	1985	1986	1987	1988	1989	1990
Solely general rate increases	72	66	67	59	57	55
Solely increases awarded individually	6	8	9	12	18	13
A mix of the two	13	14	14	19	18	23
No increases	9	12	10	10	7	9
Total	100	100	100	100	100	100

Source: Ministère du Travail, enquête annuelle complémentaire à l'enquête mensuelle sur l'evolution des salaires (Coutrot, 1992, pp. 25–6).

Table 3.3 Profit sharing: two formulas

	Optional ('intéressement', 1959 Law)		*Compulsory* ('participation', 1967 Bill)		
	Agreements	No of employees	Agreements	Firms	No of employees
1969			1,503	1,709	
1971	219		6,863	7,576	3,403,000
1974			9,291	10,443	4,666,375
1977	344	125,400	9,936	11,195	4,773,600
1980	575		10,091	11,453	4,878,937
1981	637		10,225	11,612	4,842,194
1982	845	255,800	10,360	11,795	4,832,194
1983	918	293,100	10,408	11,926	4,757,851
1984	1,086	335,200	10,483	12,090	4,698,904
1985	1,303	401,500	10,336	11,945	4,549,940
1986	2,162	589,500	10,253	12,019	4,524,282
1987	2,630	729,295	10,018	11,797	4,408,231
1988	4,600	948,811	10,111	12,001	4,478,214
1989	6,997	1,391,000	10,214	12,239	4,573,972
1990	10,717	2,000,000	10,355	12,511	4,682,566

Source: Ministère des Affaires Sociales et de l'Emploi (Vaughan-Whitehead, 1992, pp. 121–12).

From 1947 until 1975, the wage increases became less and less dependent on individual performance; job rates were what bargaining was about. During the 1980s, this trend was reversed. Within the same firm, incomes are more and more set according to individual performance or characteristics (Table 3.4). The intention is to induce higher productivity and quality. The trend is not universal because of differences between sectors in organization, technology and the possibility of measuring individual performance (Reynaud, 1993). Nevertheless, the idea that incomes should be related to individual performance is widespread among managers, both in the private and public sector. In some extreme cases, the arbitrariness of bonus payments has triggered dissatisfaction and strikes, thereby losing the projected efficiency gains.

The third break with the past concerns risk sharing. In French labour law, the income of wage-earners is traditionally conceived as immune from the risk taken by the firm: during the period of a given contract, the wage paid should be independent of the firm's fortunes. Nevertheless, two laws (1959 and 1967) had organized two (modest) forms of profit sharing, under the name of 'intéressement' and participation, not so much to respond to major economic uncertainties as to propagate 'corporatisme à la française'. A third law, implemented in 1986, was directly inspired by Weitzman's (1986) proposal for a share economy. The aim was job creation, supposed to follow from more flexible wage payments. Five times more wage earners benefited from 'intéressement' in 1990 than in 1985 (Table 3.3), though the proportion of total employee income involved is still small.

Some positive impact at the micro level but still major macroeconomic imbalances

What have been the effects of this profit-sharing? Firms which have implemented the 'intéressement' formula are found generally to exhibit larger productivity increases, and higher profitability and to have reduced turnover (Perotin, 1991; Vaughan-Whitehead, 1992). These benefits, plus the tax subsidy granted to enhance the diffusion of profit-sharing, compensate for any initial loss of profits.

Similarly, it turns out that 'intéressement' reduces direct wage increases, but enhances total earnings, i.e., the sum of wage and profit-sharing. Wage increases are more steady, but total earnings more flexible. The fluctuations of employment are dampened, as theoretical analysis would suggest (Coutrot, 1992, p. 32). In 1985, firms with profit-sharing maintained higher employment levels, *ceteris paribus* (Vaughan-Whitehead, 1992, p. 272).

Table 3.4 The various tools of income policies in France: an assessment

Type of income policy	Assumed impact	Effective implementation and impact
1. Minimum wage SMIG 1950–68	To guarantee a minimum standard of living	From 1955 to 1967, minimum wage lagged far behind wage: social protests in May 1968
2. Active minimum wage policy SMIG 1969–84	To promote more equity and reduce wage differentials	1. Incentive for productivity increases and labour-saving innovations 2. Possible negative impact upon youth and unskilled unemployment
3. Careful use of SMIC and rationalization of unemployment benefits	Try to curb the classical component of unemployment	1. Rising inequalities and poverty 2. Less inducement to rationalization
4. Implementation of a citizen wage (Revenu Minimum d'insertion)	Counterbalance rising social exclusion by general income maintenance	1. Only 30% of the persons finally get a job 2. No strong disincentive to work due to the low level of RMI
5. Committee for income assessment and policy CEAR and then CERC	1. Promote income transparency 2. Institutionalize tripartite agreements 3. Curb inflation and respond to strikes	1. Technical studies more than active role in the bargaining process 2. Vocal objections by wage-earners' unions: what about profit 3. The inflationary boom at the international level relaxes the need for such difficult arrangements
6. Leading role of the wage norms set for the public sector (for example: EDF)	Design sophisticated formula in order to institutionalize wage variations according to firm's nationwide performance i.e., total factor productivity (TFP) 'Comptes de Surplus'	1. Total factor productivity is not so easy to compute 2. No diffusion outside the public enterprises 3. Temptation to break down the formula according to pressing economic policy issues (e.g., disindexing in 1983)

Type of income policy	Assumed impact	Effective implementation and impact
7. Tax-based income policy (TIP) Prévèlement conjoncturel 1975	Remove from firms any interest to grant wage (and price) increases in excess of TFP increase	1. The tax base is so complex to compute that it was never used 2. When inflation speeds up, the process of TIP is too sluggish
8. Temporary price freeze 'Plan Barre 1976, 1978	1. Try to curb inflationary expectations 2. Use indirect taxes reduction (VAT) and monetary policy to check nominal income increases	1. The impact is short-lived 2. If maintained the price freeze may impair production (sector imbalances . . .)
9. Solemn statement by the government about new principles for wage formation 1983 Plan Delors	1. Breaking down of any indexation of wage with respect to past inflation 2. Near stability of real wage is the initial objective 3. Ultimately, decentralize wage bargaining to the firm level, in order to preserve competitiveness and employment	1. Until now, the wage cost-push inflation has been levelled off 2. Impressive restoration of profit share 3. Weak bargaining power of unions at the local level More disparities in wage increases
10. Profit sharing		
a) Loi sur l'intéressment 1959	Tax deduction for firms who negotiate bonus systems	Very limited diffusion, due to a complex legal process
b) Ordonnance sur la participation 1967	Obligation for firms over 100 wage-earners to have deferred profit-sharing plans	1. Some success in promoting wage-earners' saving 2. But little involvement in information and management of the firms 3. A very limited fraction of wage-earners' income
b) Ordonnance d'Octobre 1986 Intéressment, participation, actionnariat	1. Rationalize the previous laws 2. Make wage more flexible 3. Channel savings into Plan d'Epargne d'Entreprise	1. Explosion of participation 2. Small firms are less involved 3. Still a limited amount

But these micro effects need to be put in a macroeconomic perspective. First, for instance, recessions – that of 1992–3, for instance – are mainly Keynesian, and reduction in wage earners' incomes is only a second-best strategy by comparison with more conventional economic policies. Variation in demand remains the major determinant of employment fluctuations, whereas the elasticity with respect to wage, though significant, is moderate – around -0.33 – and the contribution to that of 'intéressement', though significant, is small. Wage-sharing funds are still small with respect to total wage bills and wage earners' income. Even if the French system is two decades old, it does not have the importance or impact of the Japanese bonus system.

Second, it is important to recognize the marginal nature of these effects on employment. When steady and long-term unemployment appears, it is too late to tackle it by the reform of income formation. It takes usually several decades to build an alternative system. These are not reasons to stop profit-sharing, but they warn that it is not a solution sufficient to cure unemployment, the major challenge for French society during the nineties.

Wage flexibility cannot be a complete substitute for adequate monetary and budgetary policies. If, for instance, high real interest rates give a premium to rentiers and little to wage-earners (CERC, 1993), if there are major uncertainties about the future of Europe or trade issues which hold back investment and if strong financial constraints as during the subsequent 1992–3 recession are the result of a previous financial bubble, it is both unfair and inefficient to ask labour to pay for the disequilibria they are not responsible for. Labour market disequilibria may derive from financial or product market imbalances, which have to be corrected quite independently from any flexibilization of wage formation.

Finally, some adverse consequences of the profit-sharing economy should be stressed. Whereas the Fordist collective agreement used to deliver great stability of wage hierarchies, complete decentralization and 'intéressement' at the firm level would trigger wide wage differentials, possibly cumulative, across sectors. This would offend common feelings about fairness: why should identical skills and competences receive unequal earnings? In the long run, this might be detrimental to efficiency, and some surveys already suggest that wage earners have negative feelings about the widening of income inequalities, which are only mitigated by the claim that the new types of labour contract are needed to fight against job destruction (Lacroix, 1990; Solow, 1990; Reynaud, 1993).

5. Three paradoxes of French economic policies

The present survey suggests some conclusions, some of them quite general and possibly applying to other European countries.

1. It would be misleading to conceive of incomes policy as a single concept, as well as to look for some optimal device which would simultaneously solve all the following problems: demand inflation, structural competitiveness, response to supply shocks and unemployment. Any given incomes policy has to be related to the 'régulation' mode and the prevailing growth regime. It is especially important to recognize the embeddedness of any such policy within the context of industrial relations.
2. France has developed a fairly sophisticated set of technical tools in order to cope with the inflationary bias of its postwar growth regime: minimum wages, wage freezes, complex pay systems in the public sector, wage norms, incentives to profit sharing, tax-based incomes policies and so on. All have been used, with varying degrees of success, in order to cure the French disease. Any system, however good, brings into existence adverse trends which progressively erode its initial efficiency. This is obviously so for temporary wage and price freezes which do not define any viable long-run incomes policy. But the same applies to another sequence typical of the French experience, i.e. the succession of minimum wage (SMIG), then growth wage (SMIC), and citizen wage (RMI).
3. Nevertheless, state power has rarely been sufficient to compensate for an inherent lack of trust between business associations and unions, firms and wage-earners. This is the first French paradox. The continuous pursuit of incomes policies by a 'strong' state has still achieved less than the broad vision of a social market economy and 'the complex set of fortuitously balanced' institutions typical of Germany.
4. Economic policy exhibits a clear turning point between 1982 and 1983, due to the conjunction of the internationalization of production and investment, financial integration, European institution-building and a new wave of technical change. In retrospect, it is quite surprising that the new orientations defined in 1982–3 have finally been accepted and have been effective in delivering an impressive decline in inflation rates. This is the second French paradox, only mitigated by the fact that unemployment is still very high despite the steady pursuit of the same strategy over a decade. Do incomes policies only affect nominal incomes, or do they shape real wage

movements? The French experience delivers a balanced view. On the one hand, the state-imposed disindexing of wages in 1983 clearly turned round the previous inflationary trend. But on the other hand, there was also an unprecedentedly high unemployment rate working to weaken the bargaining power of unions and wage earners, according to what seems like an iron law existing since the emergence of the capitalist industrial order, independently of any income policy.

5. At the firm level, a set of new principles seems to have emerged: maximum decentralization of negotiations, the individualization of pay, the remuneration of competence rather than job-related pay, the search for flexibility in wages via profit-sharing, the downgrading of the role of unions. Basically, wages have been disindexed with respect to past inflation and highly institutionalized and rigid formulae, at the sectoral or national levels, have been decaying. Both employed workers and firms seem to benefit from such a system which delivers a more satisfactory trade-off between employment and wages, between average income increases and their variability. Nevertheless, it remains to be seen if this new configuration of the labour contract is sufficient to solve the problems at the macro level. The persistence of a high unemployment and labour segmentation is especially preoccupying in France. This is the third French paradox: an impressive success may hide the coming crisis related to rising inequalities and mass unemployment. What happens to 'Liberté, Egalité, Fraternité'?

6. Last, but not least, are the new principles of income distribution sufficiently efficient to respond to the opportunities and constraints associated with European Monetary Integration? Will it be wage adjustments or, alternatively, unemployment which bears the large burden of coping with the loss of national monetary policy autonomy, when the rules of the competition game are set at the European level? This is one source of major uncertainty for the 1990s – for France certainly, and maybe for other European countries too.

References

Aglietta, M. (1982), *Régulation et crises du Capitalisme* (2nd edn), Calmann-Lévy, Paris.

Aoki, M. (1988) *Information, Incentives, and Bargaining in the Japanese Economy*, Cambridge University Press, Cambridge.

Artis, M. J. and Ormerod, P. (1991), 'Is There an "EMS" Effect in European Labour Markets?', D.P. No. 598, December, Centre for Economic Policy Research.

Benassy, J. P., Boyer, R. and Gelpi, R. M. (1979) 'Regulation des économies capitalistes et inflation', *Revue Economique*, 30(3), pp. 397–441.
Boje, T. P. and Madsen, P. K. (1992), 'Wage Formation and Income Policy in Denmark in the 1980s, paper presented at the seminar 'Les politiques des revenus' 19–21 November, Poitiers.
Bowles, S. and Boyer, R. (1992), 'Wages, Aggregate Demand, and Employment in an Open Economy: A Theoretical and Empirical Investigation', mimeo, University of Massachusetts, Amherst.
Boyer, R. (1979), 'Wage Formation in Historical Perspective: The French Experience', *Cambridge Journal of Economics*, 3, pp. 99–118.
——— (1984), 'Wage Labor, Capital Accumulation and the Crisis, 1968–1982' in M. Kesselman and G. Groux (eds), *The French Workers' Movement: Economic Crisis and Political Change*, George Allen and Unwin, London, pp. 17–38.
——— (1989), 'Wage Labor Nexus, Technology and Long Run Dynamics: An Interpretation and Preliminary Tests for US', in M. Di Matteo, R. M. Goodwin and A. Vercelli (eds.), *Lecture Notes in Economics and Mathematical Systems: Technological and Social Factors in Long Term Fluctuations*, no. 321, Springer–Verlag, New York.
——— (1991), 'New Directions in Management Practices and Work Organisation', WP Cepremap no. 9130 in Hasan, Abrar (ed.), *Technical Change as a Social Process: Society, Enterprises and Individual*, OECD, Paris.
Boyer, R. and Mistral, J. (1982), *Accumulation, Inflation, Crises* (2nd ed), Presses Universitaires de France, Paris.
CERC (1969), *Productivité globale et comptes de surplus de la SNCF*, Documents du CERC no. 3/4, La Documentation Française, Paris.
——— (1970), *Productivité globale et comptes de surplus des charbonnages de France*, no. 11, La Documentation Française, Paris.
——— (1971), *Productivité globale et comptes de surplus d'Electricité de France*, no. 13, La Documentation Française, Paris.
——— (1993), *Constat de l'évolution récente des revenus en France*, Document du CERC, no. 107, La Documentation Française, Paris.
Coutrot, T. (1992), 'L'intéressement: vers une nouvelle conventin salariale?', *Travail et Emploi*, 53(3), pp. 22–39.
Crouch, C. (1992), 'Incomes Policies, Institutions and Markets: An Overview of Recent Developments', paper presented at the seminar 'Les politiques des revenus', 19–21 November, Poitiers.
Delorme, R. and André, C. (1983), *L'Etat et l'Economie* (in particular 5th part, pp. 369–503), Seuil, Paris.
Données Sociales (1987), 'Le contrat de travail', INSEE, Paris.
Erbes-Seguin, S. E. (1980), 'Les relations collectives du travail', *Doctorat d'Etat*, Université Paris VII, Paris.
Lacroix, T. (1990), 'Le marché du travail dans les années 80, Reprise de l'emploi, chômage stabilisé et diversification des statuts', *Données Sociales*, INSEE, Paris.
Masse, P. and Bernard, P. (1969), *Les dividendes du progrés*, Seuil, Paris.
OECD (1989), *La flexibilité du marché du travail: Nouvelles tendances dans l'entreprise*, publication de l'OCDE, Paris.
Pennant-Rea, R. (1987), 'Incomes Policies', in J. Eatwell, M. Milgate and

P. Newman (eds.), *The New Palgrave: A Dictionary of Economics*, Macmillan, London, T.II, pp. 750–1.
Perotin, V. (1991), 'The Incidence and Effects of Profit-Sharing: Situation in France and Research Agenda', mimeo, CERC.
Phelps-Brown, H. (1987), 'Trade unions', in J. Eatwell, M. Milgate and P. Newman (eds.), *The New Palgrave: A Dictionary of Economics*, Macmillan, London, T.IV, pp. 672–6.
Phillips, A. W. (1958), 'The Relation between Unemployment and the Rate of Change of Money Wages in the United Kingdom 1861–1957', *Economica*, 25, pp. 283–99.
Reynaud, B. (1993), 'Travail, Formation, Emploi: la formation des salaires en France', *Problèmes Economiques*, 2315 (3 March), pp. 1–8.
Reynaud, B. and Najman, V. I. (1992), 'Les formules salariales actuelles: bricolage ou transformation radicale du fordisme?' *Travail et Emploi*, 51(1), pp. 86–97.
Rotbart, G. (1990), 'Salaires et restructuration du travail: une transformation massive et rapide', *Données Sociales*, INSEE, Paris.
Shapiro, M. D. (1987), 'Supply Shocks in Macroeconomics' in J. Eatwell, M. Milgate and P. Newman (eds.) *The New Palgrave: A Dictionary of Economics*, Macmillan, London, T.IV, pp. 556–60.
Solow, R. M. (1990), *The Labor Market as a Social Institution*, Basil Blackwell, Cambridge, MA.
Streeck, W. (1993), 'Pay Restraint without Incomes Policy: Institutionalized Monetarism and Industrial Unionism in Germany', mimeo, University of Wisconsin-Madison.
Vaughan-Whitehead, D. (1992), *Intéressement, Participation, Actionnariat*, Economica, Paris.
Webb, S. and Webb, B. (1894), *The History of Trade Unionism* (2nd ed 1920), Longmans, London.
Weitzman, M. L. (1986), *L'économie du partage: vaincre la stagflation*, Hachette, Lattes, Paris.
Worswick, G. D. N. (1987), 'Demand Management', in J. Eatwell, M. Milgate and P. Newman (eds.), *The New Palgrave: A Dictionary of Economics*, Macmillan, London, T.I, pp. 781–3.

CHAPTER 4

WAGE CONTROL AND COST-PUSH INFLATION IN SWEDEN SINCE 1960

Rune Åberg

Country statistics

Union members as a proportion of total dependent employees
    1980   89.9%   1991   96.2%
active members only: 79.9%

Public sector employees as a proportion of total employees
    1980   30.3%   1990   31.7%

Participation rates of working age population (ages 15–64)
    Men 1980   89.8%   Men 1991   88.1%
    Women 1980   75.8%   Women 1991   82.6%

Per capita GDP in US dollars (1993 exchange rates)
    1980 $14,760   1991 $27,410

Per capita GDP (PPP)
    1980 $9,517   1990 $16,867

Main collective bargaining institutions above the enterprise level

In the private sector the dominating bargaining institutions are the Swedish Employers' Federation (Svenska arbetsgivarföreningen, SAF) with 35 member federations, bargaining with the Swedish Confederation of Trade Unions (Landsorganisationen, LO) with 23 nationwide trade unions covering about 90 per cent of all blue-collar workers, and the Federation of Salaried Employees in Industry and Services (Privattjanstemannakartellen, PTK) negotiating for white-collar workers in the private sector. These white-collar workers are, together with salaried employees in the public sector, organized into two central organizations, the Swedish Central Organization of Salaried Employees (Thjanstemannens centralorganisation, TCO) and the Swedish Central Organization of Academics (Sveriges akademikers centralorganisation, SACO).

Wage negotiations in the public sector are separated into three spheres. The first of these are the negotiations between the state and its employees. The state is represented by the National Agency of Government Employers (Statens arbetsgivarverk, SAV) and the employees by the Confederation of Government Employees (Statsanställdas förbund, SF) belonging to the LO-family, TCO's section for state employees and SACO's section for state employees. The second sphere of negotiations in the public sector is that between the Swedish Association of Local Authorities (Kommunförbundet) and three employees' organizations associated with LO, TCO and SACO respectively. The third sphere is that of the Federation of Swedish County Councils (Landstingsforbundet) and corresponding LO, TCO and SACO organizations representing the employees. The employees' organizations in the public sector usually cooperate in cartels in each of these spheres in a similar way as the white-collar workers do in the private sector.

The intellectual foundations of the Swedish system: central bargaining and an active labour market policy

In conventional economic analysis the labour market is regarded as a market like other commodity markets. Wages are determined by supply and demand for labour which means that excess demand drives wages upwards and, to the extent that wage growth exceeds productivity growth, inflation will occur. When demand for labour, for one reason or another, goes down, wage increases as well as inflation will be reduced. Thus, we will observe a negative relationship between unemployment and inflation. This is the familiar Phillips curve. The idea behind this curve is an appropriate starting point for discussing the Swedish attempt to avoid cost-push inflation from the beginning of the 1950s to the middle of the 1970s.

In Sweden soon after the war, unemployment was relatively low but was expected to rise. Contemporary leading economists predicted a depression and, consequently, an expansive economic policy was advised and also implemented. However, the expected depression did not come. Inflation became the main problem and various strategies against it were proposed. One type of strategy was to use direct regulations, often practised during the war. Actually, the Social Democratic government proclaimed a wage freeze in 1949 and 1950. Another type of strategy was to let unemployment rise. Higher unemployment would mean downward pressure on wages and thus lower inflation. Neither of these strategies was accepted by the dominating unions and their central organization, the LO. A governmental incomes policy would deprive them of their main function and increasing unemployment would greatly reduce their power. Further, full employment has always been one of the main goals for social democrats and it would have been politically impossible to abandon it. Thus, there was an urgent need for new ideas about how to fight inflation without utilizing either incomes policy or unemployment.

Confronted with these problems, the labour union economists Rehn and Meidner developed what was later called the Rehn–Meidner model – the intellectual foundations for economic policy in Sweden until the end of the 1970s. They were aware of the existence of a trade-off relationship between unemployment and inflation long before Phillips published his famous article in 1958. It was this relationship they aimed to change by their proposals for economic policy. The goal was to beat inflation without unemployment, which can be expressed as an ambition to move the Phillips curve inward and downward. The following strategies were recommended:

1. Restrictive general demand policy.
2. Mobility stimulating policy.
3. Selective job creation.
4. Solidaristic wage policy and centralized bargaining.

The purpose of the restrictive demand policy was to prevent general demand exceeding the point where inflationary effects would occur. But, due to the trade-off between inflation and unemployment, that would mean rather high unemployment. To avoid that, points 2 and 3 in the above list were proposed. These two policy measures constitute what has been named active labour market policy. By stimulating the unemployed to move to those areas of the labour market that have shortages of labour, unemployment would be reduced. Further, competition for labour in these areas would be reduced with lower wage increases than would otherwise have been the case. Public employment services, retraining and geographical mobility grants were the main measures used. Selective job creation was supposed to be directed towards those of the unemployed who could not be expected to move, professionally or geographically; thus they would not compete with others for jobs. To create jobs for them would reduce unemployment without negative effects on wage competition and on inflation. The expected result was that a given rate of inflation could be achieved with a lower level of open unemployment; the Phillips curve would move inwards and downwards.

The fourth point, the solidaristic wage policy, did not originate with Rehn or Meidner. Actually, long before they developed their theories it was claimed by some unions that the norm of equal pay for equal work ought to guide workers' wage policy. This is one of the elements in the principle of a solidaristic wage policy. However, such a policy assumed some coordination of wage bargaining between different sectors of the economy. Workers in expanding high-profit sectors did not like the idea as their chances of negotiating extra high wage increases would diminish. Actually, those who were most eager to establish a centralized bargaining system were the employers. They saw centralized bargaining as a measure to stop the accelerating wage increases they faced in the overheated economy at the beginning of the 1950s. What they wanted was peace in the labour market and less wage-increasing competition amongst labour. For this purpose they were prepared to accept the idea of a solidaristic wage policy provided negotiations could be coordinated.

Another factor favouring the acceptance of a centralized bargaining system and a solidaristic wage policy was the Rehn–Meidner argument that market-determined wage flexibility was an inadequate instrument for allocating labour. Large wage differences and market-determined wages, they believed, could act against labour market flexibility. Highly paid workers would be more inclined to protect their positions by preventing others competing for their jobs. And they themselves would be less willing to move to other jobs. It was also argued that people would not let themselves be fooled by market-determined wage differences which, provided these really functioned as predicted by theory, would soon disappear after having done their job of promoting mobility.

Provided flexible wage differences do not have the decisive importance for labour mobility that neoclassical economic theory suggests, then it was argued wages could equally well be determined in negotiations following the principle of solidaristic wage policy. In practice 'equality' became a second element in this principle. It was argued that, with wage differentials as large as they were, any change to the advantage of the lower paid would move the wage structure in a fairer direction. If very high wage increases in highly profitable sectors could be partly avoided, catch-up wage demands from others could also be partly avoided. To be sure, influences from the market would not disappear and some wage drift would always occur. But the wage structure that was produced by negotiations plus wage drift would be seen as fairer than the wage structure market forces alone would have produced, and a greater sense of fairness would reduce catch-up wage demands and strikes.

It should also be mentioned that the institutional foundations for centralized bargaining were already in existence at the beginning of the 1950s, when the employers decided to follow their new strategy of centralized bargaining. The central organization for blue-collar unions, the LO, already controlled the strike funds and thus, strikes that were not sanctioned by LO could not be funded. After the agreements were signed, LO could guarantee an embargo on strikes.

One expected consequence of centralized bargaining following the principle of solidaristic wage policy is lower wages in high-profit and expanding firms than a free market would produce and higher wages in low-profit firms. This would create excess profits in high-profit firms and give them an extra financial advantage, possibly to use for further expansion. Declining, low-productivity firms have to improve or close down. Some extra unemployment in these firms is to be expected. Here the active labour market policy comes into the picture again. By these measures the expanding sectors can be helped to attract workers without using wage competition, and those workers priced out of the market helped to find other jobs by measures promoting mobility or by temporarily created jobs. Thus, a solidaristic wage policy is supposed to stimulate structural change, productivity and economic growth.

In sum, it can be concluded that government incomes policy was rejected by workers as well as employers. The role of the government in the struggle against inflation was to control general demand and reduce wage competition by active labour market policy. The role of unions and employers was to control wages through centralized bargaining following the principle of solidaristic wage policy. The expected outcome was moderate price increases, low unemployment, low conflict, decreasing wage differences and increasing productivity.

From theory to practice

Leaving the field of ideas and looking at what actually was done, the most obvious development was the building-up of the Labour Market Board from 1957. That institution was given responsibility for the active labour market policy. Except for cyclical fluctuations, expenditures on this policy gradually expanded from about 1 per cent of GDP at the beginning of the 1960s to over 3 per cent at the end of the 1980s. This is a high figure given the low unemployment rate in Sweden and compared to what other European nations spend on labour market policy. However, what especially distinguishes Sweden from other countries is the proportion spent on active policy measures compared to the proportion spent on passive unemployment cash benefits (OECD, 1992). In Sweden about two-thirds of total expenditures on unemployment used to be spent on active measures and one-third on passive. In comparable countries, the proportions tend to be the reverse. The emphasis on the 'work principle' in Swedish policy against unemployment means that the unemployed are given options whilst the pressure on them to take a job is rather high. Cash benefits cannot be received for more than 300 days (450 days for those over 55 years of age). The aim is to avoid long-term unemployment.

Centralized bargaining was practised for the first time in 1952 but it was not until the beginning of the 1960s that special emphasis was put on extra wage increases for low wage earners. This centralized system of wage negotiations was in operation until 1982, when the employers refused to participate and demanded that wages should be set at the firm level. Thereby, the era of 'the Rehn–Meidner model' came to an end.

This raises some crucial questions: Why did the model not survive longer than it did? Was it because it did not deliver the expected economic outcome? These questions are of vital political importance and consequently have been much analysed and debated. The disagreement concerns both of the pillars upon which the above model is built – active labour market policy and centralized bargaining.

Active labour market policy

Active labour market policy is supposed to promote low unemployment without wage-raising effects. Unemployment in Sweden has, indeed, been very low compared with most other nations. But is that an effect of active labour market policy, and if so, is it not at the expense of wage-cost-push inflation? It has more or less been taken for granted that labour market policy is the prime cause of the low unemployment figures but this assumption has also been questioned. Calmfors (1992) argues that active labour market policy may actually have impacted negatively upon employment. His argument is that labour market policy, when reaching the volumes experienced in Sweden, has a wage-raising effect. Those involved in labour market policy programmes are not participating in wage competition and thus wages can be assumed to increase more than if these people had been openly unemployed. This gives higher real wages than otherwise, and thus, lower employment. He argues that a reduction in unemployment caused by labour market policy has larger wage-raising effects than an unemployment reduction caused by a rise in aggregate demand. The reason is that selective measures can be expected to reduce individual unemployment risks more than a rise in general demand for labour would. Reducing unemployment by selective measures takes away incentives for people to do something about their situation.

The opposite opinion – that labour market policy has reduced unemployment and without wage increasing effects – is held by Layard (1992), among others. He, like the founding fathers of active labour market policy, stresses the fact that training the otherwise unemployed raises their qualifications and makes them more competitive on the labour market. This might reduce the number of 'bottlenecks' and thus prevent large wage increases in some labour market segments which, in the next phase, would have led to compensating wage demands and finally to substantial general increases in wages and inflation. All the other measures that facilitate the matching process between vacancies and the unemployed can also be supposed to have moderating effects on wage increases.

Further, creating jobs for those who in any case do not take part in wage competition cannot be expected to have wage-raising effects. The long-term unemployed is such a group and labour market policy can be regarded as a measure to prevent an increase in the number of long-term unemployed. If the policy is successful in its aim of minimizing long-term unemployment, total unemployment will be reduced significantly and a larger segment of the labour force will participate in wage competition. If long-term unemployment is allowed to increase, it is very difficult to get it down again and higher and higher unemployment levels will be needed in order to achieve the same downward pressure on wages.

Which of these opposing arguments finds support from the empirical facts? Let us here rely on a standard tool for analysing how the labour market functions – the Beveridge curve. This curve expresses the relationship between vacancies and unemployment. If a given unemployment rate is associated with higher and higher vacancy rates, or a given vacancy rate associated with increasing unemployment rates, the curve is moving outward and to the right. This indicates increased malfunctioning of the labour market; greater and greater unemployment is needed to fill the same proportion of vacancies. If this is the case, it

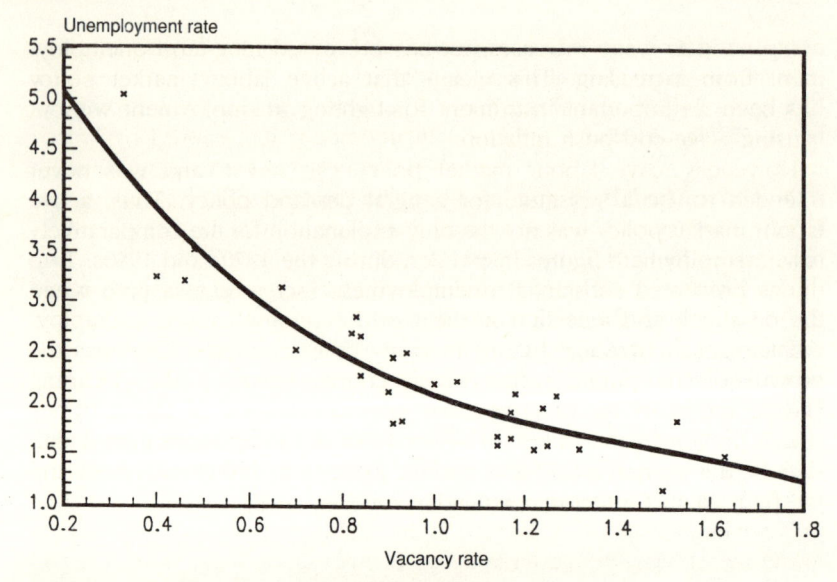

Figure 4.1 Unemployment and vacancies in Sweden between 1963 and 1992: evidence of the effectiveness of active labour market policies

can be seen as an indication of increasing labour market imbalances which can be assumed to have an upward pressure on wages. On the other hand, if the Beveridge curve is steady, and located close to the origin, increasing expenditures on labour market policy have probably not led to increasing difficulty in filling vacancies, which also is an indirect indication of a stable relationship between unemployment and wage competition.

Figure 4.1 shows the Beveridge curve for Sweden. There is no sign of movement of the curve; it is steady and located close to the origin. This is not the case in many other European countries where we often find rather dramatic changes in the curve, indicating a poorer functioning of the labour market (OECD, 1992). The reason is usually that long-term unemployment has been allowed to increase. Unemployment will continue to be high and the unemployed will, to an increasing extent, consist of people who do not compete with others for existing vacancies.

The lesson we can draw from the Swedish case is that fighting long-term unemployment does not worsen the employers' chances of filling their vacancies. Thus, such a policy probably does not have any wage-increasing effect; it is more likely that the effects are wage-decreasing. A cautious conclusion is that active labour market policy at least has not contributed to wage increases but has prevented long-term unemployment from increasing. This means that active labour market policy has been an important instrument for fighting unemployment without causing wage-cost-push inflation.

However, active labour market policy can never, and was never intended to, be a substitute for general demand policy. Thus, active labour market policy was not the only explanation for the comparatively low unemployment figures in Sweden during the 1970s and 1980s. Two things prevented substantial unemployment increases at a time when the oil shock and recession in the world economy caused unemployment to reach two-digit figures in many other countries. One was the growth of the public sector which counter-balanced the declining private industrial sector. The other was devaluation of the currency which prevented the industrial sector from declining more than it did. Clearly, the primary goal for economic policy was full employment and the fight against inflation a secondary one.

Centralized bargaining

The second cornerstone in the Rehn-Meidner model is centralized bargaining guided by the ideology of a solidaristic wage policy. As mentioned, one of the ambitions with solidaristic wage policy was to reduce wage differentials. Figure 4.2 shows that the dispersion of wages among manual workers in manufacturing decreased continuously during the 1970s. Other data, not presented here, show the same thing for the 1960s. The figure also shows that while the curve for actual wage dispersion always is above the negotiated one, the two have moved in parallel. Those who argue that the market decides in the last instance, and that attempts to change wage structures against the will of the market are futile, are probably wrong. A conclusion seems to be that centralized bargaining has produced a more equal wage structure than the market alone would have produced. Since centralized bargaining was abandoned, the wage structure has become increasingly unequal.

However, from the view of wage-cost-push inflation, it is not wage dispersion but rather the mean wage level that is of interest. Here we have, as in the case of active labour market policy, conflicting opinions about the effects of centralized bargaining. Some argue that it raises wages through an interaction effect between active labour market policy and centralized bargaining. Labour market policy itself is supposed to increase wages by accommodating the unemployment effects of too high wage increases (though a demand policy giving priority to full

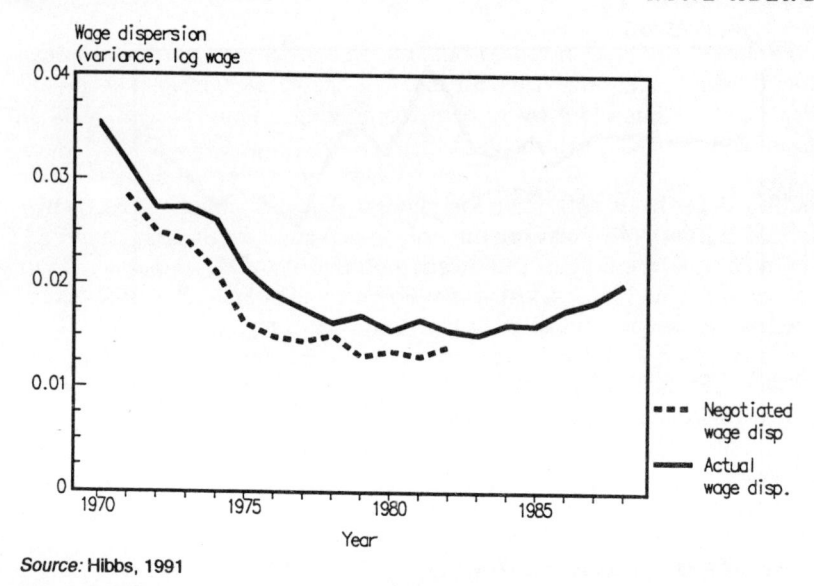

Figure 4.2 Negotiated and actual wage dispersion among blue-collar workers in Swedish manufacturing 1970 to 1990

employment is even more important in this regard). Wage negotiators do not have to bother about unemployment as that is taken care of by the government. They can negotiate for the insiders and leave the problem of outsiders to others.

That tendency to reduce the restraints on wage bargainers may be accentuated when bargaining is centralized because of the problem of satisfying many diverging interests. Everybody expects to get something and, if the ambition is to follow the goal of the solidaristic wage policy, then the low wage groups should have more than others. Therefore, the negotiators need a relatively large amount of space for wage increases. Moreover, the more the outcome of the negotiations deviates from the outcome a free market would have produced, the higher one can expect wage drift to be. These aspects of centralized bargaining drive the general wage level upward.

On the other hand, centralized bargaining prevents wage leapfrogging which was why it developed. In decentralized bargaining, all have an incentive to do better than others in their reference groups. This is rational from the individual point of view but the collective outcome is inefficient. Thus, centralized bargaining is supposed to solve a prisoners' dilemma by coordinating individual wage claims and preventing the

Source: SNEP-databas, Uppsala University, FIEF

Figure 4.3 Relative unit labour cost (RULC) 1962 to 1990 (1985 = 100)

sum of them from exceeding productivity growth in the whole economy.

Again, there is empirical evidence which bears on these conflicting hypotheses. What does it mean that wage increases have been 'too high'? Nominal wage increases might be compared with productivity changes. But changes in relative prices in significant trading partners should also be considered. This is what the measure, relative unit labour cost (RULC), does. It indicates changes in wages compared to productivity changes, and changes in terms-of-trade weighted by the relative importance of the countries' trading partners.

Looking at the development relative unit labour cost in Figure 4.3, it can be observed that these costs were rather stable until 1976. Nominal wages increased approximately 10 per cent per year, which was not so different from wage increases in other countries. Productivity changes for the whole period were slightly better (Korpi, 1992). Altogether it can be concluded that wage determination did not cause severe problems until the middle of the 1970s.

In 1975, negotiated wage increases in Sweden were extremely high. This happened after two years of low increases compared to the wage increases in, for example, the 'seven major countries' of OECD (OECD 1982, 1991). Wage drift was, despite high negotiated wages, also extremely high in 1975. In total, wage increases in manufacturing exceeded 22 per cent. This can be explained by several factors. The first is that the negotiators simply misjudged the growth potential of the economy and negotiated at a higher level than they should have done. Another reason was a new labour market policy measure introduced at this time. Employers were subsidized to produce for stock in order to keep workers employed during the downturn. This reduced the pressure on wages which unemployment would otherwise have exerted. Furthermore, profits had been high in 1974 and 1975. Workers wanted, after two years of low 'responsible' wage demands, to have their share of these profits and the conflict level went up. A year later, the relative unit labour cost increased dramatically (Figure 4.3).

This was the beginning of a period of accumulating economic problems for the Swedish economy: first, the oil-shock and then growing budget deficits, to a large extent caused by earlier commitments to subsidizing housing, for pensions, for daycare centres, etc. At the beginning of the 1980s the budget deficit had reached a level of over 13 per cent of GDP. This was covered by foreign loans, and liquidity in the Swedish economy increased. Inflation, outflow of currency and rising interest rates were the result. Exports decreased and so did production. The competitiveness of Swedish industry was severely threatened.

Sweden had come into a situation in the middle of the 1970s which undoubtedly can be characterized as a cost crisis. It could have been met by low wage increases or by reduced wage taxes and public expenditures but the primary measure used was devaluation, undertaken in 1976, 1977, 1981 and 1982. The two latest together amounted to 26 per cent. They restored the competitiveness of Swedish industry and relative unit labour cost was depressed to a level far beneath that which it was at before the problems started in the middle of the 1970s (Figure 4.3). That meant a strong, probably too strong, shot in the arm for Swedish industry.

Exports as well as profits increased dramatically in the middle of the 1980s. The stock market in Sweden became one of the most expansive in Europe. This upswing in economic activity meant increasing tax revenues and, together with some reductions in public spending, the budget deficit could be eliminated.

However, as a response to the dominating belief in the superiority of free market solutions over political control, the capital market and the banking system were deregulated. Money could now be freely moved across the borders and restrictions on credit creation were abandoned. The banks tried to increase their profits and market shares by expanding their lending. It became much easier for private persons to borrow money. Consumption increased with borrowed money, and the value of real estate especially reached unrealistically high levels. Many people became rich by dealing in stocks, also with borrowed money. This had an enormous inflationary effect. There was no feeling of emerging economic problems. On the contrary, Sweden seemed to have started a new era of economic growth.

Looking back at this period, it seems obvious that the combination of a substantial devaluation and deregulation of the banking system was very unfortunate. The economy became overheated and inflation exceeded price increases in other countries more than it had done in periods with high economic activity. It was easy to raise prices in the prevailing economic climate and the incentive to reject wage demands was low. In 1990, the relative unit labour cost had approached the level it was at before the devaluations.

The inflationary process triggered off by the above factors could have been counter-balanced by raising taxes, by reducing public spending or by moderating wage increases. None of these things happened. The government, responsible for the devaluations as well as the deregulations, did not dare to raise taxes and did not get Parliament's support for reductions in public spending. Neither did it have the power to control wages, which were no longer decided centrally. Wage demands were high and unemployment was very low; less than 2 per cent.

One conclusion that can be drawn from experiences during the period between the mid-1970s and the late 1980s is that the arrangements for wage-fixing did not deliver what a sound economic development required. After the exceptional year of 1975, the centralized bargaining system continued to yield approximately the same wage increases as before, but the changes in productivity and terms-of-trade demanded lower increases than that. Moving away from centralization in 1982 did not improve the situation at all. Neither centralization nor decentralization could solve the increasingly urgent problem of controlling general wage increases. One question that deserves to be explored further is why centralization, which seemed to have functioned so well during the 1950s and 1960s, gradually broke down.

The breakdown of centralized bilateral bargaining

The argument against incomes policy is the difficulty, even impossibility, in the long run of acting against the market. Those who are favoured by strong market positions are always tempted to break the rules and get themselves the wage increases the employers want to give them. This makes it difficult to get acceptance for incomes policy measures and, where they do work, they may well lead to increasing imbalances in the labour market and thus to increasing tensions. One can say that an incomes policy will be successful to the extent that it is regarded as legitimate, which partly depends upon the extent to which it does not create market imbalance.

In Sweden, government incomes policy has been of minor importance but, as mentioned above, centralized bargaining takes its place. It has already been concluded that this system, even in the long run, has produced much smaller wage differences than the market alone would have generated but it is more questionable what this wage determining mechanism has meant for the general wage level. It has also been concluded that the decreasing wage differences have not resulted in increasing imbalances in the labour market. This can be attributed to the intended effects of active labour market policy, but it can also be regarded as support for the argument that wage differences do not mean as much for labour mobility as is often assumed in neoclassical models of the labour market.

Centralized bargaining did not break down because of increasing market imbalances. It broke down, first and foremost, because of the employers' refusal to negotiate centrally in 1983. They insisted that wage negotiations should take place at the firm level, though they agreed to sign framework agreements at the sectoral level. There are probably many reasons behind this shift in strategy. Their own arguments were that increasing job heterogeneity, and increasing differences in the competitive situations of firms, demanded a more flexible wage system that was adapted to local conditions. The diminishing wage differentials had also, according to their view, made the wage instrument inefficient as a means of stimulating productivity. Further, it had become more and more questionable whether centralized bargaining really contributed to low general wage increases, which was the employers' original argument for demanding central negotiations.

The employers' position was also supported by the new political climate of the 1980s. Neo-liberal political values supporting market solutions gained ground and the left was put on the defensive. The employers also had political motives for their new strategy. With the break-up of the institutions of centralized bargaining, it became more difficult to preserve unity among workers and their political power was reduced. During the first five years of the 1970s, the Social Democrats together with the political left had used their political majority to enact several laws that strengthened the workers' position in the labour market. The wage-earners' fund was particularly disliked by the employers.

Second, the legitimacy of the original centralized bargaining arrangements was gradually undermined by the growing strength of white-collar employees, in the public, and to a lesser extent, private sectors. Centralized bargaining was in the first place a negotiation between the central federation of manual workers, the Swedish Confederation of Unions (LO) and their counterpart on the employers' side, the Swedish Employer Confederation (SAF). Agreements between them, based on judgements of productivity growth and the competitive situation of the export industry, were more or less followed by other sectors of the labour market. But gradually white-collar workers began to grow in number, especially in the public sector, and the degree of unionization among them steadily increased until it reached 80 per cent and comparability with blue-collar workers. Since 1966 public employees have also been allowed to strike. As their relative wages fell, they became more and more aggressive in their wage struggle. They were no longer prepared to play a secondary role in the bargaining process. Centralized bargaining therefore became increasingly complicated as more and more interests had to be coordinated. It was no longer just a negotiation between manual workers and their employers in the private sector; it also involved white-collar workers and employers in the private sector, white-collar workers and employers in the public sector and white-collar workers with academic education and their employers. Centralized bargaining simply became less centralized and increasingly difficult to carry through. Five out of six big labour market conflicts between 1966 and 1986 concerned these white-collar groups. Centralization might have been more resistant to these problems if the organizing principle of the unions, as in Germany, had been industry-based, with blue-collar workers and white-collar workers organized within the same unions.

Third, the ideology of the solidaristic wage policy was eroded. 'Equal pay for equal work' and diminishing wage differences had served as a basis for cooperation among workers. The first principle meant that it was the job not the individual which was evaluated. The second reduced wage competition: the union sought less to get as much money as possible from the employer than to get 'fair' shares for everybody or, at least, save low-income groups from being left behind.

At first, when wage differences were very large there was room for compressing differentials. But as the problem of job evaluation became increasingly acute, the smaller the wage differences became. A few attempts were made by LO to construct detailed principles for job evaluation, but it was impossible to reach agreement. Job evaluation of increasingly heterogeneous white-collar jobs – the faster growing sector of employment – became increasingly difficult, and so the 'equal pay for equal work' principle began to give way. In 1985, the public sector employers with the social democrats in government, changed the wage system in the direction of individual wage-setting instead of fixed wages for the same type of jobs. The unions' defence of the original principles was very weak and gradually the principle of evaluating individuals rather than jobs gained ground all through the labour market.

This may well have increased upward pressure on wages by strengthening individual wage claims. One's wage is seen as a measure of competence and people usually overstate their own abilities (Mayer, 1975). Feelings of unfair treatment are likely to have become more common. Moreover, the erosion of the principle of solidaristic wage policy and decentralized wage-fixing based on individual performance can also be assumed to produce a shift in people's value orientation. The system forces people to act more egoistically and this gives legitimacy to egoistic individualism.

The government steps in: incomes policy

All these factors contributed to the breakdown of centralized bargaining. From 1983 and onwards, wage agreements were primarily made at sectoral and firm level. Some central agreements were signed in 1983, 1985, 1986–7 and 1989–90 but these agreements were very general in character and more restricted than before. They were more or less to be regarded as recommendations for negotiations at the sectoral and firm levels. During the negotiations at these levels there was no embargo on strikes and lockouts as used to be the case after a central agreement had been signed. However, the need to control wage increases was even greater than before. This was a reason for the government to pursue a more active incomes policy.

The first method was 'jaw-boning'; meeting between the government and the negotiating parties where the latter were told how large a wage increase the economy could stand without inflationary effect. They were then urged to keep within this frame. Sometimes the government offered tax reductions in exchange for low-wage demands. The 'Rosenbad talks' in 1984 and 1986 had a precedent in the 'Haga meetings' of the mid-1970s. A second strategy was to use the role of the government as an employer, as in 1986. Agreements at an acceptable level were supposed to be made for the public sector in the first round. The idea was that others would then make agreements at the same level. A third strategy, used in 1988 and 1989, was to put a cash limit on wage increases for state employees.

None of these strategies worked as hoped. Between 1984 and 1990, wage increases each year exceeded what the government had estimated as compatible with the inflation goal by approximately 3 per cent; in 1989 'excess wage increase' was over 5 per cent due to exceptionally high demand for labour (Elvander, 1991).

The economic situation in 1990 was identified as exceptionally critical. Relative unit labour cost and the competitiveness of Swedish industry were deteriorating. But that had happened before. The new thing was that the traditional solution – devaluation – could no longer be used. A conscious reorientation of priorities for economic policy had occurred. The Social Democratic government seems to have become convinced that fixed exchange rates and the struggle against inflation had to be given highest priority. Why this shift in priorities?

One important reason for avoiding devaluations was the ongoing process of economic and political integration in Europe. For reasons not developed here, Sweden wanted to take part in this process and an inability to maintain stable exchange rates would have created problems in the negotiations to come. Thus, it was decided in 1991 that the Swedish currency should be tied to the ECU.

Second, the fight against inflation had become more and more important. Inflation had been reduced in other countries and if it were not similarly reduced in Sweden, devaluations to restore competitiveness would have to be ever more frequent and swingeing. Devaluations were seen as short-term solutions which could be regarded as substitutes for actually doing something about the inflation-generating mechanisms – in the first place, the process of wage-fixing and, to some extent, public sector expenditures. The government accepted the idea, for a long time preached by leading economists, that fixed norms would discipline the economic actors.

Third, it was argued that devaluation as a measure used repeatedly for adjusting relative costs had hurt the credibility of the Swedish currency. Given the deregulation of capital flows and the vast increase in their mobility (90 per cent of exchange transactions having nothing to do with trade in goods and services; Odhner 1992), borrowers had to offer a high premium to cover the risk of devaluation. Only a firm anti-inflation policy could reduce that risk, keep interest rates down and so fight unemployment.

The view that the struggle against inflation was a struggle against unemployment was shared by social democrats as well as conservatives. There was almost total agreement between the main political blocs, with no dissent from the unions, that devaluation could not, and should not, be used any more. It is difficult to explain why the political right and left had a common view about these matters. Abstaining from devaluation also has its price; most obviously, short-term unemployment with the risk of permanent elimination of firms from the market and little scope for reducing unemployment, even in the long run. With real interests rates of over 10 per cent the risk of severe depression is obvious.

In the autumn of 1990, the currency was threatened and the government proposed a cost-reducing programme. It contained proposals for price and wage stop, a reduction in social welfare spending and a law against strikes. It was also announced that the government intended to apply for membership of the EC, probably with the intention of gaining credibility for the ambition of avoiding devaluation. This was too much for the unions. After protests, the original proposals had to be modified, and the minister of finance resigned.

Soon after this political crisis, the government was reconstructed and came back with new cost-reducing proposals, among which the Rehnberg commission is of special interest here, as it represented a new type of incomes policy measure. The commission was appointed in March 1990 with the instruction to coordinate wage agreements all through the labour market, and see that these should lead to 'radical reductions in total wage increases, including wage drift, during 1991'. The government had been in contact with the unions and the employers' federation before the appointment of the commission and had their approval for the idea. The members of the commission were senior, well-reputed negotiators and the chairman was a former mediator as well as former head of the Labour Market Board. They started by analysing the economy and defined the situation as primarily a 'cost crisis'. They also developed the argument for a two-year agreement at a low level (approximately 3 per cent per year). Then they gathered representatives of the labour market organizations in order to get their acceptance of the analysis of the situation. Thereafter they formulated the text of an agreement and invited the unions and employers' federations to sign it. With few exceptions, they obtained their signatures.

These negotiations were the most centralized ever held and they were initiated by the government. It was very close to the direct incomes policy so strongly disapproved of by both labour and capital. Former attempts had ended in failure, but the Rehnberg commission talked and held discussions with the unions, something which seems to have succeeded. Wage increases were close to the frame set by the agreements. However, the commission did more than that; it also kept an eye on prices and had several meetings with representatives for retail

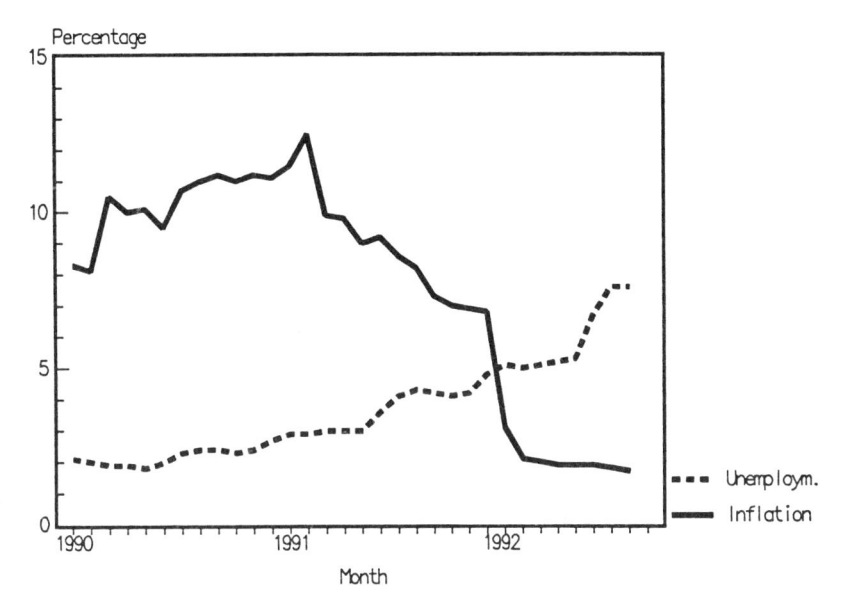

Figure 4.4 Inflation and unemployment monthly 1990 to 1992

trade and urged them to refrain from raising prices in exchange for low wage increases. The result was a dramatic decline in inflation as can be seen in Figure 4.4.

Traditional cost-inflation theories emphasize the unions' influence on wages and employment. It is often pointed out that unions, negotiating for their members, take into account expected inflation as well as expected unemployment when they formulate their wage claims. One of the purposes of the Rehnberg commission was to bring expectations of inflation well below their current level of around 10 per cent and thus create a better foundation for future negotiations. There was also a shift in the understanding of the relation between wage rises and unemployment. High wage costs increase unemployment (employers fire workers or refrain from hiring new ones), but the re-equilibrating effect of unemployment in bringing wages down increasingly ceases to work. 'Insider–outsider theory', 'efficiency wage theory' and 'internal labour market theory' are all similar attempts to explain why. 'Insiders' are not threatened by unemployment; they can press wage claims because of the privileged position they owe either to the protection of a strong union or to the fact that their employer cannot easily replace them.

It is probably true that, despite the threat of high unemployment, the sharp reductions in wage and price increases would never have come about without the work of the commission. But the dramatic decline in wage increases and inflation did not prevent unemployment from reaching levels not seen in Sweden since the 1930s. The ambition to stabilize was still incompatible with a demand policy for dealing with unemployment. If decreasing demand was seen as an emerging problem, there was no argument for a more expansionary demand policy. Unemployment, at least in the short run, seems to be unavoidable if stable prices and fixed exchange rates are to be obtained. This is what it means to make the fight against inflation a primary goal in economic policy.

The growth of unemployment in Sweden was related to the general decline of the world economy. But, as stressed already, relative competitiveness also deteriorated gradually after the devaluations of 1982, which meant that any gain in market shares was gradually lost. But other causes for the declining demand for labour can also be found. Among these the most significant are the collapse of the real-estate market and the persistent high real interest rate. The deregulation of the capital market led to accelerating property prices, which among other things made many people richer and contributed to increasing private consumption. When inflation slowed and prices fell people became poorer and the banks, after giving loans on the security of overvalued property, found themselves in difficulty. Their losses between 1991 and 1993, which the government partly covered with increasing budget deficits, can be estimated at approximately 14 per cent of GDP in 1991. This, together with a very high interest rate and low inflation, led to a dramatic decline in construction with devastating consequences for this industry and for investment in the rest of the private sector. Private consumption declined, which also slackened investment. Between 1989 and 1992, manufacturing industry lost 22 per cent of its jobs. Although the budget deficit increased, it was not enough to prevent unemployment from rising. The government's labour market policy was expanded, mostly through training programmes. In spring 1992, almost 6 per cent of the labour force was in a labour market programme. This was much more than the system had been expected to handle. Cash benefits to the increasing numbers of unemployed were another source of increasing public expenditures also contributing to the growing budget deficit.

Thus the economic problems were by no means solved by the successful work of the Rehnberg commission. In September 1992, the economic problems in Finland became acute. The currency was allowed to float, as also happened in Italy, Portugal and Britain. This meant declining relative prices in significant trading partners and negative effects on relative unit costs and competitiveness in Swedish industry. This triggered new speculation against the Swedish currency but the government did not devalue. Interest rates increased dramatically (interest charged on short-term loans from the central bank to other banks increased to 500 per cent) and the government, together with the social democrats who were now in opposition, decided on new cuts in public spending and cost reductions for firms. Again, the currency was defended by means of cost reductions and increasing interest rates; again these measures were seen as part of a strategy to avoid unemployment in the future and, again, the effect was an immediate growth in unemployment. But the krona was not devalued.

Inflation and employment: cost adjustment and demand adjustment: the paradigm of cost-push inflation and its political implications

When the fight against inflation is the primary goal for economic policy and inflation is blamed on high wage costs, then political decisions have every chance of being unpopular. It is especially so when they come from a Social Democratic government. The message to the people must be that they should work harder for less money and with higher taxes, or reduced services or transfers from the public sector. If not, they will have to take the consequence of increasing unemployment. This is not what the working class wants to hear, especially not from their own party. In September 1991, there was a parliamentary election in Sweden. Now the social democrats had to pay the price for their political reorientation. Their voters did not recognize their party and did not vote for it. The decision to make the fight against inflation the primary goal of economic policy, which among other things meant cuts in welfare programmes and a tax reform which lowered taxes for high income earners, had been taken by the party elite. Their concept of reality differed dramatically from the way rank-and-file members and ordinary voters saw the world. Many of the latter felt politically homeless and did not vote at all in the election.

Four middle-class parties formed the new coalition government and they continued the same economic policy as the social democrats had initiated. The social democrats even collaborated with the government in designing two cost-reducing programmes when the currency was again threatened. A policy against cost inflation with fixed exchange rates gives few political options. Thus, when the dominating political blocs agree on this goal it becomes difficult for the voters to find important differences between the blocs. Political activity can atrophy.

The political dilemma for social democracy is now even more severe than it was at the end of the 1940s. Then the Rehn–Meidner model was seen as a way out of the trade-off between inflation and unemployment. It worked well when productivity grew, terms of trade shifted in favourable directions and mistakes could be corrected by devaluations. If that door is closed, one way out is to find an arrangement that controls wages better than was achieved in the 1970s. One lesson that can be learned from the Swedish experience is that controlling wages and avoiding wage-cost-push inflation really is in the interest of the political left. When cost-push inflation is a reality and becomes the main target for economic policy, the measures to be taken will be painful for all, but most of all for the working class. Optimizing wages in the short run is not in its interest. Rather, it is to keep wages within the limits of productivity and to avoid unemployment.

However, it is not always so easy to decide on the kind of inflation that exists and needs to be controlled. When is unemployment caused by wages that are so costly that employers cannot afford the prevailing volume of employment? When is a level of demand for products too low to induce sufficient demand for labour? Costs, price and demand are related to each other. This means that those who have the power, and the privilege, to formulate the problem also define the direction for policy. For someone not so well acquainted with economics, it seems obvious that 30 million unemployed in Europe is a sign of low utilization of productive capacity and of a problem of insufficient demand. It also seems obvious that a single country, especially if it is a small country, cannot define its situation as a demand crisis if all the others see theirs as cost crises. The options for everybody seem to have become alternative ways of adapting costs, with the obvious result of further reduced demand. Therefore, demand management has become a matter of international cooperation.

The regime of stable prices, fixed exchange rates and cost adaptation was characterized by the present Swedish government as 'the only way'. In November 1992, money began to flow out of the country again, and this time it was impossible to continue along 'the only way'. The fixed exchange rate was abandoned. A new way will be followed. But it is still unclear what that way is.

References

Calmfors, Lars (1992), 'Lessons from the Macroeconomic Experience of Sweden', Institute for International Economic Studies, Stockholm University, Stockholm.
Elvander, Nils (1991), *Lokal lönemarknad*, SNS förlag, Stockholm.
Hibbs, Douglas A. (1991), 'Market Forces, Trade Union Ideology and Trends in Swedish Wage Dispersion', *Acta Sociologica*, 34(2), pp. 89–102.
Korpi, Walter (1992), *Halkar Sverige efter?*, Carlssons förlag, Stockholm.
Layard, Richard (1992), 'Varför överge den Svenska modellen?' in L. Calmfors (ed.), *Löner och sysselsättning*, SNS Förlag, Stockholm.
Mayer, H. (1975), 'The Pay-for-Performance Dilemma', *Organizational Dynamics*, 3, pp. 39–50.
Odhner, Clas-Erik (1992), *Ekonomi och pengar i Europa*, Tiden, Helsingborg.
OECD (1982), *Historical Statistics*, Paris.
___ (1991), *Historical Statistics*, Paris.
___ (1992), *Employment Outlook*, Paris.

CHAPTER 5

WAGE FORMATION AND INCOMES POLICY IN DENMARK IN THE 1980S

Thomas P. Boje and Per Kongshøj Madsen

Country statistics

Union members as a proportion of total dependent employees
1980   86.9%   1990   84.4%

Public sector employees as a proportion of total employees
1980   28.3%   1990   30.5%

Participation rates of working age population (ages 15–64)
　Men 1980   89.0%   Men 1990   89.6%
　Women 1980   71.4%   Women 1990   78.4%

Per capita GDP in US dollars (1993 exchange rates)
1980 $12,950   1991 $25,263

Per capita GDP (PPP)
1980 $9,830   1990 $16,570

Main collective bargaining institutions above the enterprise level

During the 1970s and at the beginning of the 1980s collective bargaining in the Danish labour market was very centralized and characterized by strong state intervention in the agreements. Parliament settled the collective agreements in 1975, 1977, 1979, 1981 and 1985. This period may be considered as a period of crisis and transition for the Danish collective bargaining system. In 1987 the normal procedure for collective bargaining reappeared. All the succeeding collective agreements have been negotiated in a decentralized manner and have been settled peacefully. Previously, collective bargaining has been dominated by the strong unions in manufacturing industries, but the rapidly growing unions for salaried employees in the private and public service industries took over the leadership in the bargaining process in the late 1980s.

Introduction

During the postwar period, developments in incomes and labour market conditions in the Danish labour market have been closely related to the creation and functioning of the welfare state. Like other parts of the Danish welfare state, the labour market is characterized by a high level of organization and a strong tradition of corporatism. Collective bargaining over wage and work conditions takes place according to a highly complicated system of procedures and normally progresses very peacefully.

The level of organization of workers is very high and the collective bargaining process is totally controlled by the labour market organizations, with the state (government and Parliament) an active negotiator as, on the one hand, the employer of about one-third of the Danish labour force and, on the other hand, as conciliator in the bargaining process.

From 1950 to 1980 income formation in Denmark has been strongly influenced by a political commitment to social and economic equality implemented by the collective bargaining organizations through a solidary incomes policy. The goal of equality has also been supported by a political redistribution of incomes through the tax system and by generous social security benefits and a system of free social services (education, health care, etc.).

Incomes policy in Denmark

Several times in the postwar period, incomes policy has been used as an instrument to steer and coordinate income formation with several aims in view. One has been to restrain inflation. Another has been to distribute incomes more equally among the different groups in the labour market. A third goal is to introduce an element of profit-sharing in order to make employers and employees cooperate instead of fighting over wage and profit shares.

It is remarkable that this whole debate on incomes policy and solidary wage formation has withered away in recent years. Meanwhile, collective bargaining has been decentralized to the level of the individual union or firm. We intend to look at the consequences of this decentralization, but first we consider the effects of postwar incomes policy.

Industrial structure and industrial relations in Denmark in the 1980s

The industrial structure

The Danish economy is highly export-oriented. Until 1960 the economy was dominated by the agricultural sector and more than 60 per cent of exports were agricultural products. This pattern has changed radically during the last decades. A combination of strong growth in the manufacturing industries and an expansion of the welfare state institutions restructured the economy completely during the 1960s. Today the Danish economy is a service economy (Table 5.1).

This shift has been accompanied by a transformation of work organization in manufacturing industries. Here employment has grown mainly in the administrative and professional grades. Mass-production and strongly hierarchical work organization has never been dominant in Danish industry and the growth of service production has emphasized the specificity of the Danish industrial structure – i.e., small production units, high demand for educated workers and flexibility in employment relations.

Compared to other EC countries, Denmark is, after the Netherlands, the most service-oriented economy in the EC, with 67 per cent of the

Table 5.1 Sectoral shares of GDP (at factor cost) and employment, Denmark, 1991 (by percentage)

Sector	GDP (factor costs)	Employment
Agriculture	4	6
Extraction of raw materials	1	0
Manufacturing industry	20	20
Construction	6	7
Private Services	47	36
Public Services	22	31
TOTAL	100	100

Source: National Accounts.

labour force in the service industries (EC average, 60 per cent in 1988 (CEC 1991, Fig. 20)).

In the Danish service industries, the public sector plays an important role. It accounted for one-third of GDP and nearly half of employment in the total service sector in 1991. For decades the strongest growth in service industries was in the public services, but the pattern was changed by political decision in the mid-1980s. Private services, especially producer services, have taken over the lead role in service sector growth.

Labour force growth has been exclusively in female participation with a decline in that of males – a growth pattern closely connected to the growth in services and particularly in public services. The majority of female workers are employed in the public sector and many have part-time jobs. Denmark has the highest level of female labour market participation in the EC and again, next to the Netherlands, the highest proportion of part-time workers (CEC, 1990).

Finally, Denmark has a small-firm economy. In 1990, 80 per cent of private-sector establishments, with 23 per cent of the labour force, had fewer than ten workers. Only 31 per cent of workers were in establishments with more than 100.

This tendency towards small firms has been reinforced by the strong growth in private services in which most firms are very small. The consequences are: (1) most vocational training takes place in the public educational system and on-the-job training is very limited; (2) job mobility frequently involves a shift of firm, but not necessarily a shift of occupational group.

The Danish size-distribution pattern is more biased towards small firms than, for example, Germany and the UK, but similar to that of Spain, Portugal and France (CEC, 1989, Figure 66).

Union organization in Denmark

The main features of the Danish union structure were established by the end of the 1800s. Union structure was organized around the traditional crafts and vocational education is still the dominant principle for union organization in Denmark today.

The fundamental unit is the local trade union. The workers are organized in more than 2,000 local unions and they constitute the basis of the central organizations. The local unions and their representatives at the firm – the shop stewards – are also the main actors in collective wage bargaining at firm level.

Danish union organization has had difficulty accommodating to change in the occupational structure. Traditional conflict within the labour movement between the unions of skilled craft workers and those of the unskilled has given way to conflict between workers and the growing number of salaried, female and highly educated workers in the service sector. Attempts are being made to shift union organization from an occupational to an industry basis, but so far this reorganization of the unions has intensified the struggle between skilled and unskilled workers rather than solved the structural problems of the unions.

On the national level the Danish Federation of Trade Unions (LO) still represents the majority of skilled and unskilled workers, but also includes the lower groups of white-collar employees in growing numbers. In the 1980s, about 70 per cent of the total wage-earner labour force was organized in LO (Scheuer, 1991). Among the salaried or white-collar workers the proportion was only about 45 per cent. Several federations have been set up for salaried and professional workers and today they include the majority of white-collar employees – mainly those employed in the public sector.

The Confederation of Employers Association (DA) is the main organization of employers in Denmark and the counterpart to LO in collective negotiations. This organization represents a smaller proportion of the employers in the Danish labour market than the proportion of workers represented by LO. On the other hand, DA is a much more centralized organization and agreements settled between DA and LO are normally standard for agreements on wage and work conditions in the rest of the private labour market.

Development in union membership

Denmark has one of the highest levels of trade union membership among the OECD-countries (Scheuer, 1991; Visser, 1991), peaking at about 85 per cent of the employed labour force in the mid-1980s. Since then a minor fall has taken place mainly because of difficulty in organizing newly entered white-collar employees – it is particularly among younger employees in the private services that the support for unionization has been declining.

Traditionally unionization has been high among male workers in manufacturing and the construction industries, where the level of membership has remained stable at about 90 per cent during the last two decades. The growth in membership has occurred among salaried employees, especially among female workers and employees in the public sector. Today we find nearly the same level of unionization for men and women and for blue-collar and white-collar workers (Scheuer 1989, p. 32 and 1991, pp. 17–20).

Two institutional factors help to explain the high level of unionization. In Denmark, Sweden and Finland – all countries with high unionization – unemployment insurance is voluntary and organized in connection with the unions. In Norway, with its public, organized and compulsory unemployment insurance system, the unionization level is lower (Visser, 1991).

Second, the Danish labour court system requires labour disputes to be solved through the collective organizations and based on the collective agreements where they exist. To be covered by collective agreements, the individual employee has to be a member of a union (Scheuer 1991, pp. 4-5).

The collective bargaining system

The organization of industrial relations and the collective bargaining system in Denmark were established at the turn of the century, a decade after the foundation of the collective action organizations. In 1899 a major labour conflict was solved by these organizations entering a comprehensive agreement that included: (1) mutual recognition of employers' and workers' rights to set up organizations, (2) acceptance of the employers' right to hire and fire workers; and finally, (3) a system of rules for the regulation of labour conflicts (strikes and lockouts).

This 'Main Agreement' of 1899 has been negotiated and revised several times – notably in 1910 – but not radically changed. Collective action organizations have to respect the peace obligation written in the 'Main Agreement' and industrial conflicts are not tolerated during the contract period of an agreement – typically for two years. Expiry of an agreement will always be accompanied by strike and lockout notices and these will be implemented unless a new agreement has been made.

After decades of purely bilateral bargaining the state slowly began to be involved. Rules for state intervention in regulation of labour conflicts were introduced by law in 1934, and a conciliation board was established. Today it is possible for the official conciliator on his own initiative to intervene in the collective bargaining before the outbreak of a conflict, if the collective actors have not come to an agreement. He may make a draft settlement, and if it is not accepted by the parties, Parliament may enforce it by embodying it in formal legislation. This practice began in the mid-1930s and since 1945 seven out of 23 collective agreements have been 'decided' by Parliament. Furthermore, in the same period several minor collective agreements covering specific groups of workers have been settled by political intervention. The 1970s and the beginning of the 1980s were specifically characterized by strong state intervention of this kind – this was the case in 1975, 1977, 1979, 1981 and 1985.

Changes in the wage negotiation pattern

The decentralized pattern of collective bargaining gave way in the 1960s to the imperative of incomes policy. Centralized bargaining with political intervention – including the enactment of the agreement into statute – began in 1963, and was accepted as necessary by the LO and the DA.

In the 1980s the decentralized negotiation pattern reappeared. Central and political steering of wages was no longer necessary because of high unemployment and rapidly falling inflation. The risk of handing over control of wage formation to the collective bargainers and market forces was limited, given the reduced bargaining position of the unions, and the unions were keen to be rid of the irksome intervention of the politician.

Simultaneously, there was a shift in the pattern of wage leadership. Previously, collective bargaining had been dominated by the strong unions in manufacturing industry – particularly the metalworkers – but the new unions took over the leadership position in the late 1980s. In the last three bargaining rounds – 1987, 1989 and 1991 – salaried employees have played a dominant role. In 1989 the office and retail sector was the first to settle and the public sector introduced pension schemes for lower-level employees and unskilled workers – schemes copied by the private sector in 1991. In the 1991 bargaining round, it was the public sector which came to an agreement first and the private sector had to follow (see Scheuer, 1993, p. 262).

This was decentralization in a further sense – a shift from standard job-related wage rates to person-related pay. In the collective agreement for 1991 the wage system for unskilled workers was changed. Previously their wages had been negotiated by the unions and fixed for the whole agreement period. Instead, the collective agreement now fixed a minimum wage level, and the major part of wages is negotiated at firm-level in a performance-linked system. Furthermore the 1991 agreement introduced different forms of flexible working time and extended the decentralized negotiations by including parts of the public sector.

Labour market, business cycle and wage development

The Danish labour market in the 1980s

Denmark's high female participation rate (75.9 per cent) is only 9 percentage points less than for males. For younger women, including young mothers, the participation rate is even higher and nearly as high as the level for men – actually the highest in the EEC area.[1]

Part-timers (70 per cent) made up 18 per cent of the employed in 1989. They are, unusually, treated equally as far as collective agreements and regulation by law are concerned. The part-time employed therefore cannot be considered as a particularly unstable and flexible kind of labour, in contrast to other EC countries.

The average number of unemployed in 1989 was 234,000 persons, or 8 per cent of the labour force. The number hit by unemployment during that year was, however, 720,000, with an average unemployment period of a little less than four months. Approximately half of them had short unemployment spells, and thus represent either frictional or seasonal unemployment. On the other hand, almost 100,000 persons in 1989 were unemployed for more than 80 per cent of the year. This figure only counts the registered unemployed, the major part of whom are receiving unemployment benefits. To this can be added a number of long-term unemployed receiving social welfare, together with those who are temporarily in a labour market training programme or receiving a labour market pension. The increasing level of long-term unemployment indicates a growing marginalization. The total number of marginalized persons in the economically active Danish population – 18 to 66 years – is, in one study, estimated to be about 600,000 persons or nearly 20 per cent of the active population. Marginalization here is defined as being supported by transfer income during more than six months within a year (Andersen and Larsen, 1989).

As for wages, with the exception of 1987, wage growth declined in the years after 1982 from 10-12 per cent at the beginning to some 4 per cent by the end of the decade. Relative wages changed only marginally.

The lowering of price inflation during the 1980s implied that the slower growth in nominal wages was not reflected in falling real wages. Actually, there were small increases in real wages during the decade; real monthly income for non-manual workers increased by 3.5 per cent, while the real hourly wage for manual workers increased by 1-2 per cent. Thus, real wages were almost stagnant over the decade taken as a whole.

The Danish business-cycle in the 1980s

The Danish economy experienced dramatic changes during the years from 1980 to 1989. As shown by the negative growth rates in GDP in 1980–1 reported in Figure 5.1, Denmark was hit severely by the second wave of oil-price increases in the late 1980s.[2]

In contrast, during the following years from 1982 to 1986 Denmark experienced an economic boom. There were several reasons for this. First, several devaluations in the years from 1978 to 1981 had improved Danish cost-competitiveness by some 20 per cent. Second, the shift from a Social Democratic to a right-wing government in 1982 meant a fundamental change in macroeconomic policy. A large fall in interest rates stimulated both private investment and consumption. This led however to a dramatic deterioration in the balance of payments. Economic policy was, therefore, tightened in 1987 – mainly through reducing the right to deduct private interest payments when calculating personal taxable income. Combined with the effect of slow economic growth in its trading partners, Denmark slid into the long-lasting recession which still characterizes the economy in the early 1990s.

As shown in Figure 5.1, the boom-period from 1982 to 1986 was also unusual in that the rate of inflation for consumer prices was steadily decreasing in spite of the economic upswing. So was wage-inflation. Partly, this reflects a general international tendency. But as we shall see later, the fall in the inflation rate also reflects new conditions in the labour market.

During the 1980s, it became obvious that the structural component in unemployment had increased. Unemployment became more and more concentrated: female, young and unskilled workers, and the average level of unemployment over the business-cycle had increased steadily since the mid-1970s.

During the upswing from 1983 to 1987, the fall in the number of registered unemployed (from 9 to 6 per cent of the labour force) accounted for only one-third of the growth in employment. This evidence of a strong structural component has since played a large role in the Danish debate on the causes of unemployment and on labour market policies.

On the political scene, a consensus was built during the 1980s around what was seen as the 'necessary economic policy'. There was a growing and widespread acceptance of the idea that tax pressure had reached a critical upper limit, and that the public sector could not grow further – even as a means of fighting unemployment.

Simultaneously, views of Denmark's international competitiveness

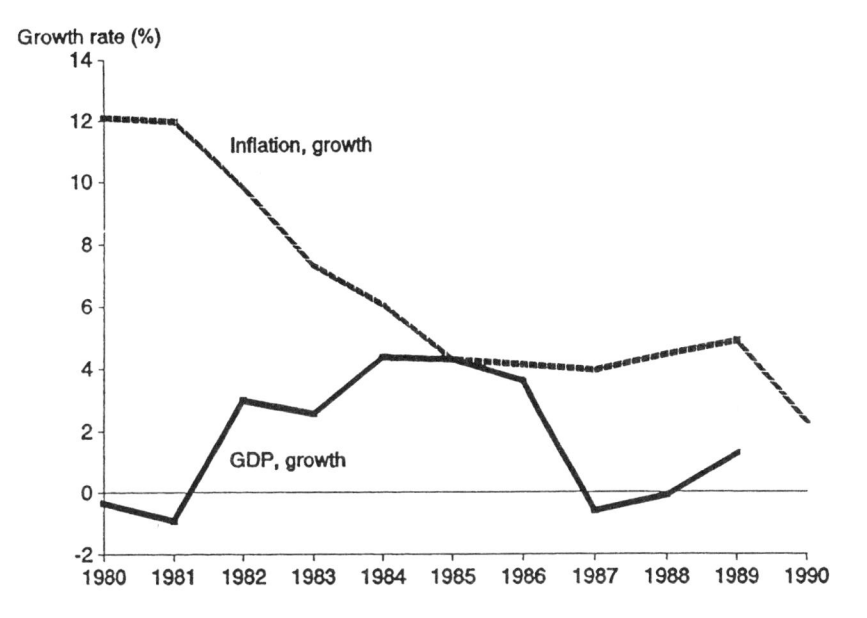

Figure 5.1 Growth and inflation in Denmark, 1980 to 1990

changed. In official reports more emphasis was put on structural problems in exports and imports, while references to wage-competitiveness were toned down. Especially during the second half of the 1980s, considerable resources were invested in an active technology policy. Finally, the plans for the Single Market caused the Danish debate on economic policy to focus much more on the problems of harmonization within the EC area, for instance in respect of levels of taxation.

As for wage formation, direct political interference was reduced during the 1980s. In 1979, 1981, 1983, 1985 and 1986, laws were passed to control general wage negotiations and rules for automatic compensation for increases in consumer prices. In 1986 wage indexation was finally abolished. Since then, general wage negotiations have been conducted without direct political interference and in a still more decentralized manner. Below we return to the question of the changing conditions for wage-formation during the 1980s.

Unemployment and wage-inflation in Denmark 1949–1991

Can one interpret falling wage-inflation of the 1980s using the traditional concept of a Phillips curve? In order to capture the long-term developments in wage-formation, the following analysis covers the whole period from 1949 to 1991.[3]

The idea of a stable relation between unemployment and wage-inflation (a Phillips curve) was very popular during the first decades of the postwar period, but in the mid-1980s the picture of a stable wage–inflation relation vanished. The combination of rising levels of unemployment and increasing inflation – labelled stagflation – was considered to demonstrate empirically the total failure of the Phillips curve. Inflation theory moved its focus away from the labour market towards monetary phenomena. Figure 5.2 shows the growth rates for hourly wages in manufacturing and the rate of unemployment in Denmark for the years 1949–91. The shift from Phillips curve in the

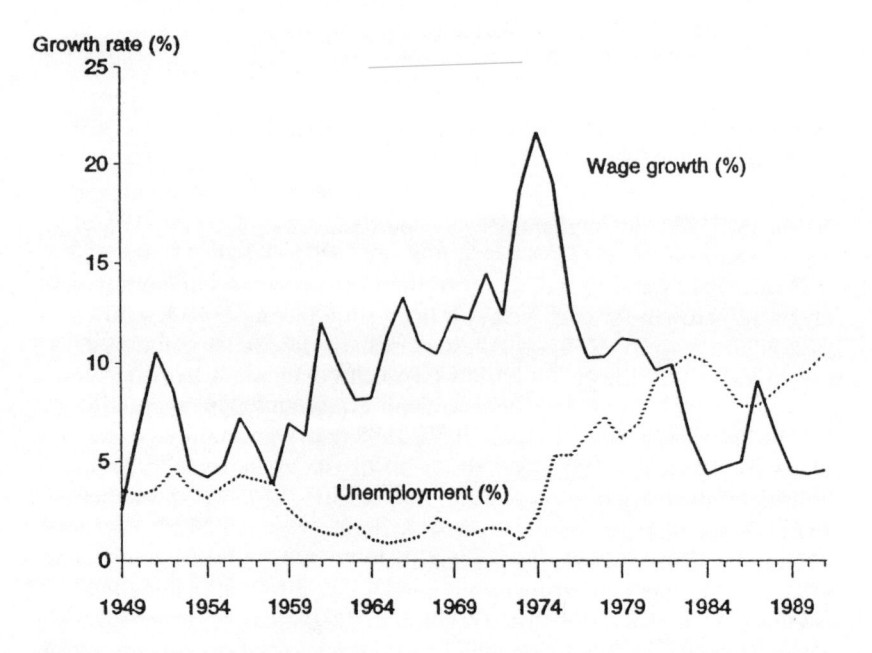

Figure 5.2 Wage growth (hourly wage of manual workers) and unemployment in Denmark, 1949 to 1991

Wage growth (%)

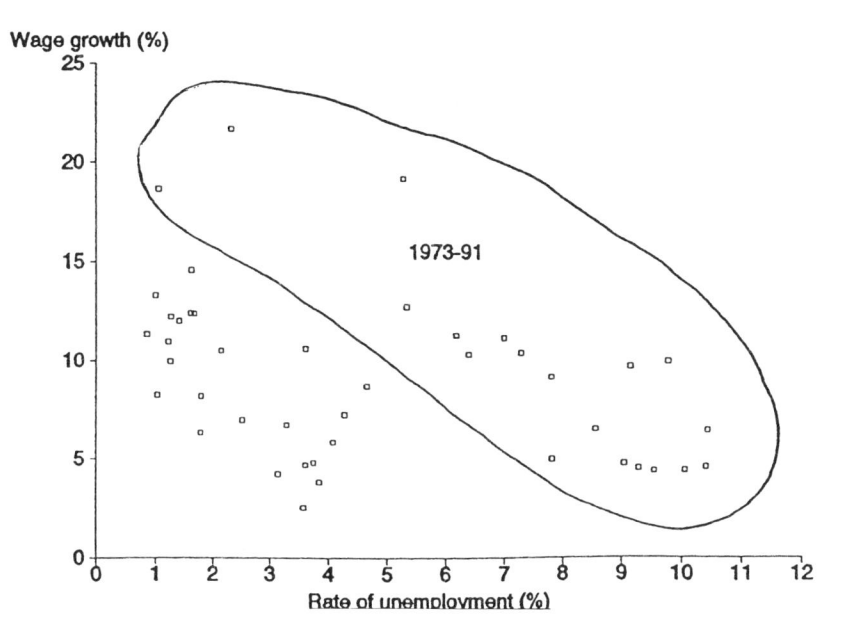

Figure 5.3 Scatter diagram of wage growth and unemployment levels in Denmark, 1949 to 1991

1950s and 1960s to stagflation in the period 1974–7 is clearly shown in the figure.

If one makes a scatter-diagram of the observations of unemployment and wage growth for each year, an interesting picture emerges however (see Figure 5.3). In the figure, the observations from the period 1949–72 are found in the lower left-hand part of the diagram, while the observations for the later years seem to form a separate downward sloping relationship at a higher level. It seems that the Phillips curve for Denmark has still been alive and well in the years after 1973 – but considerably above the level of the first decades of the postwar period. Roughly speaking, a stable Phillips curve implies that 'labour market economics matters' in the sense that the rate of wage growth is closely related to the demand and supply conditions of the labour market.

Hence, formulated directly in relation to the withering away of Danish incomes policy in the 1980s which was described above, the question is: 'Did incomes policies matter anyway?' Or can the lowering of the Danish inflation rate in the 1980s be explained mainly by the increasing level of unemployment during this period? The main conclusions from the regression experiments reported in the appendix are:

- a remarkably stable Phillips curve is found in Denmark for the whole postwar period; the only instability is found in a sharp upward shift in the Phillips curve in the early 1970s;
- the simple Phillips equation is able to explain the major part of the variation in wage-growth in the postwar period, leaving a minor fraction as unexplained variation;
- the increase in the average level of unemployment from approximately 2 per cent in the 1960s to 8-10 per cent in the 1980s, is estimated to signify a diminution of its pressure on wage increases by some 10 percentage points.[4] Wage increases in the years following 1973 were some 6 percentage points higher than before, given the level of unemployment and the historical rate of consumer-price inflation. These Danish results are consistent with the conclusions of an OECD survey that, generally:

> ... the level of unemployment 'needed' to contain inflation has risen over the past couple of decades: there was an apparent shift in the Phillips curve. (OECD, 1989a, p. 47)

The reasons for this shift (as suggested by modern theories of 'hysteresis', 'efficiency wages' and insider/outsider mechanisms) is that there has been an increase in the 'non-competitive' or structural part of unemployment. An increasing number of the registered unemployed are 'outsiders' as far as wage-formation is concerned; they are not potential employees and therefore have little effect on dampening the rate of wage increase; in Marxian terms they do not form part of the 'industrial reserve army'. Alternatively, one could point to the changing inflationary expectations of both workers and employers following the oil-price shocks. But this explanation can only be relevant for the first 3–4 years after the oil-price increases in 1973–4 and not for the whole period since 1973.

One should add that as with all econometric analysis, one should be careful in interpreting the results as a straightforward identification of an underlying structural relationship. Unemployment may be closely correlated with other variables fluctuating over the business cycle, acting merely as a proxy for these other variables, e.g., the level of profits, productivity growth or capacity utilization. Also, one could argue that the line of causation goes from higher wage-growth to higher unemployment and not the other way round as supposed in the simple reasoning of the Phillips curve – though it seems improbable that the effects of higher wages on unemployment should show themselves within the same year. A more conservative interpretation of the results could suggest that from 1973 onwards there seems to be shift in the relationship between wage-growth and other variables related to the business-cycle.

There are also possible external influences. Since 1982 the Danish currency has been closely tied to the German mark within the framework of the European Monetary system. It is very likely that an increased awareness of external constraints has had some influence on Danish wage development.

The experience from 1987 indicates, however, that internal demand pressure on the labour market still has a significant influence on the large part of wage increases – the result of decentralized negotiations. It is our view, therefore, that the level of unemployment plays an important independent role in the overall process of wage-formation and that the simple Phillips curve captures a significant trait in Danish wage-development. One could add that the small size of Danish firms and the high level of mobility in the labour market might explain the strong relationship between unemployment and wage growth in the Danish case.

DID INCOMES POLICIES MAKE A DIFFERENCE?

Using our regression, Figure 5.4 confirms the picture of a high level of labour-market influence on wage increases, but one is also able to trace some possible effects of incomes policies during the last three decades:

- in 1963–5 a rather ambitious incomes policy was implemented and can be traced in the negative difference between the fitted and the actual growth rates of the hourly wages; in the following years, however, the actual growth rates were above the fitted rates – perhaps indicating a catching-up effect on wage inflation;
- The next period of active incomes policies was from 1975 to 1985; here one can trace a slight effect for the first half of the period; the same goes for the years 1985–6, but the differences between the fitted and actual values are rather small;
- in 1987 one spots an unusually high level of wage increase stemming from a wage-agreement, where the public employees were granted rather high wage increases at an early phase of the national negotiation process.

To sum up, econometric analysis of the Danish wage formation process in the postwar years has shown that fluctuations in wage growth can

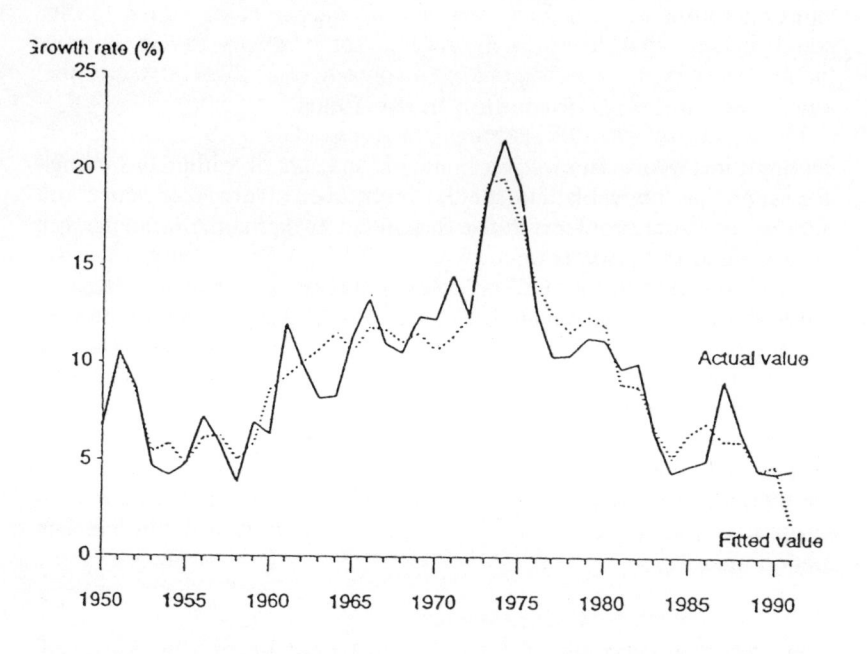

Figure 5.4 Actual and fitted values for a Danish Phillips curve, 1950 to 1991.

be largely explained within a simple Phillips curve framework. One only has to account for a sudden upward shift in the curve between 1972 and 1973. It is possible to trace slight effects of incomes policies – also in the 1980s – but the effects are minor compared with the effects on wage formation of the dramatic rise in unemployment after 1973. The most important contribution to the dampened wage-inflation in the 1980s has been made by the unemployed – just as one would expect from traditional Keynesian macroeconomic theory or from Marxian analysis of capitalist growth and crisis. The Marxian thesis of the importance of the industrial reserve army still seems to be relevant.

Given the above analysis, one must also emphasize the potential problems arising from an expansionary macroeconomic policy aimed at effectively lowering present unemployment. If an expansionary macroeconomic policy is not combined with an active labour market policy to remove bottlenecks and turn 'outsiders' on the labour market into 'insiders', the risk of wage-inflation is overwhelming. Shifting the Phillips curve back to its pre-1973 position can thus be seen as the major task of

Danish labour market policy in the 1990s. We return to this theme in our Conclusion.

Flexibility and wage formation in the 1980s

During the 1980s a lack of flexibility and considerable rigidity in wage formation has been blamed for the high level of unemployment and serious structural problems in the Danish labour market. Our analysis of the connection between unemployment and growth in wages on the macro level indicates several complex problems in this relationship.

On the basis of our analysis, there appear to be grounds for assuming the validity of the Phillips curve as an explanation of the major part of the variation in wage growth in the Danish labour market during the period 1949–91. Obviously, the rate of wage growth is closely related to supply and demand conditions in the labour market. It is the preconditions for this relationship which have changed during the period. The unemployment level in the Phillips curve required to keep wage-inflation at a certain level increased dramatically in the time period after 1973.

Flexibility and its forms

In general, the concept of flexibility can be defined as the capacity of firms to adapt to conditions in a rapidly changing product market, and the capacity of employees to adjust to changes in firm organization and in specific job functions, but it is very important to distinguish between wage flexibility and labour flexibility.

Labour flexibility takes two forms – numerical (adjustment in the number of employees or working hours) (OECD, 1991, p. 14), and functional (the ability of employees to switch job functions when production requirements change, and to adjust to the restructuring of jobs by acquiring the necessary skills).

The Danish labour market is characterized by a high level of numerical flexibility, while functional flexibility seems to be far more restricted. The large number of job shifts between firms is a clear indicator of the high level of numerical flexibility. In the period from 1980 to 1987, more than 50 per cent of employees changed firm, but most of these shifts took place within the same occupational group. Furthermore, a large proportion of the Danish labour force – primarily female workers – shifts between part-time and full-time jobs or changes the number of hours worked. Functional mobility among Danish workers is far more restricted primarily because of the strong connection between vocational education and union organization which makes it extremely difficult to cross educational lines (see, e.g., Boje, 1993).

Wage flexibility concerns mainly labour cost reduction and the firms' attempts to use some form of performance-lined pay system rather than across-the-board systems (OECD, 1989b). This kind of flexibility must be seen partly as a mechanism to initiate the other types of flexibility, partly as a means of allowing employers to hold down wage costs without reducing employment.

In the previous section, our analysis of the Phillips curve indicates a high level of flexibility in the general wage level in the Danish labour market. It is the preconditions for wage flexibility that changed in the mid-1970s through a strong growth in the level of structural unemployment. There is a lack of flexibility in the use of labour and it is towards these problems the labour market policy must turn.

Labour market rigidities in the 1980s

There are several reasons for the strong persistence of unemployment in the Danish labour market. We will briefly discuss the three most important.

First, and most important, Danish unemployment has become still more concentrated in specific groups of workers. Those between 18 and 30 and between 55 and 59 are particularly affected by high and sustained unemployment. In these age groups, unemployment experience is heavily concentrated among unskilled and female workers. The high long-term unemployment for young workers is an especially serious problem and may reinforce the rigidities in the labour market in the next decade. A large proportion of a youth generation, in 1989, more than one-third of 25 year olds, leaves the educational system without finishing vocational training (Ministry of Social Service, 1992). It is an alarming figure because the labour market future for this group most probably will be one of unstable jobs and a high level of unemployment.

For younger unskilled workers unemployment is normally caused by insufficient qualifications and low labour productivity. It has been argued that a higher differentiation in wages will give work to more low-productivity workers; a flat wage structure gives no incentives for the employers to hire unskilled workers. They prefer the more qualified and flexible, but not very much more expensive, skilled worker. The low wage differentiation has been caused by two factors. First, an unemployment benefit system characterized by a high level of compensation especially for the low-wage workers, and second, a wage policy of minimizing the wage differences between educational groups.

Second, for more than 15 years, unemployment has been very high. This has aggravated the segmentation of the labour force into a group of stable employed 'insiders' and an unstable group of 'outsiders'. This growing marginalization shows up in the increased number of long-term unemployed and a sharp rise in the number of early retired among workers in the age group 50–66. Long-term unemployment is more and more concentrated on female workers over 40 while most older men get an early retirement pension. It is for this group of workers, redundant because of requirements imposed by the labour market, that requalification and retraining has little impact on unemployment. Retraining will not change their labour market position fundamentally; they are not a part of the active labour supply, despite the fact that they still have an unutilized capacity for many kinds of jobs.

Third, and finally, the Danish labour market includes a large group of temporary layoffs, normally registered as unemployed. In the Danish unemployment insurance system, the insured could receive benefits from the first day of unemployment. This system has been changed from January 1989. Today the employer has to pay the first day of unemployment benefit and as a consequence a minor fall in temporary unemployment has occurred in the last couple of years.

Unemployment related to temporary layoff makes up about 40 per cent of all unemployment spells, and these spells account for 16 per cent of total unemployment (Jensen and Westergard-Nielsen 1989). Workers registered as unemployed as a consequence of temporary layoff cannot be regarded as unemployed because they are not looking for a new job but expect to return to their previous employer.

In addition to this type of unemployment, the Danish labour market is characterized by large and growing short-term employment. Previously job rotation was well known in the construction industry, but it has increased in most parts of the service industry in the 1980s – in hotels and restaurants and in the public sector. For many of these workers a career is a series of switches in and out of employment. A large proportion of these contract workers are the long-term unemployed in temporary employment schemes – primarily in the public sector. Altogether, the amount of unemployment related to temporary layoffs together with short-term contracts makes up 60 per cent of all unemployment spells and 17–18 per cent of total unemployment in Denmark (Ministry of Finance, 1991).

Structural unemployment and labour market policy

As suggested earlier, it is often argued that increased wage differentiation would reduce unemployment by making available new employment possibilities for the vulnerable groups in the labour market – young workers, unskilled female workers and older workers. There are several measures to accomplish a growing differentiation in wages:

- introduction of special low wages for inexperienced young workers in their first years in the labour market;
- giving up the present agreed minimum wages for low-income groups;
- reduced level of compensation for unemployment benefits – today the level of compensation is about 80–90 per cent for the low income groups.

The argument for a reduction in wages and therefore in unemployment turns out to be very problematic. In labour market research it has not been possible to show empirically that increased wage flexibility has increased the number of jobs, and thus caused higher employment (see, e.g., Rosenberg, 1989).

Experiences from other labour markets (the US and the UK) do not indicate that high level of wage differentiation has a positive effect on the employment conditions of the vulnerable groups in the labour market. These groups' difficulties in getting stable jobs seem to be determined by factors other than wages formation (see e.g. Standing 1988; Burtless 1990). On the other hand, a deregulation of wage formation through the above-mentioned measures has obvious consequences for the social structure. It creates a more differentiated income structure and as a consequence increased social inequality.

It is important to solve the structural problems in the Danish labour market without giving up wage equality and the solidary incomes policy. We must turn our attention to labour flexibility instead of wage flexibility. The aims of an active labour market policy in the years to come must be to strive for a reduction of structural unemployment through increased flexibility of employment. The efforts must be directed to increasing both numerical and functional flexibility. An increased numerical flexibility can be achieved by introducing more differentiated employment contracts and through determination of the working time in accordance with individual needs. Growing numerical flexibility cannot be accomplished without serious welfare risks unless it is accompanied by employment and job security (see, e.g., Standing,

1989). Furthermore, through flexible working time arrangements it will be possible to organize sabbatical years, time off for educational activities, etc. A precondition for more flexible work organization is growth of employment in individual firms and the placing of a large pool of qualified workers at the employer's disposal.

Numerical flexibility implies an increased functional flexibility. This means continuous education and a lessening of existing job demarcations. A reduction in segmentation has advantages for both employer and employee. It enables the employer to use the labour force more efficiently; and for the employee, it increases the number of job functions he or she can handle. It therefore creates higher employment security.

It would be an illusion to assume that all groups of workers can fulfil the requirements of a future flexible labour market. Several 'outsider' groups will be hurt by an increased flexibility unless it is combined with employment and job security and, for the most marginalized groups, a fundamental income maintenance system. Without employment, job and income security, a higher level of flexibility will lead to increased inequality and to new divisions in the labour market.

Conclusion

Apart from giving a general presentation of Danish labour markets trends in the 1980s, the aim of the chapter has been twofold. First, we wanted to evaluate the effects of Danish incomes policies since 1974. As we have shown, the main reason for reduction in the rate of wage-inflation has been the sharp increase in unemployment in the period. One is able to trace some slight effects on wages in the years of very active incomes policies, but the main downward pressure on wages seems to come from unemployment.

The relationship between unemployment and wages has not, however, been stable over the postwar period. In 1973 the Phillips curve took a sudden jump upwards, increasing the rate of wage-inflation by some 6 percentage points. But the influence of unemployment remained unchanged. It is our hypothesis that the main explanation for this must be found in a remarkable increase in the share of unemployment that we term 'structural'. Or to put the argument differently: in order to hold wage increases to a given level, a much higher level of open unemployment is needed now than 20 years ago – mainly because a large part of the unemployed at present are not in 'effective competition' in the labour market.

There are two reasons for this. One is the large share of temporarily laid-off workers registered as unemployed. The other is the large group of the long-term and unskilled unemployed for whom demand is low – and where demand will decrease even further in the years to come. Neither of these groups is competing effectively with the core-groups in the labour market. If the demand for labour increases, bottlenecks in the markets for skilled workers will soon drive up wages – even with a high level of unemployment among the unskilled groups.

The second purpose of the chapter has been to pursue the arguments about wage formation through a discussion of 'flexibility' in the Danish labour market.

Increased wage differentiation seems not to be the answer for structural unemployment; it simply creates more unstable and short-term jobs without solving the problems of labour market segmentation.

We argue for an active labour market policy which addresses the structural employment problems without giving up the goal of income equality and the solidary wage policy. The difficulties of the 'outsider' groups in getting a stable position in the labour market must be solved by creating labour market flexibility in combination with job security.

We would argue that to reduce the level of open unemployment which is at present necessary to restrain wage-inflation, several instruments are relevant:

- institutional changes to decrease the element in unemployment caused by temporary layoffs; firms should be required to improve their planning regarding the size of the labour force;
- extensive and intensive training and education aimed at improving the qualifications of the presently long-term and unskilled unemployed (especially in the younger age-groups);
- introduction of a 'third' labour market for those unemployed who are unable to obtain the qualifications needed to compete in the normal open labour markets of the public or the private sector; this third labour market could operate with permanent wage subsidies in order to keep it functioning with low-productivity labour;
- efforts to diminish the 'scar effects' of long-term unemployment by giving firms strong incentives to hire those presently unemployed; one can point to temporary wage subsidies or use of 'job-rotation' as a condition for favourable education opportunities for those presently employed (the requirement being that the unemployed should be hired as substitutes for the employed undertaking education).

If such efforts are not undertaken – and reliance is instead put on some sort of 'incomes policy' – our prediction is that this incomes policy is bound to fail. Income policies in a market economy are not able to stand the test of reality. The only way to manipulate the general wage level is through active labour market policies that aim directly at the core mechanism of the labour market: flexibility in the demand for and supply of labour.

Appendix: The econometric analysis of a Danish Phillips curve

In this appendix the relationship between wage-inflation and unemployment is explored by simple econometric techniques. Using the yearly growth rate of hourly wages in the Danish manufacturing sector as the explained (left-hand) variable (DW), linear regression equations are estimated by standard OLS-technique using the following explanatory variables:[5]

> U: the rate of unemployment for the labour force
> $DP(-1)$: the growth rate of consumer prices in the previous year
> $DUMMY$: a variable having the value of 0 in the year 1950[6] to 1972 and the value of 1 in the period from 1973 to 1991.

Also, a constant is included on the right-hand side of each regression equation. The use of the lagged growth rate of consumer prices can partly be seen as a proxy for the formal rules for inflation compensation that was part of Danish wage-agreements until suspended by law in 1986. The $DUMMY$ variable is intended to capture the upward shift in the Phillips curve in 1973. As an alternative, estimations are made for the sub-periods of 1950-72 and 1973-91. The estimated parameters and statistical test variables are shown in table 5A.1.

Looking first at the estimated parameter for the rate of unemployment, the regression result for the whole period of 1950–91 indicates that an increase in the rate of unemployment of 1 percentage point on the average will lower the rate of growth of the hourly wage rate by 1.5 percentage points. The two sub-periods show similar results.

Furthermore, the impact of the historical rate of change of consumer prices is estimated to be about 0.6 percentage points of wage-growth for each percentage point of historical inflation measured by the lagged rate of change of consumer prices.

Finally, for the regression equation covering the whole period of 1950–91, the value of the coefficient to the variable $DUMMY$ indicates that the Phillips curve took an upward jump in 1973, increasing

Table 5A.1 Estimated parameters of Danish Phillips curves for the period 1950-91 and two sub-periods

	1950–91	1950–72	1973–91
Variable			
Constant	9.65	9.69	16.0
	(14.2)	(9.46)	(8.43)
Rate of unemployment (U)	−1.48	−1.59	−1.47
	(−10.9)	(−5.56)	(−8.93)
Lagged growth in consumer prices ($DP(-1)$)	0.62	0.66	0.59
	(7.13)	(5.08)	(4.83)
DUMMY (shifting in 1972–3)	6.20	–	–
	(6.36)		
Test-values			
R-squared (R^2)	0.86	0.76	0.91
Durbin-Watson statistic (DW)	1.72	1.93	1.55

the yearly growth rate of hourly wages by 6 percentage points. This phenomenon is also shown in the similar change in the value of the estimated constant from the first to the second sub-period.

All the t-values (in parentheses) indicate that the estimated parameters are highly significant. The R^2-values are very high also, indicating that 80–90 per cent of the historical variation in Danish wage-growth is explained by the simple equations in Table 5.4. The Durbin-Watson tests for auto-correlation are satisfactory.[7]

Notes

1. Cf. CEC, 1990, chapter 6.
2. The graphic presentations and estimations in this chapter are based on our own calculations using published data from the Ten-year Surveys of the Danish Statistical Office and from the data-bank of the largest Danish econometric model (the ADAM-model).
3. The discussion in this section is based on the econometric analysis documented in the Appendix.
4. The estimate is calculated by multiplying the observed increase in the level of unemployment with the estimated coefficient for the unemployment rate in table 5A.1 in the Appendix.
5. As is well known, the Phillips curve is usually considered to be a non-linear relation between wage-inflation and unemployment. In the present chapter, however, only results from linear formations of the Phillips curve are reported. Experiments with non-linear formations have not shown significant increases in the statistical quality of the estimates.

6. The use of the lagged rate of change in consumer prices implies that the year 1949 has to be excluded from the regression period since the ADAM databank covers only the years from 1948 and onwards.
7. As an alternative test for auto-correlation, estimates were made using the lagged rate of growth of the wage rate as explaining variable. This variable however proved to be highly insignificant.

References

Andersen, John and Larsen, Jørgen Elm (1989), *Fattigdom i velfoerdsstaten (Poverty in the welfare state)*, Samfundslitteratur, Copenhagen.
Boje, Thomas P. (1993), 'Labour Market Differentiation in a Welfare State – Illustrated by the Development in Working Time Patterns in Denmark', European University Institute, January.
Burtless, Gary (ed.) (1990), *A Future of Lousy Jobs? The Changing Structure of US Wages*, The Brookings Institution, Washington DC.
Commission of the European Communities (CEC) (1989), *Employment in Europe 1989*, Luxembourg.
___ (1990), *Employment in Europe 1990*, Luxembourg.
___ (1991), *Employment in Europe 1991*, Luxembourg.
Jensen, Peter and Westergaard-Nielsen, Niels (1988), *Temporary Layoffs*, Studies in Labour Market Dynamics, Aarhus University.
Ministry of Finance (1991), *Budgetredegørelsen 1991 (Budget Report 1991)*, Copenhagen.
Ministry of Social Services (1992), *De unge: Portoet af en generation i velfoerdsstaten (The young – a portrait of a welfare state generation)*, Copenhagen.
OECD (1989a), *Economies in Transition: Structural Adjustment in OECD Countries*, Paris.
___ (1989b), *Labour Market Flexibility: Trends in Enterprises*, Paris.
___ (1991), *Employment Outlook*, Paris.
Rosenberg, Samuel (1989), 'From Segmentation to Flexibility', *Labour and Society*, 14(4).
Scheuer, Steen (1989), 'Faglig organisering 1966 til 1987: Del II: Vaeksten i funktionaer – og servicesektoren og i saerlige grupper med lav faglig organisering' (*'Unionization from 1966 to 1987'*), *Økonomi & Politik*, 62(3).
___ (1991), *Faglige organisationsgrader i Danmark og i Vesteuropa: Hovedtendenser i 1970'erne og 1980'erne (Unionization in Denmark and Western Europe: trends in the 1970s and 1980s)*, FIU-Notat, Copenhagen.
___ (1993), 'Leaders and Laggards: Who Goes First in Bargaining Rounds?', in Boje and Olsson-Hort (eds.), *Scandinavia in a New Europe*, Scandinavia University Press, Oslo.
Standing, Guy (1988), *European Unemployment, Insecurity and Flexibility: A Social Dividend Solution*, ILO, World Employment Programme, Working Paper No. 23, Geneva.
Visser, Jelle (1991), 'Trends in Trade Union Membership' in OECD *Employment Outlook, July 1991*, pp. 97–135.

CHAPTER 6

PAY RESTRAINT WITHOUT INCOMES POLICY: INSTITUTIONALIZED MONETARISM AND INDUSTRIAL UNIONISM IN GERMANY

Wolfgang Streeck

Country statistics*

Union members as a proportion of total dependent employees
 1980 42.7% 1990 31.8%
active members only 37.4%

Public sector employees as a proportion of total employees
 1980 14.6% 1990 15.1%

Participation rates of working age population (ages 15–64)
 Men 1980 84.3% Men 1991 81.4%
 Women 1980 52.8% Women 1991 57.7%

Per capita GDP in US dollars (1993 exchange rates)
 1980 $13,310 1991 $24,435

Per capita GDP (PPP)
 1980 $10,200 1990 $18,212

Main collective bargaining institutions above the enterprise level

Interconnected industrial agreements for a small number of broadly defined industries, negotiated yearly between inclusive industrial unions and employers' associations.

There is no government incomes or pay policy in Germany, and never was, the famous *Konzertierte Aktion* in the 1960s and 1970s

* All data refer to West Germany only

Table 6.1 West German economic performance: selected indicators

	GNP real growth[a]	Productivity growth[b]	Growth in unit labour costs	Real wage growth[c]	Labour share[d]	Consumer price inflation[e]	Unemployment[f]	Current account % GNP[g]
1974	0.2	1.5	9.7	3.9	63.7	7.0	2.5	2.8
1975	−1.4	1.3	5.7	1.9	63.9	6.0	4.6	1.0
1976	5.6	5.9	1.6	2.0	62.7	4.5	4.5	0.8
1977	2.7	2.7	3.9	3.7	63.1	3.7	4.3	0.8
1978	3.3	2.2	3.2	2.7	62.5	2.7	4.1	1.4
1979	4.0	2.4	3.3	1.5	62.6	4.1	3.6	−0.7
1980	1.5	−0.5	7.2	1.4	64.3	5.5	3.6	−1.7
1981	0.0	0.3	4.5	−0.5	65.0	6.3	5.1	−0.5
1982	−1.0	0.2	4.0	−0.4	64.5	5.3	7.2	0.8
1983	1.9	3.0	0.5	0.2	62.5	3.3	8.8	0.8
1984	3.3	2.6	0.8	−0.1	61.4	2.4	8.8	1.6
1985	1.9	1.1	1.7	1.7	61.2	2.2	8.9	2.7
1986	2.3	0.8	2.8	3.8	60.9	−0.1	8.5	4.5
1987	1.6	0.7	2.4	3.9	61.1	0.2	8.5	4.1
1988	3.7	2.9	0.0	2.9	60.2	1.3	8.4	4.2
1989	3.9	1.9	0.9	1.2	58.9	2.8	7.6	4.6

Definitions and Sources:
[a] GNP real growth: *OECD Economic Outlook*, Vol. 48, December 1990, p. 175
[b] Productivity growth, unit labour costs: *Jahresgutachten 1991/92 des Sachverständigenrats zur Begutachtung der gesamtwirtschaftlichen Entwicklung*, Deutscher Bundestag, 12. Wahlperiode, Drucksache 12/1618 (18 November 1991), Table 28, p. 319, own calculations.
[c] Real wage growth: Increases in nominal earnings from non-agricultural employment (ILO, *Year Book of Labour Statistics*, 1978, 1988, 1990) corrected by changes in consumer price index (*OECD Economic Outlook. Historical Statistics, 1960-1990*, 1992).
[d] Labour share: Calculated as the labour share in National Income. Source: OECD, *National Accounts. Detailed Tables Part II*, 1978 and 1990.
[e] Consumer price inflation: see Real wage growth.
[f] Unemployment: Unemployed percentage of total workforce. *Jahresgutachten 1991/92 des Sachverständigenrats zur Begutachtung der gesamtwirtschaftlichen Entwicklung*, Deutscher Bundestag, 12. Wahlperiode, Drucksache 12/1618, (18 November 1991), Table 20, p. 308.
[g] Current account as % of GNP: For GNP: OECD, *National Accounts. Detailed Tables Part II*, 1988 and 1990. For Current Account Balance: International Monetary Fund, *International Financial Statistics Yearbook*, 1991.

notwithstanding. Still, German inflation rates are outstandingly low and always have been, with real wage growth only rarely exceeding the increase in Gross National Product (Table 6.1). Moreover, interindustry, interregional and interfirm wage differentials in Germany – leaving aside the special situation of the former GDR – are also low, and yearly wage rises do not differ dramatically between individuals, firms, regions and industries.

That there is no government incomes policy in Germany is accepted and welcomed, to varying degrees, by all participants in the wage setting process – the unions, the employers and their associations, and the government itself. The operative principle is that of *Tarifautonomie*, meaning the freedom of the 'social partners' – organized employers and organized workers – to determine wages and working conditions between themselves through independent negotiations. As with all important principles in German public life, *Tarifautonomie* is enshrined in constitutional law, and both the Constitutional Court (*Bundesverfassungsgericht*) and the Federal Labour Court have emphasized its fundamental importance in defining the role of business associations and unions, and circumscribing that of government. With respect to the latter, *Tarifautonomie* clearly and unambiguously rules out any statutory incomes policy; there cannot be legislation in Germany that would place upper or lower limits on wage increases. Also unconstitutional would be any system of mandatory arbitration run by the government or backed by public power. In fact, there is an unwritten rule in German politics that the government should refrain from even commenting on ongoing wage negotiations; that norm is, of course, more often invoked by the unions than by the employers, and sometimes it is broken by the Chancellor or the Minister of Economic Affairs, who will usually express their sympathies with the employers and warn against excessive union demands.

Tarifautonomie limitations on government intervention in wage setting apply even to public sector collective bargaining. There is practically only one wage settlement for all of the public sector in Germany, covering not just the Federal government, the *Länder* and local governments, but also the universities, the armed forces, the railways and the post office. In negotiating this mammoth industrial agreement, public employers are represented by an employers' association in which the Federal government accounts only for roughly one-third of the votes. Since at least some *Länder* are likely to be governed by a party other than that which happens to hold power at the federal level – not to mention, of course, the wide variety in the political complexion of local governments – any attempt by the Federal government to dictate the outcome of public sector negotiations will probably cause disagreement within the public sector employers' association, not least since it will not make it easier to reach agreement with the public sector unions which are even more insistent on *Tarifautonomie* than their counterparts in the private sector.

'Incomes policy' in the 1960s and 1970s

The so-called *Konzertierte Aktion* (KA) between 1967 and 1978 was widely misperceived as a tool of government-led incomes policy, and was sometimes described as a German version of neo-corporatist political exchange. Today it is generally accepted that the KA was basically a symbolic exercise, and that even as such, it was by and large a failure (Adam, 1972; Hardes, 1974).

Konzertierte Aktion was introduced by the Grand Coalition Minister of Economic Affairs, Karl Schiller, who was a social democrat. The unions participated in it only on the condition that it would not lead to official 'wage guidelines', set by the government or adopted by the *Konzertierte Aktion* as a whole. Among other things, this was because their membership and lower-level officials, some of whom were vigorously opposed to the Grand Coalition, would simply not have tolerated this. Moreover, in early 1967, under the impact of the recession and in line with projections made by the Economics Ministry, the unions had accepted long-term wage agreements with predetermined, very low yearly increments. When the economic downturn was overcome faster than expected, unions were caught in their agreements, with employers refusing to reopen negotiations. Somehow this condition came to be perceived by the rank-and-file as caused by union participation in *Konzertierte Aktion*.

The situation exploded in 1969, when a wave of unofficial strikes shortly before a critical Bundestag election enabled workers to gain unprecedented wage rises outside of formal collective bargaining. In subsequent years, the foremost concern of national union leaders was to regain control over the wage bargain and in the process redress the distributional losses their members had suffered during the recession. With the rank-and-file still restive – encouraged not just by the 1969 events but also by the change of government shortly thereafter – unions were eager to emphasize even more than before the non-binding character of KA, and to demonstrate their independence by making high wage claims. Correspondingly, the government, constrained by *Tarifautonomie* anyway, was anxious not to be seen by the unions as trying to impose official wage guidelines. So when the unions withdrew from KA in 1978,[1] nobody was ever heard complaining about a useful instrument of pay policy or wage restraint having been destroyed, or asking that it be replaced by something else.

The Bundesbank: monetarism German style

A main factor that prevented *Konzertierte Aktion* becoming a tripartite forum of politically compensated wage restraint was the autonomy of the German central bank, the Bundesbank, from the Federal government, resulting in *incomplete sovereignty* of the latter over economic policy (see Katzenstein's (1987) ingenious label for the Federal Republic of Germany, 'The Semi-Sovereign State'); in a system of *divided governance* of the economy; and, during the neo-corporatist decade, in continuing *tension between attempted corporatism and institutionally entrenched monetarism*.

In safeguarding the stability of the Deutschmark, the Bundesbank is independent from the Federal government. Decisions on the key interest rates are made exclusively by the Bundesbank board, which sometimes listens to the advice of the Finance Minister or the Chancellor and sometimes does not even solicit it. The Bundesbank never considered *Konzertierte Aktion* as a viable or acceptable instrument of pay policy (on the following see Scharpf, 1991, pp. 117ff.). To the contrary, the strikes in 1969 that the KA had not prevented, and the change in the same year to a social-liberal government suspect of economic permissiveness convinced the bank that other than accommodative methods were required to bring inflation down to an acceptably low level and keep it there.

In the years immediately after 1969, West German inflation rates were unprecedentedly high. In the view of the Bundesbank, a contributing factor was the unions' 'redistributive offensive' (Scharpf, 1991, p. 135) in the aftermath of the unofficial strikes, and the expensive spending programmes of the newly elected social-liberal Federal government. In 1973, with the domestic battle against inflation still raging, the oil crisis added further inflationary pressures. Shortly thereafter, the wage negotiations in early 1974 were to become a formative event for the conduct of German industrial relations and economic policy.

Wage settlements in 1974 were around 12 per cent, which was widely considered excessive. For the first time, the wage round was led, not by the metalworkers, but by the public sector union, ÖTV, whose members have high job security and are sheltered from world market competition. During the negotiations the Chancellor, Willy Brandt, against the spirit of *Tarifautonomie*, tried to use the public sector as a tool for a national incomes policy, by publicly stating that a settlement above 'a one-digit figure' was unacceptable. When after a crippling nationwide strike the public sector gained a pay rise of 12 per cent, the Chancellor's authority was severely weakened, contributing to his resignation a few months later.

For the Bundesbank, the events proved conclusively that the unions could not be trusted and that the government could not be counted upon to keep them under control (Scharpf, 1991, pp. 129ff.). In late 1974, therefore, the bank began to apply a strategy of wage restraint that it could pursue relying exclusively on its own powers. The new approach amounted to a German version of monetarism, one that not only preceded the 'Thatcher revolution' by almost a decade but was also more effective. For every year from 1974 on, the bank would unilaterally announce a targeted rate of growth in the money supply and publicly commit itself to using all its instruments to prevent that rate being exceeded, *whatever the consequences*. Allowable increases would equal 'the expected growth of real productive potential, including unavoidable inflation', a measure that had originally been proposed by the Council of Economic Advisors (Scharpf, 1991, p. 137). It is important to emphasize that the bank considers its target to be non-negotiable, either with the Federal government or with anybody else. Indeed it is precisely the policy's credibly established non-negotiability – and the implied rejection of any trade-off with other objectives, in particular full employment – which is regarded by the bank as its most important condition of success.

The impact on German industrial relations was profound. The powers of the Bundesbank being what they are, after 1974 the Federal government found itself relieved, or deprived, of the 'Keynesian' dilemma between accommodating or not accommodating overshooting wage settlements. Moreover, the unions knew that, as far as monetary policies were concerned, they were dealing with a government – that is, the Bundesbank – that was not subject to electoral pressures and could not therefore be bound to a political full employment guarantee. Not having to be concerned about unemployment, that government was unwilling to compensate unions for wage moderation; if unions chose to settle above the rate of potential growth, it was for them to live with the consequences. By making its monetary target public, the bank left no doubt what these consequences would be, and that was as much as it was prepared to do for the unions.[2]

German unions were *de facto* dealing with a monetarist government already by the mid-1970s and in spite of the accession to power of the Social Democrats. German monetarism was not infallible, and certainly the unions never believed it was.[3] Union experts continued to quarrel with the technicalities of the Bundesbank's macro-economics, and above all insisted that there were other factors in addition to excessive wage settlements that could cause unemployment under the bank's new approach. All of this, however, did not change the fact that from the mid-1970s on, with a Federal government unable or unwilling to use fiscal policy to counteract the Bundesbank's monetary policy, the pursuit of monetary stability in Germany had become effectively insulated from political counter-pressures, and had become free to proceed regardless of its impact on other economic objectives such as growth or employment.

Industrial unionism: interconnected industry-wide wage setting

To understand fully the effectiveness of the Bundesbank's stabilization policy, one has to take into account the organizational and institutional dynamics of industrial unionism and industrywide pay bargaining. 'Voluntary' wage restraint in the face of hard monetarism is most likely where collective bargaining is centralized and unions have strong organizational capacities at national level.[4] Structures of this kind force unions to internalize the effects of excessive wage increases, while enabling them to constrain irresponsible behaviour of groups of members with above-average bargaining power. German unions and collective bargaining, although on the surface sectorally rather than nationally based, have an encompassing *corporatist structure* that happened to mesh well with the *constitutionalized monetarism* of German economic policy in making possible *uncompensated yet self-interested wage moderation* on the part of unions.

That German unionism and collective bargaining are in fact encompassing is not a moot point. Much of the literature (e.g., Scharpf, 1991, p. 199) tends to classify German industrial relations as only intermediately centralized, in light of the fact that bargaining is sectoral; the main union federation, the DGB, has no authority over it; and there are three national federations rather then just one. Closer inspection, however, reveals much higher cohesion and coordination than the formal structure suggests. While the DGB consists of 17 industrial unions, most of these do not independently bargain. Five unions take part in negotiating the general agreement for the public sector. A number of others are too small, and their industries too insignificant, to make a difference. It is only very few unions, above all the metalworkers (IGMetall or IGM), the chemical workers and the construction workers that, together with the leading public sector union, ÖTV, have the capacity to be significant independent wage bargainers.

Also, while it is true that the DGB has no power to coordinate its affiliates' bargaining strategies and behaviour, there is a strong functional equivalent to authoritative coordination, in the form of long-established *wage leadership* by the largest and most powerful union, IGM. In almost all yearly 'wage rounds' since the formation of the present collective bargaining system in the 1950s,[5] it was this union that was the first to set its demands, negotiate, go on strike if necessary, and settle. The others followed suit and, apart from marginal variations on the edges, faithfully transferred the metal agreement to their sectors.

The reason for this lies in the organizational structure and the sectoral conditions of both IGM and its potential rivals for wage leadership. IGM is huge, comprising both metal engineering in its entirety and steelmaking. Its membership amounts to more than one-third of all unionized workers in Germany. Moreover, IGM has been through more successful strikes than any other German union, making it reasonable for the others to expect it to set the best possible precedent for them. Note that strikes in the public sector are easy to organize but unpopular; strikes in construction, if they have to have an effect for the entire industry, are difficult to organize; and strikes in chemicals tend to be unpopular with the membership. And while, for example, the textile workers' union would often prefer lower wage settlements, to protect employment in its industry, its members will not do with less than the 'going rate' (Swenson, 1989).

In short, other unions usually follow IGM because they lack the capacity to settle higher while being unable to afford settling lower. Moreover, given the wide variety of conditions within sectors as broadly defined as those organized by German unions, a national 'going rate' established by the largest union offers itself as a convenient wage norm for industrial unions torn between segments of their membership with high bargaining power and others preferring a lower settlement to safeguard employment. Industrial unions can maintain their organizational cohesion only if they manage to avoid internal battles over relativities. They therefore require a *uniform settlement for their entire sector.* Acceptance of wage leadership is an important way of relieving industrial unions' political process from the quandaries of setting their own wage targets.[6]

This, of course, raises the question how IGM determines its wage demands and level of settlement. Three points are important here:

1. The industrial sector represented by IGM is larger and more heterogeneous than that of any other DGB union. In setting its bargaining

targets, the leadership has to take into account widely different sub-sectoral conditions and employer abilities to pay. It also knows that other sectors are likely to follow its lead, and that the employment of its members depends to a large part on the propensity of businesses in these sectors to invest. IGM is thus *forced by self-interest* to conceive its collective bargaining strategies in a macroeconomic context. Indeed in defending its wage demands, IGM typically refers to the conditions, not just in the metal sector, but in the entire economy.[7]

2. Unlike the public sector, workers in the metal industry do face a risk of unemployment resulting from monetary constraints. Unemployment may also result because the German metalworking sector is exposed to strong international competition in foreign as well as domestic markets; for example, more than two-thirds of the cars built in Germany are exported. Just as the Bundesbank's non-negotiable tight money policy, the international exposure of its industries forces IGM to moderate its wage demands, especially since as an industrial union it cannot hope to divert unemployment in its sector to members of other unions or workers in non-unionized firms.

3. While there are strong pressures on IGM to be macro-economically 'responsible', overshooting does occur, sometimes because the economic situation is misread, and sometimes because the union's internal politics result in a wage settlement in excess of what the leadership might have preferred. IGM's wage demands are set in a long internal discussion process involving a large part of the membership. The result may not always be moderate, especially since IGM has never renounced the idea that wage bargaining should contain a redistributive component. Occasionally, the leadership is forced by the rank-and-file to take that claim seriously.[8]

German unions, and IGM in particular, are well aware of the precariousness of their organizational capacity to contain rank-and-file wage pressures within the limits set by Bundesbank monetarism. It was in the face of rising unemployment in the 1980s that unions increasingly complemented their wage demands with a wide array of other, 'qualitative' demands, *potentially enabling them to trade-off the former against the latter*. As early as the late 1970s, IGM made reduction of working hours its main policy, the objective being to reduce unemployment through work sharing. While the membership remained unwilling to accept an absolute decline in their incomes, insisting on wage increases for their reduced working time that were high enough to keep take-home pay constant, the gradual implementation of working time reduction in the 1980s and its implicit coupling to productivity increases took much of the heat out of wage bargaining. As usual, other unions followed IGM's lead, implicitly endorsing for a number of difficult years an alternative pay formula designed to prevent unemployment from being further driven up by a collision between union strength under *Tarifautonomie* and a *de facto* monetarist government.[9]

Summing up, the remarkable uniformity of wage settlements in Germany is not primarily the result of unions and employers being committed to norms of 'fair pay'. While German wage bargaining does follow an *implicit principle* that intra- and inter-sectoral wage differentials should not be allowed to change dramatically, that principle is not established by experts in government-appointed commissions, nor is adherence to it the outcome of a moral discourse on distributive justice. While it is true that largely identical wage rises for everybody are sometimes defended with reference to the egalitarian norm that nobody should fall drastically behind, the reason why there are so few defections from that norm is not primarily that it is viewed as morally compelling. Even where it is not, for actors constrained and enabled by an institutional structure like the German one, roughly identical settlements that make the wage structure highly inert correspond to strong political and organizational imperatives.

Wage drift: co-determination as safety valve

Up to now, I have accounted for the willingness of German industrial unions to take the Bundesbank's announced money targets seriously; settle for macroeconomically responsible wage increases; and do so simultaneously and uniformly, following the lead of IGM. What still needs to be explained is why national union leaders are in fact able to impose identical wage settlements on their highly heterogeneous 'industries', and why union workplace organizations seem to content themselves with what is in practice a national wage bargain unresponsive to their inevitably widely divergent economic conditions and interests.

More specifically, there are two separate problems here. Industrial unions need a capacity to impose uniform wage increases on marginal firms that may not be able to pay them, and on workers in these firms that must be afraid of undifferentiated wage raises endangering their employment. At the same time, they must be able to prevent their members in prosperous firms and sub-sectors from seeking additional wage increases above the industrywide settlement, from employers whose ability to pay is as high as their interest in uninterrupted operation in favourable market conditions is strong. As to workers in marginal firms, German industrial unions remain convinced that workers should not subsidize with lower wages an employer that is unable to operate profitably at a high wage level. This is seen as an important reason why industrial unions are preferable to company unions, which cannot afford to distance themselves from the fate of individual employers. To the extent that industrywide wage increases do result in unemployment on the margins, a union like IGM believes that it is the task of public labour market policy to train and retrain displaced workers and help them find new and more productive jobs. Rigid wage bargains combined with good public policy are regarded as a 'productivity whip' increasing the economy's overall performance and thereby underwriting, as it were *ex post*, 'redistributive', i.e., initially too high, wage settlements.

While high unemployment has made it more difficult in the early 1980s, and especially after unification, to stick to these principles, it has hardly relieved the equally complicated problems of preventing wage drift in above-average firms. Unions urgently need such firms inside industrywide bargaining units since their presence adds to labour's aggregate bargaining power. At the same time, there are strong temptations for workers in prosperous firms to seek their own wage bargains, using their full bargaining power for themselves without having to share it with workers in weaker firms or moderating their demands to enable such firms to survive. This is reflected in what sometimes appears an almost paranoid vigilance on the part of industrial union officials against any sign of incipient sub-sectoral separatism, and in a permanent preparedness to act ruthlessly to suppress it (Streeck, 1984).

German industrial union leaders have been spectacularly successful in preventing their members with high bargaining power from seceding. In part, this is because employers in prosperous firms have no interest in cultivating breakaway unions formed to seek higher-than-average wage increases. Being members of their employers' association, they are bound by the industrial agreement negotiated on their behalf. If they sign a separate agreement, the association will expel them. The only way for a breakaway union to get an agreement would be to organize a strike powerful enough to make the employer resign from the employers' association and cease dealing with the industrial union. Such a strike would have to be won against the resistance and the resources of not just one employer, but of the employers' association as a whole. It goes almost without saying that leaders of a breakaway strike against an employer covered by an industrial agreement would be expelled from the union; that strikers would receive no strike support; and that the union would withhold legal protection from them. No such strike has ever been attempted.

The most effective mechanism containing centrifugal tendencies in German industrial unions, however, is plant-level *co-determination* and its core institution, the *works council* (Streeck, 1992; Thelen, 1992; Turner, 1992). In Germany, organizational support for unions during the neo-corporatist 1970s was provided mainly in the form of expansion of co-determination. Co-determination legislation responded to the shopfloor unrest at the end of the preceding decade by offering workers a channel at the workplace for airing grievances and influencing managerial decisions on technology, work organization, training, restructuring, hiring and firing, etc. To this extent, co-determination relieved national unions and centralized collective bargaining of potentially explosive 'qualitative' matter that might have been difficult or impossible to address centrally.

Also, in keeping with a tradition that went back as far as the Weimar Republic, wage bargaining remained excluded from the jurisdiction of co-determination, confirming the monopoly of industrial unions over wage setting and the strike. In subsequent years, unions and employers' associations learned to use co-determination as an outlet for local discontent with a potentially overcentralized bargaining system, devolving to works councils and individual employers circumscribed rights to modify central agreements on non-wage matters in line with local conditions, without weakening central authority over the wage bargain. Co-determination thus contributed to the extraordinary stability of industrial unionism and sectoral collective bargaining in Germany at a time of increasingly heterogeneous workplace conditions.

In particular, co-determination and the works council system supported in at least two ways the integrity of sectoral industrial agreements. As the rights and resources of works councils were expanded, union workplace organizations increasingly moved into and merged with the works council system. With industrial unions regularly winning about 80 per cent of the seats in works council elections, works councils, while formally union-independent and based in law, became the chosen organizational form of the union at the workplace. Once incorporated in this way, workplace unions became, not legally but for all practical purposes, subject to the general prohibition on works councils negotiating wages and calling strikes.

In addition, however, works councils in prosperous firms make industrywide wage agreements stick by circumventing them. While there are *de facto* no independent union workplace organizations in German firms that could generate wage drift legally, there are works councils that can do so, strictly speaking, illegally. Where the gap between an employer's ability to pay and the industrial agreement is very high, works councils will sometimes ask for additional bonuses, upgrading of specific categories of jobs or workers or the like. Such demands may be backed by signals that in the absence of, formally unilateral, concessions the council will exercise its legal co-determination rights in ways highly uncomfortable to the employer. While this is certainly not legal, it is difficult if not impossible to prevent with legal means. To the extent that the employer gives in, wage drift results. At the same time, since works council demands for additional pay cannot be backed by a strike threat, such wage drift remains moderate. And since it is produced tacitly and is difficult to observe, it does not or only rarely give rise to comparability claims and as a consequence saves the face of the industrial agreement.

Wage drift of this kind is *not* dysfunctional for industrywide collective bargaining, but to the contrary supports it. Moderate wage drift, as generated under co-determination, reduces dissatisfaction with central regulation, and thereby contributes to its legitimacy. Slightly deviant local implementation of an egalitarian wage bargain may thus serve egalitarian objectives better than a more rigid regime that might give rise to potentially destructive discontent. *Nota bene* that wage drift in Germany has declined in the period of high unemployment in the 1980s,[10] not least apparently as a result of industrial union policies focusing on qualitative matters and in particular on reduction of working time – keeping works councils busy negotiating the details of complex work organization and working time regimes and making them expend their limited bargaining power on issues other than wage increases in excess of the industrial agreement.

Economic performance

By the mid-1980s, after several years of struggle with the aftereffects of the second oil shock, West Germany's institutionalized monetarism, supported by the wage restraint built into industrial unionism and encompassing collective bargaining, had virtually eliminated inflation (Table 6.1). Simultaneously, a current account surplus was reached that for several years exceeded 4 per cent of the Gross National Product, higher than at any time since the early 1970s. While real growth and overall productivity increases were modest, the former reflected low population growth, declining participation rates and considerable reductions in working hours, whereas the latter was associated with a high absolute level of productivity, as evidenced by West Germany's outstanding export performance in spite of comparatively very high wages.[11]

In its pursuit of zero-inflation the Bundesbank was helped by low real wage growth. In 10 of the 15 years from 1975 to 1989, real wages grew less than the economy as a whole, contributing to a fall in the labour share to an unprecedented low. Unit labour costs also rose only slowly, especially after 1982 when unions re-directed their primary attention from wage increases to reductions in working time. Nevertheless, unemployment stabilized at between 8 and 9 per cent of the labour force for most of the 1980s. High unemployment thus became the characteristic weak spot in West German economic performance, persisting in spite of very low inflation, a positive current account balance, continuing success in international markets, and radical redistribution of income in favour of capital.

Could West German unions have increased employment by lowering their wage demands? Between 1974 and the onset of high unemployment in 1982, real wage growth exceeded economic growth in no more than three years, 1975, 1977 and 1982 (when wages declined at a slightly lower rate than the GDP).[12] As Scharpf has noted (1991, p. 138), Bundesbank-style monetarism may result in unemployment even if unions strictly observe the limits for wage increases set by the growth potential of the economy and the bank's corresponding monetary targets. But while it would be difficult to attribute West German unemployment in the 1980s to excessive yearly wage *increments*, the *high level* and, in particular, the comparatively *flat structure* of wages in West Germany may be a different matter. To the extent that especially the latter reflects the same organizational imperatives for industrial unionism under centralized collective bargaining as does sensitivity to monetarist government policies, the German syndrome in the 1980s of low inflation, high external competitiveness and high and stable unemployment may have been more than just accidental.

To the extent that German unemployment in the 1980s was caused by a high-wage regime that intentionally curtailed employment opportunities for unskilled workers by keeping wage differentials narrow,[13] it confronted the unions with a painful dilemma. Unemployment might in the short run have been reduced by a new union wage policy allowing for significantly more differentiation between skill groups, firms and industries.[14] However, any such policy would have severely tested the intra- and inter-organizational cohesion of industrial unions, and would have required an extremely difficult search with uncertain success for a new pay formula capable of ensuring orderly wage setting under *Tarifautonomie*. Moreover, greater wage differentiation would have weakened the economic constraints on German employers that had in the past contributed to making them invest in workforce training, product development and social consensus, and would have reopened for a growing number of firms especially small firms the opportunity to survive and prosper as low-wage and low-skill producers. Such relaxation of the wage regime on its margins might then have caused erosion in its core, with low-wage competition threatening the short-term viability of high-wage producers and confronting them with a permanent temptation to defect from economically virtuous strategies of upmarket production.

Refusing to yield to growing pressures to abandon their traditional policies of high wages and low wage differentiation, West German unions in the 1980s tried to fight unemployment through a combination of working time reduction, pressures on employers to train even more, and demands for an active labour market policy by the government and the unemployment insurance fund aimed at moving the unemployed up to a skill level that would allow them to share in the existing opportunities for high-wage employment. As the statistics show, this was at most partly successful.[15] While more or less effectively defending both the relative flatness of the West German wage structure and their own organizational stability, already before unification German unions were puzzled by the political and moral problem of how much unemployment they could ask the workforce to bear, in defence of high wages and an egalitarian wage structure for those lucky enough to have found employment in ever more demanding workplaces.

Future prospects

Will Germany continue to enjoy the benefits of low inflation, a relatively egalitarian wage structure and orderly collective bargaining in spite of and in combination with *Tarifautonomie* and without a government pay policy? The high performance of the West German economy before unification was supported by a complex set of fortuitously balanced institutions and policies, partly complementing and partly constraining each other, and more often than not generating their beneficial outcomes unintentionally or as a result of conflict, contestation and compromise. Throughout its existence, this 'German system' – the autonomy of the Bundesbank, the inclusiveness of industrial unions and sectoral collective bargaining, the 'social partnership' between business and labour, the abstention of government from direct intervention, the involvement of workers and unions in management through co-determination – has been under pressures to change, from dissatisfied constituencies as well as newly emerging contingencies.

And, indeed, change was continuous. Historically, what may with hindsight appear as a well-designed and finely tuned set of integrated institutions was always in flux, underwent permanent transformation with uncertain event, and required for its adaptive survival risky decisions of skilful leaders. It is true that the system's basic parameters were preserved. Yet the challenges, from the first lockout in 1962 to the strike more than three decades later in the East German metal sector, were formidable.[16] Far from being guaranteed, the survival of the system depended in critical moments on the *fortunes* of organizations and individuals, constrained as well as enabled in their actions by past experience and its institutional sediments. While prudent leadership was somehow always supplied, although sometimes only at the last minute, this need not be so forever. On the other hand, given past performance, there is no reason to be categorically pessimistic about the system's ability to continue its balancing act along its established evolutionary path.

Today industrial relations in all developed industrial economies have come under strong pressures for decentralization. However, such pressures play themselves out differently in different settings, depending on the institutions that are already in place. In Germany, co-determination at the plant and enterprise level, and its intersection with industrial unionism and sectoral collective bargaining, has provided an institutional infrastructure for a version of decentralization that was *centrally coordinated* (Thelen, 1992). While extending the role of local negotiators and bargaining arenas, coordinated centralization does not destroy, and indeed arguably reinforces, the capacity of central agents to influence local events, through devolution of competence and subject matter; more pronounced differentiation between wage bargaining and qualitative bargaining; mandates for lower-level bargainers to implement central agreements; and centrally circumscribed discretion for local agents in doing so.

This, however, was before unification. Since 1989, new pressures for decentralization have built up, posing problems of institutional adaptation that are without precedent and seem to become more rather than less severe as time passes. Originally unification was perceived as nothing more than a transfer of West German institutions to the East and the united country as a whole, *without such institutions being importantly affected or modified in the process*. Unions, employers' associations and the government agreed early and without visible controversy to work together in extending co-determination and industrywide collective bargaining to the 'new *Länder*'. Works councils were set up, employers' associations were founded, the West German unions recruited members in the East, bargaining districts were established, and industrial agreements were signed as part of the West German yearly wage round. Neither the conservative government nor the employers attempted to use the opening offered by unification to attack the position the unions had gained for themselves and their members in the West German system; if anybody ever felt a temptation to build East Germany into a 'free enterprise zone' with a large non-union sector and low-skill, low-wage production, this was certainly never proposed in public.

In fact, on the surface at least there was consensus among all parties that any development of this kind had to be avoided and jointly prevented. The first industrial agreements for the Eastern part of the country, negotiated as usual under the leadership of IGM, provided for pre-established, rapid yearly wage increases designed to bring wages in the former GDR up to the West German standard within a few years. While the agreements recognized that productivity, and to some extent the costs of living, in the East were below West German levels – and as a consequence allowed for a considerable initial wage differential – East German wages were from the beginning expressed as a percentage of West German wages, providing a measuring rod by which to gauge progress towards equalization.

Three years later, it has become apparent that the easy consensus of the time of unification was premised on unrealistically optimistic assumptions on the economic prospects of the new *Länder*. Unemployment in East Germany remains high and is still rising; investment is far lower than projected; and productivity has not even begun to approximate the Western part of the country. Today it is understood that the East will, well into the next century, require gigantic injections of public funds. As a consequence, strong pressures have begun to converge on the unions to reconsider their demand for rapid wage equalization, with employers and the government demanding a revision of the escalator clauses in East German industrial agreements. In addition, employers in particular have called for 'opening clauses' to be included in industrial agreements in the new *Länder* under which individual employers may, with the consent of their workforce or their works council, pay their workers below the industrial agreement if this helps them keep their plant or firm in business and protect the employment of the existing workforce.

For the unions pressures like these have become increasingly difficult to resist. Since the costs of unemployment in the East are picked up by the West German taxpayer, a high-wage union policy that may contribute to unemployment is bound to be unpopular. Indeed it may be less than welcome even to the workers in the East who ostensibly are to benefit from it. Where employers can convince their workers that their firms, and the jobs they offer, can survive only if they are allowed to pay lower wages matching lower productivity, unions may find it hard to convince their newly recruited members of the merits of industrywide wage setting. It was knowing these mounting internal difficulties that Gesamtmetall, the national employers' association for the metalworking sector, stated its intention in the early phases of the 1993 wage round no longer to honour the escalator agreements on wage equalization in the new *Länder*, for the first time ever breaking an industrial agreement and leaving IGM no choice but to call what was perhaps the riskiest strike in its history.

IGM and the unions that follow its lead would probably have been quite willing to agree to an extension of the deadline for wage equalization, although this would have met with resistance from those of their members in the East that are safely employed and are now doing the same work as their much better paid Western counterparts. In fact, unions were likely to accept deferment if only to defuse the pressure for opening clauses. While a change in the equalization calendar is a temporary device that does not affect the wage setting system as such, the 'flexibility' introduced by opening clauses could be difficult to retract later, and may in the longer term be impossible to confine to the Eastern part of the country. In early 1993, fears like these could find themselves confirmed by the rhetoric that accompanied employer demands for what would essentially have been downward flexibility in wage setting for individual firms – a rhetoric that emphasized the alleged competitive disadvantages caused by 'rigid standardization', and the specificity of the conditions of firms and plants that was claimed to require tailor-made wage regimes locally negotiated between the individual employer and 'his' workforce.

To understand the sense of alarm with which German unions observed the emerging discussion, one must know that opening clauses are not a new invention. Ironically, the concept was first used in the 1960s by militant factions inside IGM representing, essentially, workers in prosperous sub-sectors and firms. For them, opening clauses were to offer works councils, or preferably workplace unions, an opportunity to start a 'second wage round' after the conclusion of the industrial agreement, enabling them to get closer to their employers' above-average ability to pay and bring wage drift under the control of binding collective contracts. National union leaders successfully resisted these demands, with the tacit and less-than-tacit support of employers' associations, arguing that opening clauses would make the wage setting process ungovernable, undermine the role of industrial unions, weaken the interest of workers in prosperous firms in the outcome of industry-wide negotiations, and thus result in lower industrial settlements and higher wage differentials between firms. Later, in the 1970s and 1980s, unions and employers' associations used opening clauses in industrial agreements to delegate qualitative matter to negotiations between works councils and employers under the ground rules of co-determination; wages, however, remained excluded, and one reason why opening clauses were introduced on a large scale was precisely to divert the attention of shopfloor militants from wages to other, macroeconomically less precarious subjects.

Present concerns of unions over opening clauses allowing downward wage flexibility are the same as those that made unions resist upward flexibility in the 1960s. While the IGM leaders had warned their members that employers would use opening clauses to demand lower wages in marginal or badly managed firms, they now remind employers of the possibility that opening clauses could in favourable conditions be used by militant shopfloor activists to win wage rises above the industrial agreement level. Either way, the result would be a loss of control of unions and employers' associations over the wage bargain; a 'Balkanization' of labour markets; higher interfirm wage differentials; and a focusing of worker interests on their present place of employment, as a source either of aggressively negotiated above-average wages or of precarious employment.

Resistance to 'flexibility' and 'reasonable' local wage cuts ostensibly demanded to protect employment in East Germany is difficult for German unions to sell in the present economic crisis. One way in which IGM tried to contain employer enthusiasm for opening clauses was to demand that before a wage reduction can be agreed, a firm has to open its books and show that no other method is available to preserve jobs. If the crisis in the East continues, however, unions may have to retreat and limit themselves to seeking guarantees that opening clauses will be discontinued after a certain time, and will not be transferred to West Germany. Whether they will succeed in this may well be the most important question in German industrial relations in coming years[17].

Opening up industrial agreements to allow for more differentiation of wages in line with the economic performance of firms and the bargaining power of their workforces would introduce fundamental change in German industrial relations and wage setting. Similar to what happened in many other countries in the 1980s, opening clauses as demanded by the employers would reduce the hold of institutional governance over the German labour market and would expose wages, employment and unions much more than before to market pressures. Not only would the wage spread increase, but for the first time there might develop a substantial low-wage and low-skill sector in the German economy. The pressures for this are strong, and are caused not just by the crisis in the new *Länder*, but also by unabating immigration, East European labour market competition, and the defeat of the 'Social Dimension' of the European Community at the hands of European business and the British government. Ultimately they may be irresistible. At this point, German governments may finally have to embark on the, very probably futile, search for a public incomes policy to replace and succeed *Tarifautonomie*.

Notes

1. In response to the employers taking the 1976 Co-Determination Law to the Constitutional Court. Employers knew both that their prospects of prevailing there were poor, and that it would be impossible for the unions to continue with *Konzertierte Aktion* if the employers went to the court. Nevertheless, by doing this they showed how little importance they attached to the KA.
2. 'Thus union economists were right when they criticized the Bundesbank's new concept as reprivatizing the risk of unemployment . . . That was its whole point' (Scharpf, 1991, p. 138)
3. As Marsh (1992, pp. 345ff.) shows, of the 17 years from 1975 to 1991, the bank's monetary target was met in only nine, and was missed by more than one percentage point in no fewer than five.
4. Centralization of collective bargaining requires also strong employers associations interested in and capable of taking wages out of competition. In Germany, employers associations are almost as encompassing as the unions with which they negotiate, and historically they have shown remarkable cohesion in spite of frequent internal dissent on wage policy.
5. Most industrial agreements have a currency of about one year, and are timed to run out in the spring which is considered the best season for unions to go on strike. Synchronization of collective bargaining is not formally institutionalized, and sometimes unions have tried to move bargaining in their industry to the autumn. All of them have, however, returned to the flock, for the same reasons that make them accept IGM wage leadership.
6. Another factor is that IGM does not take it easily if smaller unions try to outdo it. Sometimes at least the appearance of identical settlements is

preserved by unions and employers in 'deviant' sectors hiding above-average settlements in the technicalities of their, very complex, industrial agreement. Generally, however, the most important factor is that no single union is both small enough macroeconomically and strong enough industrially to be an effective 'free rider' on IGM's leadership.

7. Information on macroeconomic prospects is provided by a variety of sources in Germany, above all the Council of Economic Advisers (*Sachverständigenrat zur Begutachtung der gesamtwirtschaftlichen Entwicklung*), a number of research institutes that together issue a yearly economic forecast, the regular reports of the Bundesbank, the research departments of the leading banks, etc. The major unions in addition have sizeable research departments. The *Konzertierte Aktion* did not add much to this, which was one reason why it could so easily be abandoned. It is generally understood in Germany that numbers cannot be completely accurate, that they may be politically biased, and that the best predictions may be overturned by events. No single assessment is therefore taken as gospel. Together, however, they more or less reliably describe a funnel of possible trajectories within which union leaders usually want to situate their policies, 'kept honest' although not infallible by the effective responsibility bestowed on them by the large size of their bargaining units.

8. While normally IGM is willing to settle for a wage increase that amounts to the expected increase in productivity (by and large for the manufacturing sector as a whole) plus the expected rate of inflation, in some years it adds to this a so-called 'redistribution factor' (*Umverteilungsfaktor*) from capital to labour, to make good for a conjunctural decline in the labour share or generally to increase the labour share.

9. Other 'qualitative' issues in the 1970s and 1980s that helped defuse the tensions and dilemmas of free collective wage bargaining under non-negotiable monetary targets were work organization – or 'humanization of work' – training and retraining, employment protection, and redeployment of workers. That unions turned these into prominent subjects of collective bargaining served not just to help them contain wage settlements at a level where unemployment did not undermine their power and legitimacy; it also redirected industrial relations to production issues and thereby made them contribute to the restructuring of the German economy.

10. In the 1980s yearly increases in negotiated and actual hourly earnings differed usually by less than one half of a percentage point, with the former in some years exceeding the latter (Sachverständigenrat, 1991, p. 103). As a consequence, absolute differences between negotiated and actual earnings remained constant or declined slightly; reliable data on these are hard to find. Overtime in Germany is low by Anglo-American standards, and its use declined in the years before unification as a result of union efforts to make cuts in working hours stick.

11. Throughout the 1980s, West Germany, Japan and the United States each accounted for about 18 per cent of total exports from OECD countries, with Japan's population being twice as large as West Germany's, and the population of the United States being twice that of Japan.

12. Note that in 1984, the year of the successful six-week strike by the metal-

workers for reduction of working hours, real wages remained constant in spite of 3.3 per cent growth in the economy (Table 6.1).
13. Stalling growth in industries that depend on low wages, especially in the service sector. See the low level of employment in Germany in private services, as compared to the still extraordinarily high employment share of manufacturing.
14. Although this would appear far from certain. Compare Britain, where declining wages and rising wage differentiation in the 1980s, and explosive growth in low-wage and low-skill employment, went together with a level of unemployment that was consistently higher than in Germany – not to mention lower international competitiveness as well as higher inflation rates.
15. Determining the reasons for this goes beyond the scope of this chapter. To the extent that they may point to inherent limits of an upgrading response to industrial change, in the capacity both of individuals to adjust to ever growing skill demands and of markets to absorb ever more quality-competitive products, the matter raises fundamental strategic questions especially for unions and the social-democratic left.
16. Other crises include the recession in 1966–7, the Grand Coalition, the strike waves of 1969 and 1973, the high inflation between 1970 and 1973, the attempted Keynsianism of the Brandt and Schmidt governments, the co-determination legislation of 1972 and 1976, high unemployment throughout the 1980s, the strike for reduction of working hours in 1984, subsequent attempts by the government to limit unions' strike capacity by changes in the unemployment insurance system, the 1992 strike in the public sector, etc..

References

Adam, H. (1972), *Die Konzertierte Aktion in der Bundesrepublik*, Bund Verlag, Cologne.
Hardes, H.-D. (1974), *Einkooemnspolitik in der BRD. Stabilität und Gruppeninteressen: Der Fall Konzertierte Aktion*, Herder, Frankfurt.
Katzenstein, P. J. (1987), *Policy and Politics in West Germany: The Growth of a Semisovereign State*, Temple University Press, Philadelphia.
Marsh, D. (1992), *The Bundesbank: The Bank That Rules Europe*, Mandarin Paperback, London.
Sachverständigenrat zur Begutachtung der gesamtwirtschaftlichen Entwicklung (1991), *Jahresgutachten 1991/92*, Deutscher Bundestag, 12. Wahlperiode, Drucksache 12/1618 (18 November 1991).
Scharpf, F. W. (1991), *Crisis and Choice in European Social Democracy*, Cornell University Press, Ithaca, NY.
Streeck, W. (1984), *Industrial Relations in West Germany: The Case of the Car Industry*, Heinemann, London, St. Martin's Press, New York.
___ (1992), 'Co-Determination: After Four Decades', in idem, *Social Institutions and Economic Performance: Studies of Industrial Relations in Advanced Capitalist Economies*, Sage, London and Beverly Hills, pp. 137–68.

Swenson, P. (1989), *Fair Shares: Unions, Pay and Politics in Sweden and West Germany*, Cornell University Press, Ithaca, NY.
Thelen, K. (1992), *Union of Parts: Labor Politics in Postwar Germany*, Cornell University Press, Ithaca, NY.
Turner, L. (1992), *Democracy at Work: Changing World Markets and the Future of Labor Unions*, Cornell University Press, Ithaca, NY.

CHAPTER 7

CORPORATISM AND INCOMES POLICY IN AUSTRIA – EXPERIENCES AND PERSPECTIVES

Alois Guger and Wolfgang Polt

Country Statistics

Union members as a proportion of total dependent employees
  1980   58.5%   1990   57.1%

Public sector employees as a proportion of total employees
  1980   17.3%   1991   20.5%

Participation rates of working age population (aged 15–64)
  Men 1980   81.3%   Men   1990   80.1%
  Women 1980   48.7%   Women   1990   55.4%

Per capita GDP in US dollars (1993 exchange rates)
  1980 $10,184   1991 $20,958

Per capita GDP in PPP's
  1980 $8,664   1991 $17,280

Main collective bargaining institutions above the enterprise level

In Austria, wage bargaining is embedded in the institution of social partnership which is a system of permanent, voluntary and informal cooperation between labour, business, and government on virtually all aspects of economic policy. Wage policy is thus coordinated with fiscal and monetary policy.

Although there is no national wage round in Austria the bargaining process is highly centralized; in part this is due to the fact that both employers' and employees' organizations are highly centralized, but also there is a *de facto* wage leader, the Metal Workers Union. The degree of organization is high on both sides: membership of the chamber of labour and business is compulsory and about 60 per cent of the employees are trade union members.

Although the bargaining structures have by and large been stable in the eighties, there is less coordination between the social partners and government policy today than in 1980.

An exception to social deregulation

The 1980s has been a period of widespread reappearance of market solutions. Deregulation has been the key-word and corporatist institutions have become suspect among economists as well as politicians. This holds true especially for incomes policies, which have been replaced in many countries by market oriented approaches and unemployment has taken over the function of preserving the value of money.

But looking at macroeconomic indicators like price stability, growth and employment, we will learn that the overall economic performance of the more corporatist countries compares still quite favourably. This is reflected in, for example, the favourable position of the corporatist countries in the 1980s according to the Bruno and Sachs' ranking of countries (measuring the degree of corporatism) and an enriched misery index[1]. The economic problems of the recent past thus gave rise to a renewed interest in corporatistic intervention, although focusing mainly on supply-side policies like industrial and technology policy.

The subject matter of this chapter is the analysis of the Austrian economy with respect to its institutional arrangements and economic policy against the background of these developments.

The chapter is organized in four parts: first, we shall give a brief account of the development of the Austrian economy since the 1970s in comparison with international developments; then a description of Austrian economic policy and its underlying institutional arrangements will be given; followed by a more detailed treatment of the labour market and incomes policy; finally, we shall turn to the problems and prospects of the Austrian model of corporatism.

The performance of the Austrian economy in the 1970s and 1980s

Austria's economic development compares well with that of other countries during the stagflationary periods of the seventies and eighties.

When, in the aftermath of the two oil crises, the world economy experienced a marked decline in growth and a substantial rise in inflation and unemployment Austria experienced a more or less continuous catching-up process.

After the war, rapid productivity growth had been the result of the reconstruction boom and of bridging the technological gap, but soon government policy enhanced growth. After the breaking of the postwar price–wage spiral in 1953, economic growth received the highest priority in Austria's economic policy. Since growth was limited by labour shortages throughout the sixties, a comprehensive system of investment promotion was introduced to foster capital accumulation and productivity growth. Furthermore, the labour market was opened to foreign workers. Their share in the labour force increased from 0.5 per cent at the beginning of the sixties to 7per cent in 1973/74.

In 1970, Austria's GDP per capita was still about 5 per cent lower than in OECD-Europe on average and 20 per cent lower than in Germany. In the seventies and eighties, however, Austria's economy improved its relative position significantly. In 1990, Austria's GDP per capita was about 18 per cent higher than in OECD-Europe and 9 per cent lower than (West) Germany's.[2] While 20 years ago the productivity levels in manufacturing (including energy production) were 30 per cent lower than in Germany, there is no difference today according to national accounts statistics.

In the aftermath of the first oil crisis, economic policy gave full employment the highest priority and accepted a higher deficit as an automatic stabilizer. Thus, while labour market participation and employment increased, unemployment rates remained under 2 per cent despite a considerable growth in the labour force up to 1980. This employment policy was also supported by some labour hoarding in the nationalized industries in the late 1970s. In fact, private firms were also rather cautious in their layoff policies, since unemployment remained at a very low level and business expectations were fairly optimistic[3] throughout the seventies. Furthermore, on the supplyside a reduction of the legal working time in 1975 and a more restrictive foreign labour policy contributed to this favourable development on the labour market.

After the second oil crisis, the policy response was different. All main trading partners, and Germany in particular, followed a more deflationary course than in the 1970s; and Austrian policy-makers moved further and further away from the idea of 'diving through the recession'.

A number of factors which coincided in the early eighties led to this change in policy. In the aftermath of the second oil shock, the effects of the world-wide recession were reinforced by a substantial effective appreciation of the Austrian schilling. Rapidly rising unemployment and the structural crisis in the nationalized iron and steel industries put heavy strains on the federal budget.[4] At the same time, a steep rise in interest rates increased the costs of financing the budget deficit considerably. In this environment, the anti-state and anti-activist ideologies of the time found readier acceptance than in the seventies. Furthermore, the increasing share of interest payments in government expenditures and the deflationary international environment gave some substance to these objections by weakening the multiplier effects of expenditures. Thus, the coalition governments that followed the majority rule of the Socialist Party after 1983 gradually ceased to give absolute priority to full employment.

Hence, in the eighties, the development of the Austrian economy indicates a gradual abandonment of the policy of the seventies. While the hard currency approach and moderate incomes policy has been maintained, fiscal policy has been significantly less expansionary or even contractionary. The 'consolidation' of the federal budget has gained priority over full employment, and the unemployment rate increased from 1.6 per cent in 1980 to 4.7 per cent in 1990.

The rise in unemployment may seem moderate by international standards, in particular when we take into account seasonal unemployment which is high and rising with the growing tourist sector. But the unemployment figures do not reflect the labour market situation correctly; on the one hand, early retirement schemes, special allowances for particular groups of older workers, and a lower recruitment of foreign labour reduced open unemployment. On the other hand, in some regions, the structural crisis of the large iron and steel industries has led to much higher unemployment figures.

Summing up, the growth and labour market performance of the Austrian economy was quite remarkable in the 1970s. In the 1980s, unemployment figures increased substantially, though they have remained well below the average European rates. Although employment has increased in recent years with rates of about 2 per cent, unemployment figures have still been rising. Also, the prospects are rather gloomy; the economy is in recession with an expected decline in economic activity of about 1 per cent in 1993 while labour supply is still growing both through an inflow of foreign labour and increased participation rates.

The performance of Austria's economy in the 1970s has often been attributed to its institutions and policy; the question arises, therefore, whether the deterioration of the 1980s is caused solely by the abandonment of the former strategy or whether the strategy itself was not viable in the longer run.

The Austro-Keynesian model

In the late 1970s, Austria's economic institutions and policy approach attracted widespread interest. (Arndt, 1982; Flanagan, Soskice and Ulman, 1983). While most industrialized countries gave highest priority to the fight against inflation, Austria pursued a special type of Keynesian full employment strategy, despite inflationary pressures from abroad.

The main characteristics of the Austrian economic strategy, which has ex post proudly been labelled as 'Austro-Keynesianism' (Seidel, 1982), are:

- the social partnership as a form of voluntary, informal, and permanent incomes policy to control wages and prices and international competitiveness;
- an expansionary fiscal policy to foster growth and employment;
- a hard-currency policy to fight inflation; and
- absolute priority to full employment and growth.

This Austro-Keynesian model differs from 'standard Keynesianism'; it is not confined to anti-cyclical demand management, but represents a long-term device to stabilize business expectations with the help of incomes and exchange rate policies, thus fostering investment and growth; in fact, Austro-Keynesianism focuses extensively on stabilizing the private sector. [5]

Austro-Keynesianism is, on the one hand, based on rather fundamental Keynesian notions such as uncertainty and volatile business expectations (Tichy, 1984), and on the other hand, on the corporatist institutions of the Austrian Social Partnership.

Furthermore, there is a specific assignment of instruments and goals that takes into account the openness of the country, its institutional situation, and the inflationary environment of the time. In the period of high imported inflation, the traditional assignment did not seem adequate for a small open economy. While the traditional fiscal policy of compensating for fluctuations in demand was extended to foster growth by investment promotion, exchange rate policy was assigned to price stability, and incomes policy to external equilibrium by checking the price–wage spiral and preserving international competitiveness. Thus, moderate incomes policies had to soften the combined effects of hard-currency and expansionary fiscal policy on the balance of payments.

As Austria's institutions have been widely discussed in the international literature on corporatism and economic policy (Katzenstein, 1984). we shall confine ourselves to a rather short summary and raise some special issues.

The social partnership: a nexus of chambers, commissions and boards

The social partnership (see Suppanz and Robinson, 1972; Marin, 1982; Gerlich, Grande and Müller, 1985) has been widely considered as the centerpiece of Austria's postwar economic policy. Its scope is much wider than an institution of wage bargaining; it is a system of institutionalized cooperation between labour, business, and government which is involved in all important aspects of economic and social policy. It was formed on a voluntary and informal[6] basis by the Austrian Trade Union Federation and the Chambers of Agriculture, Commerce, and Labour to control postwar inflation in the early fifties. The Austrian chamber system as the highest level of interest representation with compulsory membership secured a high degree of centralized bargaining. The chambers are legal representatives of their members in the legislative process, i.e., the government has to obtain the appraisal of the chambers on draft legislation before it is submitted to Parliament. There are chambers for various professions, but only the Chamber of Commerce, the Chamber of Labour and the Chamber of Agriculture are of political importance from a macroeconomic point of view and, hence, are represented in the Parity Commission for Wages and Prices. The Chambers also play an essential part as intellectual brains trusts for the two large political parties in the general process of policy and strategy formulation. At the same time, they constitute, together with the Austrian Trade Union Federation (ÖGB), the nationwide, top-level bargaining institutions for wage and price policies. Today, the Trade Union Federation represents some 60 per cent of all Austrian employees, and in large industrial companies this percentage is much higher.

The Parity Commission is the most important formal institution of social partnership and is the top-level bargaining institution of incomes policy in Austria. It is formed by the above-mentioned Chambers, the Austrian Trade Union Federation and the relevant ministers on a voluntary basis. All decision have to be unanimous. The Parity Commission has no legal authority nor means of applying direct sanctions. The threat to impose sanctions is left to the government, but has hardly ever been used.

The Parity Commission has formed sub-committees on prices and wages to handle its task of curbing prices and wages: The Prices Sub-Committee authorizes price increases which have to be justified by substantial cost increases and applied for by individual firms or branches. Since the Sub-Committee has no authority to examine firms' accounts, its effects are limited and more or less confined to postponements of price increases. In the late 1970s, the Prices Sub-Committee covered about 20 per cent of consumer prices and about 50 per cent of industrial prices; officially regulated prices and tariffs, which cover another 15 to 20 per cent of consumer expenditures (Nowotny, 1989, p. 138), and import prices are excluded. Today, the coverage of both the Prices Sub-Committee and the official price regulation is much lower (Pollan, 1992a). Since, with the reduction of trade barriers in the process of European integration foreign competition has intensified and many industries became price takers. Thus, price regulation has more and more been considered as outdated and the social partners are considering whether to transform the Prices Sub-Committee into a Sub-Committee on Competition.

The Wages Sub-Committee exercises its control on wages by approving or refusing the opening of wage negotiations. Its task is to combine both wage-bargaining autonomy at the branch level and the introduction of macroeconomic considerations in the wage formation process. To start wage negotiations, individual trade unions have to apply through the Trade Union Federation. Thus, although wage negotiations are conducted by the subordinate sectoral trade union bodies, the Federation has a voice in fixing the dates and coordinating the individual wage claims. There is a Working Party on Wage Policy at the trade union headquarters to formulate common objectives of wage policy. Although individual trade unions are autonomous in their wage negotiations, bargaining processes have to be authorized and are coordinated by the Trade Union Federation and the Wages Sub-Committee (Suppanz and Robinson, 1972, p. 11ff.).

In this context, it seems that the power of the Austrian Trade Union Federation vis-à-vis its subordinate sectoral trade unions – at least some of them – is somewhat overestimated in international studies on wage bargaining and corporatism. For one thing, the high and growing wage differentials indicate that one needs to be careful not to put too much emphasis on the high degree of centralization of bargaining in Austria. By having control over finances, the Trade Union Federation is potentially very powerful, but has given much autonomy to the individual unions.

The Parity Commission – apart from being the main institution for wage and price control – has also become 'an instrument which gives the employers' and workers' organizations a voice in government economic policy in general and conversely enables the Government to make sure of co-operation from these organizations in its economic policy measures' (Ibid., p. 17). Thus a third permanent Sub-Committee, the Economic and Social Advisory Board, was established to extend the activities of the Commission beyond incomes policies and to broaden the scientific basis of economic policy. The Advisory Board is composed of representatives of the social partners and ministries as well as of experts. Its task is to prepare a scientific basis for policy recommendations to the government. Compared to similar institutions abroad, the Advisory Board has to be seen, on the one hand, as an instrument for finding consensus by providing a common assessment of important features of the economy but, on the other hand, it has also served to suppress the discussion of crucial issues such as the problems of environmental protection.

In short, the Austrian social partnership, whose institutions and climate of consensus grew out of the history of the country, can be characterized by a rather high degree of centralization, a wide scope of policy involvement, a cooperative mode of industrial relations, the absence of direct government involvement, and by informality.

When trade unions suggest a hard currency policy

Price stability has traditionally been assigned to monetary policy. Taking into account the conditions of a small open economy and the origin of inflation, Austria has assigned price stability to the exchange rate and external equilibrium to incomes policy since the seventies.

Since 1976 the Austrian schilling has been closely tied to the German mark; the consequence has been an effective appreciation of the schilling. This policy has been widely considered as a precondition for the expansionary demand policy in the face of high inflationary pressures from abroad.

Interestingly enough, this policy was suggested by the trade unions to foster incomes policy, on the one hand, because it would slow down the increase in import prices, but also because it may have made it easier for the trade unions to explain their moderate wage policy to their members by exchange rate policy reasons (Winckler, 1988).

In the early seventies, fiscal and monetary policy had been well coordinated in following a rather expansionary course. The National Bank aimed at stable nominal interest rates as well as a stable price level and exchange rate. Then, since the mid seventies the Austrian schilling has been tied to the German mark. Yet, mainly due to capital market imperfections, Austrian monetary policy managed to combine its policy of stable interest rates with a roughly constant exchange rate to the German mark till 1979. Then, with growing capital market integration and rising German interest rates this policy became unsustainable and the National Bank gave up its stable interest rate policy. The decision to keep to the fixed schilling–DM rate has since narrowed the room for manoeuvre of monetary policy and Austrian monetary policy has to a high degree been determined by both the Deutsche Bundesbank and the difference in inflation expectations between Austria and Germany. Nevertheless, there is no indication that Austrian monetary policy has had particularly restrictive effects on the real economy (Handler, 1989).

Incomes policy: a component of a long-term social partnership

In many countries, governments resort to incomes policies as short-term measures to cope with accelerating inflation; incomes policy is normally confined to wage and price regulation and is backed up by legal force. In contrast, the Austrian social partnership represents a long-term, voluntary strategy incorporating virtually all aspects of economic policy. This means that incomes policy in Austria is embedded in a national economic strategy and tied to the developments of monetary and fiscal policy.

The present-day pattern of wage bargaining has evolved since the late sixties when in this period of rapidly rising prices the large unions of construction and of metalworkers recognized the responsibility which they bore for the whole economy by setting the key bargains. 'Without any formal agreement between the Social Partners, the unions themselves pursued a policy of wage restraint to ensure low inflation and international competitiveness. One of the instruments used by unions to moderate wage increases was to retard wage settlements for several months; two clear examples of this strategy were the wage bargains in the recession of 1967/68 and the slowdown of 1978.'[7]

There is no national wage round in Austria. Although wage bargaining takes place at the industry level the bargaining process is highly concentrated: the three largest wage bargains (Public Sevices, white- and blue-collar workers in trade and blue-collar workers in metal and engineering including small-scale industries) cover more than 50 per cent and the five largest about 75 per cent of the labour force in Austria. A mere 7 per cent are not covered by any collective agreements (domestic services, non-profit institutions) (Pollan 1992b). Wage settlements are binding for all employees of the sector or the industry.

There is also no official wage guideline in Austria because trade unions avoid such standards which could be viewed as minimum increase and would foster unhealthy inter-union rivalry (Kienzl, 1973, pp. 230–1). Despite the absence of formal wage norms the negotiated increases in the wage rates are remarkably uniform. There are three tiers of wage negotiations in Austria; at the sectoral or industry level, at the plant level between the works council and the employer and often also at the individual level between the individual employee and the employer.

There is another peculiarity of Austrian wage policy: wages actually paid often differ markedly from negotiated rates; in some industries overpayment or 'wage drift' is quite substantial. Hence, in the large wage bargains of industrial production there are two wage settlements one for contractual or minimum wages and a second one for wages actually paid. In 1992 for instance, the settlement of the metalworkers' union provided that contractual wages increase by 5.2 per cent and paid wages by 4.5 per cent. If business expectations are not too gloomy there will be a positive wage drift in Austria, since there is some room to manoeuvre at the plant level.

The Austrian Trade Unions have not formulated explicit distributive goals; their policy has been based on a firm growth ideology. Trade union leaders argue that wage policy is not an effective redistributive instrument; it would lead to lower investment and reduce long-term productivity growth and real wage increases.

Progressive taxes and high public expenditures are seen as more appropriate redistributive instruments.[8] Since the seventies, trade union leaders and the politicians of the labour movement have emphasized uniformly that maintaining full employment is the most effective distributive policy. Generally, the wage policy of the Trade Union Federation has been oriented both to compensating for inflation and to long-run productivity growth. In the period since 1960 both real wages and productivity have on average been growing about 3¼ per cent per year (Table 7.1).

In the sixties, the unions pursued an explicit countercyclical wage policy, which implied rather moderate wage claims during business upswings and some pressure during a recession. Hence, wage policy had overall stabilizing effects.

In the early seventies, the trade unions aimed at promoting growth and full employment and formulated a new guideline, which aimed at a long-run real wage growth of 3 per cent. Since productivity growth

CORPORATISM AND INCOMES POLICY IN AUSTRIA

Table 7.1 Wages, productivity, the real wage gap and inflation (average annual increase in %)

	1960-70	1970-80	1980-90	1960-90	1991	1992
Productivity [a]	5.0	3.0	2.0	3.3	1.2	1.0
Real producer wage [b]	4.3	3.3	1.1	2.9	2.9	1.1
Real consumer wage [c]	4.8	3.3	1.3	3.1	3.1	1.4
Real wage gap [d]	0.2	−0.1	1.2	−0.4	1.7	−0.1
Wages per employee						
gross wages [e]	8.6	9.9	5.0	7.8	6.5	5.5
real net wages	4.0	2.6	1.2	2.7	2.2	0.4
Minimum wages [f]	7.0	10.2	5.0	7.4	6.9	5.6
Inflation [g]	3.6	6.3	3.6	4.5	3.3	4.1

Notes:
[a] Real GDP per person employed.
[b] Gross wage income per employee divided by the GDP-deflator.
[c] Gross wage income per employee deflated by consumer prices.
[d] Real wage increase minus productivity increase minus deterioration of terms of trade (average of the period).
[e] Gross wage income per employee at current prices.
[f] Contractual (minimum) wage increase.
[g] Deflator of private consumption.

Source: ÖSTAT: National Accounts, Contractual wage index; Austrian Institute of Economic Research (WIFO).

ranged between 4 and 6 per cent at that time, this implied the acceptance of a shift in the functional distribution in favour of profits.

Since it soon became clear in the seventies that a unilateral stimulation of demand would clash with external equilibrium, current account considerations were more and more taken into account in wage claims.[9] The comparison of wage equations of the periods 1964–84 and 1970–90 reveals that the coefficient of the current balance in percentage of GDP increases from 0.6 to 0.8–1.0.

Actually, the wage explosion of 1975, which was mainly due to grossly overoptimistic forecasts, was soon scaled back by moderate wage agreements in the following years. In fact the development of wages was such that the international cost competitiveness of manufacturing has improved again since the mid-1970s despite a substantial revaluation of the Austrian schilling (see Table 7.2).

Despite the corporatist institutional setting, which has often been considered as an obstacle to flexible market adjustments, nominal and real wage flexibility in Austria is relatively high by international standards.

Table 7.2 Labour costs and productivity in industry (average annual increase in %)

	1960-70	1970-80	1980-90	1991	1992
Total wage costs per hour	8.9	11.4	5.7	6.1	6.1
Productivity per hour	6.4	5.5	4.8	5.3	3.9
Unit labour costs	2.3	5.6	0.9	0.7	2.2
Exchange rate:					
weighted trading partners	0.3	−2.8	−1.4	0.8	−1.9
Germany [a]	1.3	0.0	−0.1	0.0	0.0
Relative unit labour costs to:[b]					
weighted trading partners	−0.8	0.6	−0.5	−4.7	0.4
Germany	−1.9	0.1	−0.7	−3.0	−3.3

Notes: [a] denotes a revaluation; [b] Austria/weighted trading partner resp. Germany in a single currency.
Sources: Austrian Institute of Economic Research (WIFO), OECD: Main Economic Indicators.

Taking into account our foregoing analysis, Austria's corporatist institutions have, however, to be seen as an important reason for this high wage flexibility.

Wage equations show that Austria is one of the few countries where the Phillips relation still holds, although there has been a remarkable shift in the 1980s. In the 1970s the unemployment elasticity of nominal wages came close to that of Japan and was then one of the highest in the OECD countries. A comparison of wage equations for the periods 1964-84 and 1970-90 reveals that unemployment elasticity of nominal wages has decreased somewhat (from −1.8 to −1.01). But, since price increases have also been compensated to a smaller degree in the second period, real wage rigidity is about the same, namely 0.5. Thus, if we follow this (OECD) reasoning this would mean that in Austria a rise in the unemployment rate of half a percentage point suffices to counter-balance the wage-inflationary effect of a 1 per cent rise in inflation.

A comparison between the seventies and eighties also reveals that wage flexibility has risen in the 1980s when unemployment started to rise significantly, which might be due to the fact that the Metal Workers Union, which acts as a quasi wage leader, was hit most severely by the crisis in the nationalized industries.

The two major limits of Austrian corporatism

In the 1980s, it has become more difficult to pursue expansionary policies, particularly in the restrictive environment imposed by the German economic policy; so Austro-Keynesianism has lost many of its instruments. Unemployment started to rise and public debt and interest payments on that debt increased rapidly. When, in the mid-1980s, the deep crisis in the nationalized industries also became a big burden for the federal budget there was a rather radical change in economic policy. Since then budget consolidation has had high priority in fiscal policy and federal budgets have been rather restrictive[10] and have no longer been an instrument promoting growth and employment. In fact, expansionary fiscal policy, a crucial element of the policy of the 1970s, has been given up.

Although the restrictive international environment and the burden of public debt may have been the actual reason for these important changes, the question remains whether endogenous flaws in Austria's policy of the 1970s may have reduced its long run viability. For some time the contention has existed that Austro-Keynesianism suffers from allocative inefficiencies (Guger, 1978, pp. 19ff.; Aiginger, 1983; Walther, 1984; Winckler, 1985). And Tichy writes: 'If Austro-Keynesianism should fail in the longer term, it will probably be because of the fact that industrial policy is definitely conserving old and outdated structures' (Tichy, 1984, p. 382).

Allocative inefficiencies

The Austro-Keynesian policy of the 1970s was essentially a macroeconomic strategy which aimed at growth and full employment. First, there was a crucial lack of allocative instruments in this strategy. Industrial policy was more or less confined to indirect investment promotions such as accelerated depreciation, investment allowances, and low-interest credits affecting all industries across-the-board and favouring particularly capital-intensive industries. While this policy fitted in with the macroeconomic strategy of fostering overall growth and a high level of employment, it more or less ignored the long-run allocative effects and hampered the process of structural adjustment and technological progress.[11] By lowering the costs of investment, this policy increased labour productivity to close to (West) German levels, but capital productivity remained rather low in international comparison (Hahn, 1991). The catching-up process in labour productivity was achieved by a relative rise in capital intensity and not by the use of leading-edge technology. Capital–output ratios in industry continued to increase in the 1980s, whereas in some other countries they declined (at least in the most advanced sectors of industry) due to growing success in technological modernization and a higher speed of diffusion of new technologies.[12]

Second, there is another important aspect to the inefficiency in Austrian corporatism: There are numerous regulations, such as the *Gewerbeordnung*, protecting substantial numbers of goods and services producers, in particular the professions, against new competitors (Szopo, 1986). Hence, although the wage level is relatively low by international standards, in Austria services are rather expensive.

Thus, Austria seems to be a good example of 'defensive corporatism'. Landesmann (1992) has pointed to the fact that industrial policies are generally less conducive to centralized agreements and are therefore less often part of the tripartite negotiations of Austrian corporatism. Offensive measures like policies fostering structural change, the promotion of R&D and the redirection of education and training have only 'potential' advocates, while the protection of well-established interests is often pursued by coalitions between trade unions and entrepreneurs.

In comparison to other small corporatist countries such as Sweden, Finland and the Netherlands, the subsidies to industry have been focusing very much on help to endangered firm and branches, while in the aforementioned countries the emphasis has been shifting to R&D, regional and innovation policy (Glatz *et al.*, 1991).

High wage differentials and slow structural change

Due to the extent of the social welfare system and the large share of public expenditures on social affairs, Austria has often been compared with Sweden as a country with a high degree of equality. But the structure of primary incomes in Austria differs substantially from other corporatist economies; wage differentials are very high in Austria. According to total labour cost and earnings data for manual workers, Austria shows the highest inter-industry wage differentials in Europe. Among industrialized countries, inter-industrial wage dispersion is only higher in Japan, the USA, and Canada (Guger, 1990; Rowthorn, 1992).

Segmentation in the Austrian labour market is generally relatively high; also, wage differentials according to social status and qualifications are much higher than in the Scandinavian countries and higher than in Germany.

The Austrian wage structure has been rather sensitive to market forces (Pollan, 1980). In fact, two elements seem to have been of outstanding importance; the general labour market conditions and the opening of the labour market for foreign labour. In the last 30 years, inter-industrial wage differentials have widened substantially as the changes in the coefficients of variation indicate. In the early 1960s, the inter-industrial wage dispersion of manual and non-manual workers had been quite similar, i.e. less than 15 per cent of average income. Then, in the late 1960s and early 1970s, when labour demand increased rapidly, the dispersion of blue-collar earnings widened with the influx of cheap foreign labour, while the structure of salaries remained stable.

From the mid-1970s to the late 1980s, the dispersion of both wages and salaries increased. Over this period, overall labour market conditions deteriorated and general wages policy has followed a rather moderate course. Both factors may have been of importance for the explanation of the tendency to rising inequality; since low contractual wage increases have left ample room for wage drift in industries where either demand conditions and profitability have been better or the trade union organization has had a stronger position, as it had in the nationalized industries till the mid-1980s. Furthermore, in Austria, the concept of 'soldaristic wage policy' has more or less been confined to broadly equal increases in contractual wage rates. The actual development of effective earnings has been left to branch- or firm-specific negotiations. Till lately, there was hardly an attempt to reduce absolute wage differences. Since the wage-round of autumn 1989 there have already been some activities in reducing wage dispersion within some industrial wage contracts.

While wide wage differentials and a flexible wage structure have often been considered as instrumental to labour market flexibility and productivity growth, the Austrian experience teaches rather the contrary. The large and widening inter-industrial wage differentials have rather hampered the process of structural adjustment; first in the 1970s, by keeping labour and capital too long in marginal production, and second, in the mid-1980s, by impeding the process of reallocating labour from high-wage but deficitarian (nationalized) industries to profitable industries paying lower wages. In addition, there were for too long public subsidies to ailing industries which have weakened competitive pressures and slowed down the process of restructuring.

A more solidaristic wage policy with higher wage increases in the low wage sectors would probably have led to greater wage and labour market rigidity, but certainly also to higher capital mobility and, thus, to faster structural adjustments in the period of high employment till 1981.

The principle of a solidaristic wage policy was also abandoned when at the 10th Trade Union Congress (1983) sector-specific reductions in working time per week were recommended, and the well-organized high wage sectors were able to push ahead to reduce weekly working hours. For example, the employees in the printing industries already have a 36 hour week, while in the public sector the working week is still 40 hours.

Some threats to Austrian corporatism

From a macroeconomic perspective, corporatism has been rather successful in Austria, despite some adversities. In the fifties and sixties, the promotion of economic growth and, in the seventies up to 1983, full employment had highest priority in the national economic strategy. In the increasingly deflationary environment of the 1980s, when public debts and interest payments increased rapidly, the fiscal policy has been changed from an expansive course to budget consolidation.

From a microeconomic perspective, Austrian corporatism has been less successful. There has been a lack of allocative efficiency and the process of structural adjustment has – at least until recently – been hampered by an industrial policy which favoured large capital-intensive enterprises rather than small businesses, as well as by high and growing wage differentials which kept capital and labour too long in marginal production.

In recent years, some improvements on the supply side of the economy have been initiated; first, some parts of the nationalized industries have been successfully restructured – but huge problems remain to be resolved and will be on the agenda for the next few years; second, there have also been moderate steps to reduce and redirect subsidies towards R&D and technology diffusion programmes – but these still occupy but a modest part of industrial policy efforts; third, the new tax system favours the enlargement of a firm's capital base. In addition, some deregulation has recently taken place in the agricultural and food production sector. Finally, the trade unions themselves have become aware of growing inequalities and tend to narrow wage dispersion in new wage contracts, which is likely to have positive effects on the speed of structural change.

Austria's economic performance has been above the OECD average again in the last years. Corporatism and its institutions, however, have been losing influence and popularity in the last decade. On the one hand, due to the changes in the employment structure, i.e., shifts from large-scale manufacturing production to services, and the crisis in nationalized industry organized labour has been gradually losing some of its authority and influence. On the other hand, the social partnership has also failed to take up new problems of general interest, such as environmental protection.

Concerning incomes policy in particular, the power of centralized bargaining institutions has declined over the years while the power of individual bargaining units and of works councils has risen. There are economic reasons for this development: First, the marked rise in unemployment since the early eighties, second the decline in employment in heavy (nationalized) industries, and third, the easing of labour market regulations in 1990 which has made entry to the labour market easier for foreign workers from the Eastern European countries (very recently, these regulations have been tightened again).

On the other hand, there are also important political reasons. An erosion of the main political camps in response to shifts in the occupational structure, particularly the growth of white-collar employment and the service sector, has paved the way for an 'individualization' of values. This trend causes both a dramatic increase in the proportion of floating voters and a rising opposition to compulsory membership in chambers.

The main threats for Austrian corporatism will be on the one hand the influx of cheap labour and products from the Eastern European countries that will continue to exercise pressure on the ability of the social partners to control labour market conditions. So far, the social partners have reacted mainly with protectionist measures on both markets.

On the other hand, the integration into the EC will limit the influence of the social partners on economic policy in general as many areas of economic policy will be shifted to a central European level. All these tendencies strain the governance capacity of macro-corporatism in general and the power of the unions in particular.

These developments may re-concentrate the activites of the social partners on incomes policies and bring distributional questions to the forefront again – but with a reduced set of measures to cushion these conflicts.

Notes

1. Which is composed of the rate of unemployment plus the rate of inflation minus the rate of growth of productivity minus the rate of growth of employment plus the rate of growth of population. While the often used Okun index consists only of unemployment and inflation this index also takes into

account of productivity growth and participation in the labour market.
2. According to purchasing power parities of the OECD.
3. Austria's high investment rate may be mentioned as an indicator: Gross fixed capital formation was 26.4 per cent of GDP on average between 1974 and 1979, 23.6 per cent in the period 1980 to 1990 (OECD: *Historical Statistics 1960–1990*). Only Norway, Japan, Iceland and Finland show higher figures in the OECD area. Austria's relative position had been significantly higher in this period than in any period since 1960.
4. Employment programmes and claims on the social budget had to be financed; and the net borrowing increased from 2.2 per cent in 1981 to 5.0 per cent in 1983, and in 1992 fell to 2.9 per cent.
5. In his discussions of the economic plans for the after-war period in the Treasury, Keynes stressed the importance of this point (Guger and Walterskirchen, 1988)
6. The voluntary and informal nature of the Austrian approach has been imposed by the Austrian constitution.
7. For a short history of union bargaining in Austria compare Pollan (1992b) p. 4.
8. In fact, the overall tax system is not progressive in Austria, because of a large share of indirect taxes it is rather proportional cf. Guger (1987).
9. According to wage equations for the period 1964–84, an increase of the ratio of the current account deficit to GDP of one percentage point dampened the growth of contractual wage rates by half a percentage point; see Biffl, Guger and Pollan (1987).
10. Although, in 1989, the income tax reform which led to a large loss in tax revenues bolstered disposable incomes substantially.
11. For a more comprehensive treatment of Austrian industrial policy, see Landesmann (1992).
12. This development can not be ascribed to the attitudes of the Austrian trade unions towards technical change, which is very positive in general, but by the 'defensive bias' of Austrian corporatism.

References and bibliography

Abele, Hans, Nowotny, Ewald, Schleicher, Stefan and Winckler, Georg (eds.) (1989), 'Handbuch der österreichischen Wirtschaftspolitik' (3rd edn; 2nd edn 1984), Manz, Vienna.

Aiginger, Karl (1983), *Labor Relations and Industrial Policy in Austria and their Influence on Macroeconomic Activity*, Conference paper, Stresa.

Airndt, Sven, W. (ed.) (1982), *The Political Economy of Austria*, American Enterprise Institute for Public Policy Research, Washington DC.

Biffl, Gudrun, Guger, Alois and Pollan, Wolfgang (1987), 'The Causes of Low Unemployment in Austria', Occasional Papers in Employment Studies No. 7, University of Buckingham.

Bruno, Michael and Sachs, Jeffrey (1985), 'The Economics of Worldwide Stagflation', Harvard University Press, Cambridge, MA.

Flanagan, Robert J., Soskice, David W. and Ulman, Lloyd (1983), 'Unionism,

Economic Stabilization, and Incomes Policies: European Experience', Studies in Wage-Price Policy, The Brookings Institution, Washington, DC.
Gerlich, Peter, Grande, Edgar and Müller, Wolfgang C. (eds.) (1985), *Sozialpartnerschaft in der Krise. Leistungen und Grenzen des Neokorporatismus in Österreich*, Böhlau, Vienna.
Glatz, Hans, Latzer, Michael, Polt, Wolfgang and Schedler, Andreas (1991), 'Kleinstaaten im wirtschaftlichen Strukturwandel. Industrie- und technologiepolitische Strategien ausgewählter Industrieländer'. Studie im Auftrag des Bundesministeriums für öffentliche Wirtschaft und Verkehr. Vienna.
Guger, Alois (1978), 'Ist die Beschäftigungspolitik am Ende?', *Wirtschaft und Gesellschaft*, 4(1), pp.9–26.
—— (ed.) (1987), 'Umverteilung durch öffentliche Haushalte in Österreich', *WIFO-Gutachten*, WIFO, Vienna.
—— (1990), 'Verteilungspolitik als Strukturpolitik', in Beigewum and Memorandum-Gruppe (eds.), *Steuerungsprobleme der Wirtschaftspolitik*, Vienna and Bremen, pp.94–104.
Guger, Alois and Walterskirchen, Ewald (1988), 'Fiscal and Monetary Policy in the Keynes–Kalecki Tradition', in J. A. Kregel, E. Matzner and A. Roncaglia (eds.), *Barriers to Full Employment*, Macmillan, London.
Hahn, Franz R. (1991), 'Kapitalproduktivität in der österreichischen Industrie 1970 bis 1989', *WIFO-Monatberichte*, 64(11), pp. 641–7.
Handler, Heinz (1989), *Grundlagen der österreichischen Hartwährungspolitik*, Manz, Vienna.
Katzenstein, Peter J. (1984), *Corporatism and Change: Austria, Switzerland, and the Politics of Industry*, Cornell University Press, Ithaca, NY and London.
Kienzl, Heinz (1973), 'Gewerkschaftliche Lohnpolitik und Stabilität', in Wolfgang Schmitz (ed.), *Geldwertstabilität und Wirtschaftswachstum, Festschrift für Andreas Korp*, Springer, Vienna.
Landesmann, Michael (1992), 'Industrial Policies and Soccial Corporatism', in Pekkarinen *et al.*, pp. 242–79.
Marin, Bernd (1982), *Die Paritätische Kommission. Aufgeklärter Technokorporatismus in Österreich*, Internationale Publikationen Ges. mbH, Vienna.
Nowotny, Ewald (1979), 'Verstaatlichte Unternehmen als Instrument der Beschäftigungspolitik in Österreich', *Zeitschrift für öffentliche und gemeinwirtschaftliche Unternehmen*, 2(3), pp. 252–76.
—— (1989), 'Institutionelle Grundlagen, Akteure und Entscheidungsverhältnisse in der österreichischen Wirtschaftspolitik', in Abele *et al.*, pp.125–48.
Pekkarinen, Jukka, Pohjola, Matti and Rowthorn, Bob (eds.) (1992), *Social Corporatism – A Superior Economic System?*, Clarendon Press, Oxford.
Pollan, Wolfgang (1980), 'Wage Rigidity and the Structure of the Austrian Manufacturing Industry – An Econometric Analysis of Relative Wages', *Weltwirtschaftliches Archiv*, 116(4), pp. 697–728.
—— (1992a), 'Preisregelung in Österreich', *Wirtschaftspolitische Blätter*, 1/1992, pp.33–44.
—— (1992b), 'Austria's Collective Bargaining System Under Strain', (unpublished paper).
Polt, Wolfgang et al. (1992), 'Perspektiven von Technologie und Arbeitswelt in

Österreich', Studie im Auftrag des Bundesministeriums für Wissenschaft und Forschung, Vienna.

Rowthorn, Bob (1992), 'Corporatism and Labour Market Performance', in Pekkarinen *et al.*, pp. 82–131.

Seidel, Hans (1982), 'Der Austro-Keynesianismus', *Wirtschaftspolitische Blätter*, 1982(3), pp.11–15.

Suppanz, Hannes and Robinson, Derek (1972), *Prices and Incomes Policy. The Austrian Experience*, OECD, Paris.

Tichy, Gunther (1984), 'Strategy and Implementation of Employment Policy in Austria', *Kyklos*, 37(3), pp. 363–86.

Walterskirchen, Ewald (1990), 'Unemployment and Labour Market Flexibility: Austria', mimeo, ILO, Geneva (forthcoming ILO Study).

Walther, Herbert (1984), 'Einige mikro- und makroökonomische Aspekte der Preisregelung durch die Paritätische Kommission', in Abele *et al.*, pp. 399–411.

Winckler, Georg (1985), 'Sozialpartnerschaft und ökonomische Effizienz', in: Gerlich *et al.*, pp. 295–312.

—— (1988), 'Hartwährungspolitik und Sozialpartnerschaft', *Wirtschaftspolitische Blätter*, 35(1) pp. 58–67.

CHAPTER 8

PROCEDURES AND INSTITUTIONS OF INCOMES POLICIES IN ITALY

Tiziano Treu

Country statistics

Union members as a proportion of total dependent employees
   1980   54.4%   1986–87   45%
active members only 58.6%

Public sector employees as a proportion of total employees
   1980   14.5%   1990   15.5%

Participation rates of working age population (ages 15–64)
   Men 1980   80.6%   Men 1991   75.5%
   Women 1980 38.9%   Women 1991 44.3%

Per capita GDP in US dollars (1993 exchange rates)
   1980 $6,190   1991 $20,159

Per capita GDP (PPP)
   1980 $7,790   1990 $15,953

Main collective bargaining institutions above the enterprise level

c.1980

Three national union federations (CGIL, CSL, UIL) differentiated by political party affiliation plus historical institutional accident and inertia.

    Sectoral federations, each linked to one of the three centres. Members of more than one union frequently found at each enterprise, with representative structures of great and ill-institutionalized complexity.

    National level bargaining between three union federations,

Confindustria and other smaller employer organizations and government over main features of pay such as *scala mobile* inflation adjustment. Sectoral contracts for 2-3 years, in which sectoral federations of each centre bargain together. Additional enterprise-level bargaining of varying structures, growing in importance.

1993

Little change except:

1. Ending of *scala mobile* automatic inflation adjustments.
2. Revival of activity at the national level.
3. Further reduction through amalgamations in the number of sectoral contracting units to 17.
4. Lengthening of the contractual period of sectoral agreements.
5. Increasing importance of enterprise level bargaining and some institutionalization of the forms of workplace representation.

Tripartite consultation and cooperation in the field of economic and social policies have quite a significant tradition in Italy, in spite of the fact that the nature of Italian industrial relations has not been traditionally conducive to these practices.

Most of the traditional features of the system have made tripartite cooperation difficult[1]. These include: the relative fragility and low level of institutionalization of industrial relations and collective bargaining, a characteristic which is linked to the country's late economic development, the fragmentation of industrial structures (a high proportion of small firms) and the tensions within the political system which hamper the already difficult task of building a national and social consensus. Italian trade unions have been characterized by deeply rooted political divisions. The three main national centres each have party links; the CGIL (a little over 5 million members in 1990) primarily with the Communist Party (now the PDS) and secondarily with the socialist PSI; CISL (3.5 million) with the Christian Democrats, and UIL (1.5 million), chiefly linked to the Socialists, but also with the Social Democrats and the Republicans.

Equally important is the in-built tradition of confrontational attitudes which, particularly in the eight years after the 'hot autumn' of 1969 and the subsequent Statute of Workers' Rights which confirmed the adversarial structure of industrial relations, made highly conflictual bargaining the only technique used by Italian trade unions and prevented the development of long-term responsible relations between management and labour.

But after 1977 there was a change – towards concertation. The main reason was the economic crisis following the oil shock – an explosion of inflation even worse than in other OECD countries, a profound restructuring of industry and increased unemployment.

Developments within the political system itself also favoured concertation. On the one hand, the instability of government coalitions precluded 'interventionist' solutions to the economic crisis. On the other hand, laissez-faire liberalism was also not an option because the major Italian political parties, including the Christian Democratic Party, were too closely linked to large factions of the labour movement. The trade unions, for their part, were too strong and too widely represented in institutional structures to be ignored. (Apart from the moribund CNEL, the National Council of Economy and Labour – a constitutional body deriving directly from prewar corporatist traditions with the power to submit bills to Parliament – unions had the power to appoint representatives to the main social security institutions, the employment services and so on.) Hence even employers, particularly their national-level representatives, were reluctant to consider a strategy of union exclusion.

There was, in fact, a widely shared perception that something had to be done to deal with the root causes of the crisis in the economy responsible for inflation and unemployment – rigidities in the labour market and industrial relations, the fall in the rate of profit, the growth of the service economy and the associated decline in the growth rate of productivity. Even the Communist Party was one of the major supporters of social concertation in 1977, concerned as it was, in the era of the 'historical compromise', to be recognized as a major partner in economic and social policy, if not as a fully fledged partner in government.

The series of national-level agreements between 1977 and 1984 were *ad hoc* agreements, conducted outside existing tripartite bodies such as the CNEL. Their main aim was to set up a concerted incomes policy to combat inflation and unemployment, but they also sought to stabilize the industrial relations system and reduce the level of conflict. And the record of the 1980s suggests that they made a considerable contribution in this direction.

The 1980s: growth in the build-up to crisis

Indeed, the overall performance of the Italian economy has greatly improved during the decade. GNP has grown substantially. There has been an increase in productivity, particularly in the industrial sector, second in Europe only to West Germany. The balance of payments has improved, and there has been a substantial reduction of unemployment. (Almost to vanishing point in northern Italy, by 1991, though the recession has had an impact here too.)

A major turning point was the entry into the ERM and the acceptance of Bundesbank discipline. After 1983 inflation rapidly came down from the near-20 per cent of 1981 to below 5 per cent in 1987; the value of the lira against 14 industrial-country currencies, which had fallen by 11 per cent between 1981 and 1983, strengthened by 6 per cent from 1988 and 1991. The expectation of lower inflation and of pressure to hold down prices, fed through rapidly into smaller increases in wages. It also increased pressures for rationalization of production, technical innovation, and locally negotiated agreements for more flexible use of labour which led to productivity growth rates of 4-5 per cent per annum, a figure which, from 1982 to 1987 allowed both for a steady growth in real wages and a decline in the wage share from 67 to 62 per cent of GNP. This trend was reversed thereafter; the possibility of easy productivity gains had been exhausted; the stronger lira diminished export competitiveness. Pressure on profits increased towards the end of the decade as did productivity growth rates, and a big public sector wage increase in 1990 increased the tensions in private sector wage negotiations.

Bargaining structures continued a process of decentralization. Italy had evolved a three-tier structure. The peak-level national agreements referred to above gained and retained their importance because they established the *scala mobile* (sliding scale), which made partial (lagged) compensation for inflation universal. What lost in importance was the second-level national collective agreements. These have steadily covered larger and more heterogeneous groups of workers – 16 of them now, compared with 150 much more sectorally specialized agreements in 1947. These, especially the contract in the pace-setting engineering (*metalmeccanica*) industry, attract considerable press attention. They set (usually for three years at a time) minimum standards for whole sectors, but their importance has been declining steadily compared with that of the third tier – decentralized bargaining at the plant or enterprise level with managers or owner-managers (there are still a lot in Italy) on one side of the table, and worker representatives on the other. The structure of such bargaining groups is complex and full of potential for conflict. They are generally based on the delegates or works council committees sanctioned by the 1970 Statuto dei Lavoratori, but are of a rich variety and uninstitutionalized complexity insofar as concerns their integration with, or independence from, outside union officials – of the three major confederations, of the sectoral bargaining units at national or regional level, of the local Chamber of Labour, of political parties – and also of regional and local governments and sometimes the local Prefect, as patterns of informal mediation in work-stopping disputes have gradually been semi-institutionalized. It is generally recognized that some legal formalization of local bargaining structures – on the lines of the reform of public sector bargaining carried out in 1992-3 – is overdue.

Predominant employer opinion once favoured national-level bargaining (which would apply also to small non-unionized firms) and sought to restrict the scope of plant-level agreements. In the 1980s, however, employer opinion shifted and the plant-level agreement became an important means of gaining the flexibility on which productivity growth depended. A measure of the shift in the bargaining centre of gravity is given by figures for 'wage drift' – the variation of locally bargained wages from central collective agreements. Wage drift increased markedly through the decade; from 17 per cent in 1982 to 36 per cent in 1990 in engineering, from 40 to 61 per cent in chemicals, from –1 to +9 per cent in construction, and from 3 to 16 per cent in the food industry. (In textiles, the wood industry, and public shops and hotels, wages remained below centrally bargained rates, though not by much.)

But what brought a sense of crisis at the beginning of the 1990s was not so much current wage trends or problems of industrial relations as concern with the fiscal problems of the welfare state. The tripartite agreements of the 1970s had come home to roost. As in other Latin Mediterranean countries, the welfare policies created as part of the social bargaining had consumed more public resources than expected and led to large public deficits.[2] One reason for this was the very weakness of the social pact experiments. Social conflict was 'fiscalized': i.e., consensus had to be 'bought' by immediate concession of welfare provisions, because the unions had little trust in the ability of government to ensure that any immediate sacrifice by the workers through restraining their exercise of bargaining power would be rewarded in the longer term by gains to workers through improved growth and economic stability.

The situation since 1984

The new situation did not end concerted social and income policies, but it led to a lesser degree of centralization and institutionalization.

In 1984, agreement on wage increases was reached with great difficulty and led to a serious split of the labour movement precisely on the method and merit of concerted incomes policies. This dramatic experience led to changes. First direct regulatory intervention of the state was as far as possible avoided, but it remained important in wage issues, particularly in the 1986 agreement which modified the *scala mobile* to reduce the degree of automatic cost-of-living indexation of wages.

Second, there was a change in the scope of bilateral negotiations between the central confederations of employers and unions. They concentrated more selectively on matters concerned with improving the performance of the industrial relations system and human resource management (HRM): the promotion of vocational training through 'education contracts'; a 'guided' use of atypical – and less secure – labour contracts (fixed term, part-time) needed to make flexible the use of manpower; the improvement of conflict resolution procedures, particularly in the essential public services; guidelines aimed at coordinating decentralized collective bargaining practice in accordance with national economic objectives.

Government lent informal support to the negotiations by continuing to implement the labour legislation called for in the 1984 agreement (particularly as regards youth employment, part-time working, solidarity[3] and education contracts, etc.) and by adopting fiscal policies favourable to the labour movement (fiscal drag reduction, taxation of treasury bonds, etc.).

In the following years, informal consultations continued to be held by government with the central union confederation and the central employers' associations separately, especially on issues of fiscal policy, particularly in preparation of the budget law, which lays down yearly the major guidelines of economic and fiscal policy.

On 26 January, 1989, for example, a bilateral agreement was signed between the government and the central union confederation which provided that fiscal drag should be neutralized automatically rather than after a time lag in return for union agreement to raising the rate of value added tax (VAT) to align it to European standards.

Formal tripartism re-emerged in 1990. In January, unions and employers agreed bilaterally, among other things, to press the government to reduce social security contributions to bring these indirect labour costs in line with European standards. This was intended to facilitate the renewal of national industry-level collective agreements which had expired in 1989.

Then, in July 1990, in face of persistent difficulty in renewing the collective agreements, a pledge to reduce these labour costs at state expense was solemnly confirmed in a formally tripartite agreement, which also committed the social parties to a new reform of the escalator clause by December 1991.

The new phase

Recent events mark an even more dramatic turning point. The worsening of the world economic situation and the specific weaknesses of the Italian economy brought back into focus key problems which for some years had appeared overcome or forgotten: the need to control inflation and to reduce the huge public deficit (largely accumulated in order to pay for social consensus).

Other related structural problems re-emerged too: skewed distribution of employment and new unemployment; increasing export difficulties and the low competitiveness of Italian industry; the persistent inefficiency of the public administration.

New efforts for concerted centralized action were increasingly seen to be necessary. In a first phase (1990/91) unions and employers sought to reassert their autonomy vis-à-vis the state, explicitly and polemically rejecting the excessive dependence on state action, which had characterized the concerted action of the previous decade.

The bargaining agenda concentrated on issues within the competence of the two parties, issues discussed earlier; the joint administration of vocational training, the regulation of special training contracts (which had proved a good instrument for hiring cheap young labour, but according to the union was less useful for real training), improvement of consultation procedures on issues of industrial restructuring, new regulation of plant union representatives, and better coordination between bargaining levels.

But it was clear from the beginning that the core issue was the regulation and control of wage bargaining. Faced with growing international competition, employers have kept the need to hold down labour costs at the centre of attention, and were successful in getting that need recognized by the public opinion and politicians. It became almost an axiomatic starting point.

Given this pressure, and given that state handouts were not ruled out, the unions had only narrow opportunities to bargain positive concessions in return for wage moderation – concessions which employers, not the state, could grant. The issues they took up had recurred in earlier negotiations: the role of union representatives at plant level; better procedures for the election and functioning of those representatives, and for giving them a wider bargaining competence;

greater involvement in consultation and participation within the enterprise.

Plant level representation was the key issue, but the compromise proposals elaborated by the unions did not even reach the stage of serious negotiation, largely because of divisions among the unions over the system of election. Some unions favour open 'slates', allowing any employee to be nominated; others sought greater control over employee representation by confining representatives to union members.

There were also divisions over consultation and participation. Not all the unions gave it sufficient priority to make it a meaningful *quid pro quo* for wage concessions; employers for their part, while open to some improvement of existing information procedures, were reluctant to concede to union plant representatives significant powers of participation in matters of critical importance for management prerogatives.

The third issue presented by the unions (CISL in particular) was one for which they were prepared to agree to the employers' prime request, the abolition of what remained of the *scala mobile*, the escalator clause, namely the recognition of unions and the right of collective bargaining (either directly at plant level or at the territorial level for groups of firms) in those small and smallest firms where unions were traditionally absent or scarcely active. This proposal was rejected outright by employers owing to its implications for the balance of power in industrial relations: it would have reduced the unilateral control of employers in a vast area of the Italian economy essential to keep it totally flexible.

Nor were the unions able to offer enough to employers to gain such concessions. Employers had no faith in the central unions' power to control local wage bargainers. Between 1977 and 1983 the unions had proved able to restrain the wage push of their local representatives. But this experience was still too partial and short-lived to overcome a long history of conflict and 'indiscipline' of Italian industrial relations at plant level, particularly given the increased decentralization of collective bargaining. Hence, it was not possible for the social partners themselves to find viable terms of exchange on issues within their own respective powers of control. Nor was there much room for manoeuvre when they sought to bring in the state for additional bargaining counters. The necessary resources were not available, given the state of public finances.

Tax reductions granted in earlier years for the lowest-paid employees, to compensate them for the reduction of indexation, had reached the limit after the government had introduced, in 1989, a (quasi) automatic neutralization of fiscal drag for employees.

The burden of social security contributions was still the highest in

Europe, but the state budget could not stand further social security costs, and any actual reduction of social security benefits (pensions) was *a priori* refused by the unions. The recruitment of retired people as union members had grown to the point of making them the largest single component in the three main confederations.

One proposal from the unions, to increase fiscal control so as to reduce the huge tax evasion which plagued the Italian economy, failed to get sufficiently united support from the employers to overcome the traditional resistance of the political and economic lobbies.

Finally, it was hardly possible for the unions to 'offer' the employers specific measures to increase labour flexibility and consequently productivity. Major rigidities (both legal and customary) in the use of the labour force had already been removed, and the effects were shown in the increased mobility and industrial productivity during the second half of the 1980s. Further deregulation was not within the trade unions' power capacity, even if they were willing to try, and it was equally difficult for the legislator, due to the prevailing mood of Parliament and the political parties.

In short, even though they were willing to relinquish their devotion to bilateralism, the lack of public resources was a major obstacle to reaching a 'balanced' agreement, or even any agreement. This explains why the negotiation remained substantially blocked for over two years. Only a series of ambiguous postponing documents were signed, leaving as the increasingly salient central issue the automatic escalator clause, still the main source of wage increase. The employers argued that its abolition was the only way to restrain wages, given the persisting disorder of the Italian bargaining system.

The three major union confederations were divided and so were the political parties which backed them. Some insisted on dogmatic defence of the escalator clause as the last symbol of labour guarantees. But generally such opposition weakened. There were vague proposals for modification of the escalator provisions. Others proposed the alternative of legislation to establish a minimum wage (fully indexed) similar to that existing in France.

The weakness resulting from this uncertain and largely defensive position was already clear in the protocol of 10 December 1991, which hinted in obscure terms at the future termination of the escalator clause. That termination finally came in the following July.

The election of April 1992, and the widespread realization of the depth of the fiscal crisis – induced by the Maastricht Treaty and the conditions for monetary union which it set – created an atmosphere which allowed the new Amato government to mobilize support for a series of drastic expenditure cuts and tax increases. It was accepted that Italy had (a) to control inflation if the lira was to be kept in the ERM, and (b) to reduce fiscal deficits to avoid being a 'second league' country excluded from eventual monetary union. This was the background for further intense pressure on the unions by the government and employers which led to the turning-point tripartite agreement of 31 July 1992.

The central feature of that agreement was wage control, with none of the traditional welfare counter-benefits. Its purpose was defined as securing a programme of inflation reduction; from a current 5.4 per cent to 3.2 per cent in 1993, 2.5 per cent in 1994 and 2 per cent in 1995. The escalator clause was definitively abandoned. Private sector wages were to be frozen until the end of 1992 (with some possibility of inflation compensation in industries where contracts had expired and their renewal was still being negotiated). For 1993 there was to be a small flat-rate monthly sum, equal for all, and there were to be no plant-level negotiations for higher salaries. The total public sector wage bill was to increase at only the programmed rate of inflation. Prices were to be monitored and price control powers would be sought if necessary. Protection of the real wage was to be guaranteed.

An all-night bargaining session, a near-split in the CGIL, the biggest federation, and the prime minister's threat of resignation, a governmental crisis and perhaps fresh elections – which nobody wanted to have to take responsibility for – created the atmosphere of high drama deemed appropriate for major accords of this kind. The CGIL Secretary, to whose personal charisma the press attributed the final decision of his union's executive to sign, resigned the next day in recognition of the strength of opinion against his position. (The (successful) motion not to accept his resignation thus became the focus of the debate over the accords at the delegates' meeting the following September.)

The opposition was considerable. Wildcat strikes were declared by some hundreds of works councils of large northern enterprises. The blocking of industrial and plant-level bargaining was, indeed, the most difficult part of the accords for the unions to accept. It reversed the decentralizing trends of the 1980s. But at the same time, the escalator clause which had been the main *raison d'être* for continued central bargaining, was now abandoned, leaving the leaders of the national confederations – in the absence, now, of any possibility of increased welfare spending – with nothing to secure compliance from the industrial unions except shared party loyalties, their moral authority, and their claim both to have safeguarded workers' essential interests (e.g., the guaranteed maintenance of the real wage) and to have achieved certain institutional reforms.

These last, however, were not reforms with much public appeal. The first was gradual equalization of public and private pension systems to reduce the considerable privileges of workers in the public sector – an 'equalization downwards' which public sector unions naturally opposed and which did not arouse much joy in the private sector either, particularly as it was seen as part of a general move to reduce pension benefits which, since 1969, have been higher in Italy than elsewhere in Europe.

The main concern of the trade unions with respect to the public sector (with 4 million employees) has been to reduce the role of legislation and increase that of collective bargaining in setting terms and conditions of employment. This is generally seen as having the public interest justification that, as in the private sector, 'delegalization', more bargaining and fewer rigid rules, will contribute to the better use of human resources and greater efficiency. For the unions, it is also a means of beating off the threat from the unofficial *Cobas*, the militant 'grass roots committees', which in some areas – the railway and teaching, for example – have gained enough support to threaten the legitimacy of the established unions. The two aims are not necessarily interdependent, and the unions may lose popular support if they achieve the second without effective action to achieve the first.

A second area covered by the agreement had more popular appeal and has long been a preoccupation of the unions; measures – including a minimum 'presumed income' system – to reduce tax evasion among artisans, small shopkeepers and those in the liberal professions. The subsequent directives produced strong reactions from these groups and the political lobbies which support them, but if the public administration is strong enough to implement them they promise the most 'redistributive' effect of all efforts at concerted action – a clear case of the unions acting as representatives of the public interest to achieve a more equitable income distribution and raise fiscal revenues, partially counter-balancing pressures to cut social expenditures.

There were also – the third area – provisions in the accord which promised measures to maintain employment – implementation of measures which had for some time been discussed to improve the working of *cassa integrazione* layoff subsidies, and to use them more effectively to further the productive restructuring of firms in difficulties. As the lira crisis which came soon after the accord raised interest rates to levels which intensified concerns about employment, the government also moved to vote quite large sums for employment creation.

The entrenchment of tripartism

The 1992 accord does not quite belong to the category of 'union concession bargaining', given that the real wage was guaranteed (insofar as the state was in a position to guarantee anything). But the unions were required to give promises (including the promise of control over their component unions) in return for none of the economic, social welfare benefits which had marked previous agreements – indeed, at a time when social benefits were being reduced, drastically for the public sector, but also for the private sector as well.

Tripartism in the Austrian or Swedish 'neo-corporatist' mode has the state representing a public interest (in inflation control, employment maintenance, improved competitiveness, etc.) which embraces and transcends that of the other two social partners. In Italy a state which was not sufficiently strong and independent of the parties to play that role was reduced to the role of providing expensive concessions out of the public budget. A shift from tripartism to bilateralism was seen as the only way to break the habit. But the deepening crisis has brought the state back in – and this time in a much stronger 'public interest' role.

But it was still a matter of 'concertation'. There had to be an agreement. There was no question of imposing an incomes policy by statute – partly because long years of coalition governments have bred a strong preference for consensus creation, partly because not even the Amato government – stronger than most previous ones – could be confident of administering an imposed policy over the social opposition which could be expected.

But formal concertation by peak-level organizations is ineffective (in, say, controlling inflation) unless those organizations have the capacity to deliver the consent of their members. That capacity is in doubt even for the employers' Confindustria. It is even more in doubt in the case of the unions, as the demonstrations and strikes of the weeks following the accord made clear. Hence the device of freezing collective bargaining completely for a period, instead of relying on the peak-level organizations' powers to control it, particularly at the enterprise level.

This is partly to be attributed to the weak institutionalization of the *bargaining structures* which determine those links between peak organizations and their peripheral constituents. Earlier, at the time of the Statute of Workers' Rights (the 1970 Statuto dei Lavoratori), for example, the state had intervened massively, but in recent years local industrial relations structures have been seen as a matter properly left to bilateral bargaining. However disagreement over the role of plant representatives has led to the drafting of a new state initiative – which many in the unions support too: a law to codify systems of election and to clarify the effects of agreements on non-union-member dissenters. The state has also entered the field, sometimes, as in the 1990 Law No. 146 on strikes in essential public services, to supplement, rather than to supplant bilateral bargaining. The act requires unions and employers to reach agreement on the level of public service to be maintained in a strike. It provides guidelines, but entrusts to the social partners the definition of the 'public interest'.

This strengthening of collective institutions with increasing state support is a significant feature of the present phase of social policy in Italy. It represents a 'positive' term of exchange for unions in an emergency situation where all other terms are negative. Neither peak-level bilateralism, nor laissez-faire decentralized collective bargaining has been seen as a viable option in Italy. Nor are there many employers who hanker after emasculated unions and employer unilateralism, or state officials who contemplate a statutory incomes policy. Tripartism is alive, and stronger than in France or Britain. Its latest manifestation in the 1992 emergency accords had a stronger 'public interest' flavour than at any time since the emergency reconstruction period immediately after World War II.

Postscript

In an Italy still gripped by a sense of crisis, a second accord was finally reached – after 40 days of bargaining, and frequent media predictions of imminent breakdown – in June 1993. It went well beyond the emergency freeze measures of the previous year to the creation of new institutional arrangements. Wage contracts at national or regional level will be for four years and will be based on an explicit forecast of expected inflation over that period. Their wage provisions will be revised at the end of two years in the light of actual inflation experience. Where renegotiation at the end of four years has not been achieved, there will be automatic wage increases compensating for past inflation – but only to the tune of 30 per cent after three months and 50 per cent after six.

At the enterprise or establishment level: (1) unitary one-per-establishment bargaining structures were formalized; two-thirds of worker representatives were to be elected from the plant, and one-third appointed by the higher-level industry union organization which represents that plant in national bargaining; (2) wage increases bargained at this level are to be linked to productivity performance.

A number of other measures of lesser import occupied the agreement's 29 pages – a reduction in the 'temporary' lay-off subsidies (*cassa integrazione*) and a shifting of funds to other active labour market policies, the legal regulation of contract-worker agencies, etc. Immediate media comment spoke frequently of 'a new era' in Italian industrial relations. The practical effects of the new arrangements remain to be seen.

Notes

1. In general on these features, see Treu (1990); and more specifically, Treu (1987), pp. 357–63.
2. These changes have been considered by many scholars, not only in Italy, preclusive to the continuation of central concertive action or neo-corporatist practices. See in general Salvati (1992), pp. 57–64.
3. Company agreement which, in order to avoid collective dismissals or layoff because of a labour surplus, or in order to permit the hiring of new personnel, provides for a reduction in the working hours and pay of all the company's employees. The job-security agreement concluded to avoid staff cuts, known as a 'defensive' agreement, attracts assistance from the Wages Guarantee Fund equal to 50 per cent of the loss of pay, for a maximum period of 24 months. If, however, the purpose is to permit the hiring of new personnel, i.e., the 'offensive' job-creation agreement, the employer is paid a contribution for each new employee hired and is also allowed to use recruitment 'by name', rather than being required to accept employees nominated by the public employment office.

References

Salvati, M. (1989), 'A Long Cycle in Industrial Relations or: Regulatory Theory and Political Economy', *Labour*, 1, pp. 57–64.

Streeck, W. (1992), 'From National Corporatism to Transnational Pluralism: European Interest Politics and the Single Market', in T. Treu (ed.), *Participation in Public Policy-making*, de Gruyter, Berlin and New York. pp. 100–11.

Treu, T. (1987), 'Ten Years of Social Concertation in Italy', *Labour and Society*, 12, pp. 357–63.

—— (1990), 'Monograph Italy', in *International Encyclopaedia for Labour Law*, Kluwer, The Netherlands.

CHAPTER 9

INCOMES POLICIES, INSTITUTIONS AND MARKETS: AN OVERVIEW OF RECENT DEVELOPMENTS

Colin Crouch

State, Markets and Institutions

We are, it is hoped, now emerging from the lengthy period during which 'market forces' and 'state intervention' were opposed as the main alternatives in the conduct of economies, not only in relation to incomes policy, but generally. When Andrew Shonfield wrote his *Modern Capitalism* (1965), for example, he could deal conceptually with the German economy largely by describing it as 'planning by banks'. This was certainly an improvement on the conventional wisdom about West Germany at that time: no major macroeconomic state intervention, therefore it must be a free-market economy. But it still demonstrated the dearth of concepts available for describing the institutions of a complex economy. Far worse was to come – and with less excuse, since institutional economics had advanced a good deal by the 1980s – when Milton Friedman described Japan as an example of pure laissez faire. The logic was simple. In a Manichean world where there is either laissez faire or state control, the absence of the latter implies the presence of the former.

But we now have a richer conceptual apparatus at our disposal. The neo-corporatist literature was able to demonstrate the capacity of non-state, non-market institutions, provided certain environing conditions affecting the logic of action were met, to act in ways other than as mere impediments to trade. The French 'régulation' school, and also the research of the group around Maurice, Sellier and Silvestre (1982), demonstrated the variety of forms of arrangement for capitalist economies, influencing the powerful popular presentation of the theme in Michel Albert's *Capitalisme contre capitalisme* (1991). Italian writers, starting with Arnaldo Bagnasco's seminal work on *La terza Italia*

(1977), have described the local, sometimes informal, sometimes local state-sponsored, institutions of inter-firm cooperation that support competitiveness among small firms in many regions of Italy. In doing so they have ironically re-invented a concept first used to describe a phenomenon in what is usually presented as the ultimate free-market economy of late nineteenth-century Britain – Alfred Marshall's idea of industrial districts. Some authors have identified similar processes at work in the most dynamic parts of the German economy, primarily Baden–Württemberg. Wolfgang Streeck (1992) has demonstrated the role of institutions, political, social and community-based, in general in Germany, and with Egon Matzner (1991) he has shown how the absence of formal state intervention and Keynesian demand management in the postwar German economy did not mean that the state was economically passive; its connections with firms and business associations were complex and varied.

We now have therefore an array of knowledge about institutions that reinforce, change and redirect market forces, and about the circumstances in which these can improve rather than worsen economic outcomes (in terms of income/unemployment trade-offs, effects on balance of trade, effects on growth rates). Sociology has joined economics and political science in the analysis of political economy. By institutions I mean here stable networks of relations among social actors that influence their behaviour in more or less predictable ways – other than as direct responses to either state direction or pure market stimuli. (A more general concept of institution clearly includes states and markets; the point of separating them out here is in order to focus on other institutional forms, given the dominance of these two in conventional discussion of incomes policy.)

Market conformity

To be fair, debate over and practice of incomes policy usually recognized this. During the 1960s and 1970s, these policies usually comprised some tripartite arrangement rather than simple state intervention, and collective bargaining is clearly not pure market determination.

But what has been the relationship between the intended outcome of an incomes policy and market forces? Policies that have merely interfered with or tried to prevent the working out of demand and supply pressures have a poor record. An attempt to prevent firms solving problems of labour shortage by bidding up wages is unlikely to be successful in the long run (unless accompanied by labour supply measures). Often they have simply 'dammed up' pay claims until the policy is removed, creating an inflationary pressure that, some have argued, may well be more intense than the problem the policy was originally trying to resolve. (Not that increasing wages solves the original problem if there are no clear mechanisms linking wages with the provision of training for the occupations in which there are shortages – mechanisms which, given the complexity of the organization of training, are unlikely to be merely market forces.)

On the other hand, if a policy solely ensures that the outcome of collective bargaining is the same as would have occurred had the organization of labour and capital not originally interfered with market forces, we have a difficult problem of institutional inefficiency: incomes policy institutions would then be being used to cancel out the effect of bargaining institutions. Would it not be more efficient simply to abolish collective bargaining? Many trade unions of course saw incomes policy in that light and therefore refused to cooperate with it. Politicians and business people of the New Right made a similar analysis, but decided that energy which might have been devoted to developing incomes policies would be more effectively engaged in breaking trade unions and collective bargaining.

So what do unions which cooperate in neo-corporatist incomes policy arrangements achieve that is different from what would be achieved by their disappearance – since such unions seem to be primarily engaged in stopping the conflict and inflation that their members would probably cause if top-level unions did not restrain them (Crouch, 1985). When I raised this question earlier (Ibid.), Castles (1987) responded as have several others since (see Dell'Aringa and Lodovici, 1992; Crouch, 1993, ch. 1), that neo-corporatist unions seem to secure lower unemployment and higher social benefits than those which concentrate on conflictual bargaining or outright contestation.

In other words, if we may return to the metaphor about 'damming up' pay claims, we must accept that merely trying to disrupt or prevent the flow of market forces is doomed to failure: the stream will insist on flowing. On the other hand it does make sense to talk of diverting the river. Markets, like rivers, must flow; but they might be able to flow through more than one channel; and some potential channels might give outcome mixes that are preferable, both to other available 'artificial' ones and to the so-called 'natural' one that would dominate were we to do nothing at all. Incomes policy institutions thus become mechanisms for diverting the flow. They can be judged in terms of their effectiveness in improving outcomes, but in securing such outcomes they will need to correspond to, rather than simply attempt to impede, some kind of market force.

This leads us to consider the range of constraints and incentives that would lead unions and employers' groups to adopt objectives of this kind, rather than simply use the power of organization, as Adam Smith would have expected, to form conspiracies against the public. The mechanism that has been most widely discussed is that derived from Mancur Olson's idea of encompassingness (1982); where an interest organization represents more than a small proportion of the total population that will be affected by its actions, it is less likely to distinguish between the universe of its membership and that of the wider society, since it can no longer risk externalizing its 'collective bads'. We know from the evidence of the neo-corporatist literature that, from the 1970s to the end of the 1980s, systems with effectively centralized labour market organizations pursued strategies which enabled them reasonably effectively to optimize the trade-off between inflation and unemployment.

But there are other circumstances in which organized actors may be forced to come to terms with market constraints. It emerges clearly from Streeck's contribution to the present volume that the strength of the German system lies in the combination of a highly corporatized labour market and a central bank that stands entirely beyond the reach of either organized interests or the political forces within government. Far from being contradictory, corporatism and the Bundesbank play complementary roles; organizations within the former, knowing that the latter cannot be brought within their influence, accommodate to its requirements. Without the Bundesbank's guaranteed autonomy, it is likely that such a heavily organized economy as the German would slip into protectionism, as did the old Bismarckian economy.

A similar function can be performed in small open economies where, again provided that organizations capable of responding strategically are in place, labour market actors are forced by the obviousness of the need to be competitive in export markets not to try to solve their problems by protectionist behaviour. This situation has been analysed in detail by Katzenstein (1985), though he perhaps sees market-conforming behaviour as a kind of *functional* necessity, automatically achieved irrespective of the capacity and form of interest organizations. For this reason he has difficulty accounting for major parts of the income determination histories of Ireland, Finland, Belgium and, recently, most of Scandinavia.

Finally, market sensitivity may be provided at the micro-level. This requires either institutions at the level of the individual company or a complete inability of organized labour to operate within companies. In the latter case all relations between social partners are kept strictly at national and/or sectoral level. Strong, problem-internalizing organizations might look after the macro-level, while within the basic minima thereby set, firms are left free to adjust and ensure that aggregate labour costs are market-competitive. The problem with such a model is that trade unions that are very weak at the company level are rarely capable of behaving in an encompassing way. They are more likely to try to demonstrate as much strength as they can at these higher levels in order to increase their doubtful weight within the society, their small scope enabling them to ignore any wider consequences of what they are doing.

The only exceptions to this are likely to occur when government, or employer organizations, accord unions what Katzenstein (1984), thinking specifically of Switzerland, has called 'social promotion'. Faced with a weak union movement, government and/or employers grant it a level of importance and a role that it would, paradoxically, be unlikely to obtain if it had to struggle for it. The unions reciprocate by exercising a moderating influence, paralleling the similar influence being achieved at company level through organized labour's weakness. This option, which at least in theory should be associated with exceptionally stable and favourable outcomes, has the disadvantage of being 'non-obvious'. Most governments and employers, faced with a weak union movement, will merely want to make it weaker still, rather than offer a social promotion.

Incomes policies apart, can there be company-level institutions which enhance the likelihood that wage-determination will be market-compatible – more than if there were no union bargaining mechanisms at all? It is a question on which there is not much evidence, given that the whole history of trade unionism is about attempts at organizing workers above the company level so that they might limit market exposure and the instability it brings. (Intervention in product and labour markets to constrain competition, and attempts, through political pressure for Keynesian and similar policies, to affect the overall macro-economic context within which pay-determination takes place.)

Finally, there are cases where the government and certain major companies have particularly close relations, the latter becoming involved in national economic strategy and not just normal corporate behaviour. These firms may then play a role within, or even outside, employers' associations to impose some kind of conformity with defined national economic policy goals on the labour market.

Institutions and market conformity: a model

We thus have two variables for the analysis of incomes policy: the strength and character of the institutional structure of the policy, and the extent to which a particular form of policy works with, rather than against, some forms of market force (*marktkonform*, as Germans would put it) or tries to impede them. Figure 9.1 presents these two dimensions, locating various alternative policy forms in relation to them.

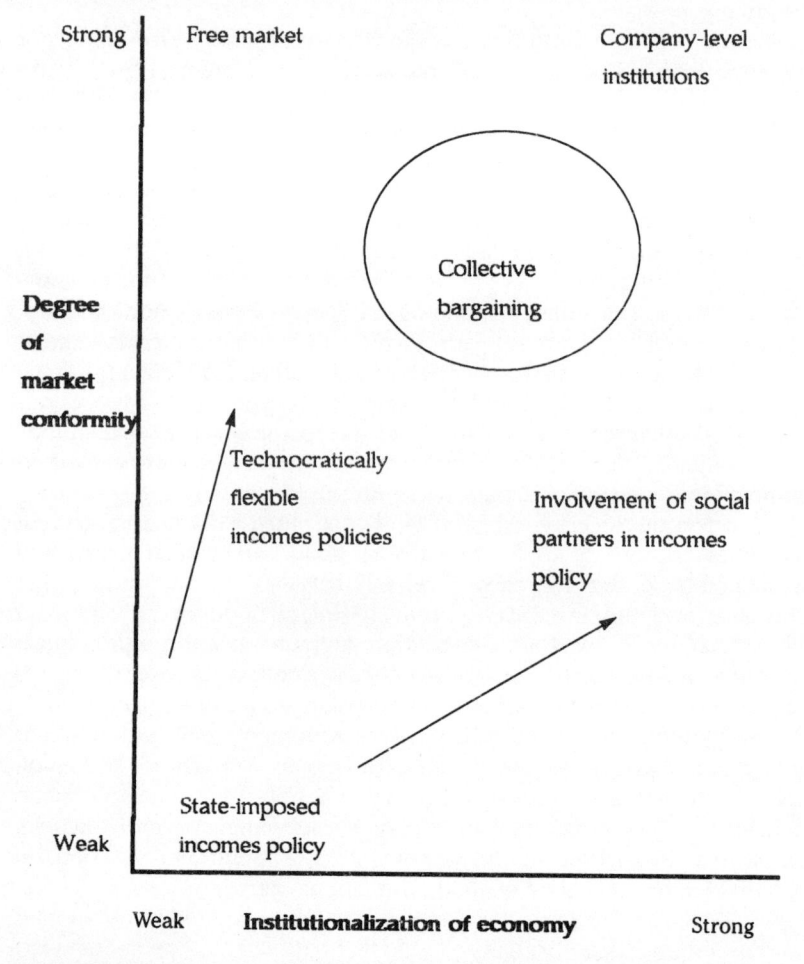

Figure 9.1 Markets and institutions in different systems of income determination

A simple market force model is included as a limiting case, representing the high extreme of closeness to market in its outcomes, and the low extreme of institutional development. The simplest form of incomes policy, unilateral state intervention to impose a pay freeze or pay norm, is at the other extreme on the dimension of proximity to market, as these emergency, sometimes panic, measures, are designed to impede, to dam up, the operations of the market. They are however not much further away from an extreme lack of institutions than the free-market model: simple state intervention implies a relative absence of institutional mediation between government and market, which is why straightforward state intervention is the form of incomes policy most readily understood, if not particularly favoured, by market economics.

It has long been part of the conventional wisdom of state incomes interventions that, like military interventions abroad, they are easier to start than to stop. This is because of the damming-up effect. Pent-up claims are waiting to be resolved once the strong state action is withdrawn. Governments therefore usually try to replace their unilateral interventions with more durable mechanisms that permit market forces to operate in a restrained way, often calling on tripartite institutions to try to achieve this. Moves of this kind clearly represent diagonal moves across Figure 9.1 from the state intervention position, the slope of the line depending on whether the moves towards market proximity or institutional involvement predominate. It is of course possible for the government to retain control, not sharing it with social partners, but to seek, through technical devices, to bring policy into closer conformity with a market solution. On the other hand, it may bring in the social partners in order to solve the political problems of running a policy alone, but find that they take it no closer to, and perhaps further from, a market-compatible solution.

Devices for the involvement of social partners in incomes policy will follow the various outlines discussed above. Institutionalization will mark a diagonal rather than a merely horizontal (left to right) movement across Figure 9.1 only where it combines a growing strength of institutions (necessary to give discipline and achieve Olsonian encompassingness) with mechanisms for requiring organizations to come to terms with market forces (independent central bank; export competitiveness for small, open economies; company-level institutions; state-company relations, etc.).

To speak of a growing importance of institutions at the level of the firm therefore requires an examination of what happens to the various extra-firm mechanisms. Do skilful company-level strategies by management destroy extra-firm autonomous non-employee labour representation? On balance, probably, most commonly among non-manual workers, whose numbers are increasing; and the decline of trade unionism in the giant US economy has led to the growth of purely intra-firm mechanisms among manual workers too.

Such managerial strategies raise, though at the other end of the scale, the same problems as a political social promotion: if certain forms of labour are so weak that they cannot organize nationally, why should employers bother to build company-level institutions to deal with them, rather than simply use managerial authority and market mechanisms? That is often exactly the conclusion that employers reach, which is why it has been much easier to find examples of 'macho-management' than of clever human resource management in these recent years following the decline of trade unionism. But, as with social promotion, sometimes employers do build company institutions for a form of workforce representation, and these examples make an interesting study.

For complex institutions binding the company level to higher levels of worker organization to survive or strengthen, highly articulated bargaining and union organization structures are needed. The German and Austrian dual systems of worker representation, linking extra-firm unions with works councils, are examples of just such a rare phenomenon. Particularly in Germany, this structure is very important in the explanation of wage stability in a context of relatively strong unionism and no obvious incomes policy as conventionally understood. Does it simply force workers to face the market? Rather, it allows a rechannelling of market forces. Workers' representatives, both in the works councils and in the linked union and collective bargaining system, are able to influence in various ways precisely how market forces will affect jobs, working hours and working conditions.

Different again is the pattern of company unions within large Japanese firms. There is considerable debate in the literature as to whether these more closely resemble employer-created bodies subservient to management or a genuinely autonomous representation linked to a wider union structure of the German kind. It is clear that they are somewhere along this continuum, and also clear that they operate in the manner predicted here to contain wage inflation.

Finally, we need to locate straightforward collective bargaining within this theoretical framework. It occupies a large potential space at the centre of the diagram. Large because it can take such varied forms; and at the centre because it is a half-way house on both our dimensions. There cannot be collective bargaining of any stability without recognized institutions; but the institutions do not have to develop very far if their main role is just to cope with conflict. Bargaining clearly marks a move away from market determination, because one of the unions' main aims in pursuing it is to try to secure better outcomes for their members than the market would be likely to give them individually. But it is still a form of market contract.

Overall this model gives us a picture compatible with the thesis and evidence of Calmfors and Driffill (1988), that the relationship between the organization of the labour market and a favourable combined inflation and unemployment performance is a U-shaped curve. Optimal outcomes take place at (a) where there is virtually no organization, or free-market conditions; and (b) where there is a very high level of encompassing organization. Soskice (1990) has challenged this argument by claiming that the two main examples of good performances without strong encompassing unions (France and Japan) are not in fact cases of free-market wage determination. There is, rather, in the former state coordination; and in the latter coordination by government departments and extensive corporate groups. He therefore proposes *coordination* in various forms as the variable in what becomes a unilinear rather than a curvilinear relationship.

Some recent examples

We can now put flesh on this abstract model by looking at how actual cases of incomes institutions fit into the space of Figure 9.1.

There are of course very many instances of the limiting case, of pure market determination. It is most often found at both extremes of the labour market: among employees so skilled or so highly placed in the company hierarchy that they do not need any non-market assistance in advancing and stabilizing their pay and conditions; and among those so marginal and low-paid that they have no ability to secure it.

Emergency repairs to once-stable systems

State-imposed incomes policies continued to make their appearance as short-run emergency packages during the 1980s, at various times in Belgium, the Netherlands and throughout the Nordic countries. In each case government has been rather anxious to hand over to tripartite institutions as soon as it can. In all these instances this action represented something of a crisis for the system, as they had been accustomed to working through sophisticated institutions that produced market compatible outcomes with very little state intervention, if any. Belgium was always an exception to this; the regional–cultural tensions required more state involvement. In the Netherlands, the collapse of union membership and of the *verzuiling* structure which held Dutch society together could well have provided a lurch toward free-market solutions, but, after emergency state intervention, attempts to rebuild bi- or tripartite models (with a strong element of social promotion) have appeared.

The Scandinavian countries have had a less happy experience. Their institutional legacy has been a primarily macro-level tripartite (more usually bipartite) cooperation model. A rich institutional network led workers and firms to cooperate in a whole set of articulated relationships, the economic outcomes of which were for a long period competitively successful. The policy mix was both heavily institutional and market-compatible. Particularly important have been active labour market policies that have tried to raise the level of employment capable of being achieved in a context of highly organized labour markets (see the papers by Åberg and by Boje and Madsen in this volume). But in recent years there have been two major problems with this well-known model. First, changes in occupational structure made it increasingly difficult for manual workers in the export industries to continue bearing the institutional brunt of the pressures to internalize the system's costs (Lash, 1985; Crouch, 1990). They were becoming a smaller minority of the labour force, while the growing ranks of white-collar workers and public-service employees were never quite part of the social partner (or labour market partner, as it is more often called in the Nordic countries) system.

Second, although these industrial relations patterns were highly institutionalized, with strong regional and local components, the level of the company as such was never truly built into the calculations of the union side. This became highly problematic as the demands of both industrial structuring and employers' attempts to build 'whole company strategies' demanded a more important autonomous role for the firm. The industrial relations systems came less and less to suit the needs of the changing economies; in particular their outcomes were decreasingly market-compatible; inflation rates became higher and economic growth lower.

The initial responses to these problems – which in Denmark date back to the 1960s, in Norway and Sweden to the mid-1970s – were for emergency direct state intervention and attempts at incomes policy of the most obvious kind. According to my hypothesis these interventions are a sign of institutional weakness, and this is how they have been interpreted in Scandinavia. The labour-market parties see it is a form of defeat when their bipartism becomes tripartite.

The present situation in the other Nordic countries is also difficult to summarize with confidence. In the early 1980s Denmark was faced with the familiar difficulty of moving out successfully from a state intervention mode. Government and employers seemed to favour the straightforward free-market route of achieving market compatibility through thoroughgoing deinstitutionalization. That is a long route in a country where not only are institutions thoroughly entrenched, but have considerable achievements to their credit. However, the decentralization was always 'managed' by Danske Arbejdsgiverforeningen (DA), the central employers' federation (Due *et al.*, 1994). The federation indicated to firms when it considered that there should be a move to wage formation at company level, and when it wanted to reassert some central control. The DA in no way collapsed, though its membership, concentrated in the industrial sector, was accounting for a declining proportion of the Danish workforce. More recently, but before the change of government in early 1993, there have been clear signs of a new involvement of the social partners in the context of restructured organizations on both sides of the labour market.

Swedish employers and government seem however only now to be embarking, and with less apparent hesitation, on the thoroughgoing deinstitutionalization path. Svenska Arbetsgivarföreningen (SAF), the central employers' organization, in particular wants to demolish virtually all cooperative institutions in the labour market (Pestoff, 1991). Employers and the new non-social-democratic governing forces seem impressed with the economic success of the United Kingdom and wish to imitate its recent policies. One wonders whether this attempt at a 'vertical strategy' will not, as in its southern neighbour, revert before long to the 'diagonal', though an important difference has to be noted between the two countries. Danish firms are mainly small, and need the services of an association to help with much of their labour management and other issues. The Swedish economy is dominated by large companies which, although they find it easy to combine when they want to do so, have less need of associational support services.

Norwegian developments have been less dramatic, but have shown similar patterns of movement: that the former institutional structure is no longer working effectively has become clear; there have been instances of a reversion to state policy to cope with the emergency; and both vertical and diagonal moves away from that position, with the latter currently dominating (Foss, 1992).

Social pacts and social promotion

Different from all these cases, though perhaps similar to Finland in the late 1960s, have been the attempted 'social pacts' seen mainly in Spain, but also though often less explicitly in Italy, Greece and Portugal. Here governments are trying both: (i) to get a grip on a labour market that is either inflationary or (more recently) too costly given the situation in competitor countries in the Far East where trade unions, welfare states and democracy are not much of a problem; and (ii) to reinforce a more general social order that is felt to be fragile. Problem (i) might indicate a simple move to pure markets, but the consciousness of problem (ii) leads both to fears of the consequences of widespread opposition to such a strategy and to a desire to build up institutions as a protection of civil society. In Spain, Portugal and Greece this need results from the recency of democracy; in Italy from the recurrent instability of the country's geographical divisions, sporadic violent social movements, and entrenched criminality within some regions. The economic ends of incomes policy become mixed, and interact, with much wider goals.

For example, it may seem that governments in countries with weak unions (which is the case in all except Italy) have little incentive to keep experimenting with tripartite forums in order to involve unions that do not have much control over their members, and when in fact the main effective policy towards the labour market is 'Thatcherite'. But whereas Conservative governments in the country where Thatcherism originated believe they can take a number of risks given the deep and rich stability of British social institutions, that is a very questionable proposition in southern Europe. There is therefore a continuing social promotion of unions. At the very least this is in order to prevent them from allying with threatening sources of regional or political instability; at best they might help build a settled fabric of civil society at the national level. Similar strategies can be seen at work, even more desperately, in the former Czechoslovakia, Hungary and Poland, and perhaps elsewhere in Eastern Europe. What one observes are weak and ineffective tripartite devices. They are not irrelevant to incomes policy; but that is not all that they are about.

Italy is really a case apart from the other southern and eastern European ones (see Treu, chapter 8 in this volume). In all these latter government is engaged in the ostensibly puzzling task of building up the unions' national position in order to make them behave themselves, while in other respects pursuing demand-management and labour-market strategies that would be easier were unions not to exist at all. In Italy in contrast there is no doubt about the importance and strength of organized labour; nor indeed of the willingness of much of its leadership to participate in social pacts. They are prevented from moving along the diagonal from pacts to richer institutions and/or greater market conformity by the inability of the official union level to coordinate lower, and in particular company, levels. This is of course the same 'defect' in managing the awkward transition between institutions and companies that has recently caused such trouble in Scandinavia, though without the historical background of long years of successful cooperation in the northern countries. If solutions to this problem are found in Italy they are likely to be – as with so much in Italian public life – when the 'centre' is located below the level of the Rome-based state. Part of the story of the Third Italy in the 1980s concerned the considerable capacity for tripartite cooperation at city or provincial levels.

The situation in France is different again; but like the foregoing, concepts of weak social partnership and of social promotion assist the analysis (see Boyer, chapter 3 in this volume). In retrospect I think we can now see a distinct shift in state policy in France away from a Jacobin remoteness from organized social interests to one of trying to integrate them in various ways, dating back to 1968 (possibly even earlier if one considers attempts at incomes policy in the public sector in the early 1960s). The legislation of the first years of the Mitterrand governments here only accelerated a pattern begun some years earlier (in which Jacques Delors, it is relevant to mention, played an important part as a civil servant). In motive the strategy has not been so different from that in southern Europe: a mixture of social promotion and weak social partnership to incorporate a labour movement that, though weak, can be troublesome.

More recently initiatives in accordance with this model have been increasingly taken up autonomously by French employers' organizations – which is itself an indication of the success of the initiative. Both the Patronat at the national cross-sectoral level and individual branch associations of employers have been reaching agreements with unions on a wide range of issues, usually framework agreements of some kind. This has been taking place at a time of great weakness for French unions, whose numerical strength has declined while the established confederations have been undermined by the rise of small autonomous unions. Further, the CGT has refused to sign most of the agreements.

Views of the significance of these arrangements vary. Some regard them as skilful attempts by the employers to both divide the union movement (given the CGT's reluctance to sign agreements) and force it into unfavourable deals at a time of weakness. These observers also see little evidence in practice of the new 'enlightened' personnel policies that French employers claim now to be pursuing. Others say the changes do mark important if much delayed progress towards an institutionalization of French industrial relations. They are of little immediate significance to incomes policy, disturbance and conflict in French labour markets being held down and kept remarkably moderate primarily by organized labour's weakness and the high level of unemployment. Meanwhile, the tranquillity of labour markets and of French society in general are being shaken by new social movements and semi-violent protests of various kinds. While these might seem to make the formal actions of employers' associations and unions less relevant, they at the same time (as in Italy) raise their importance as institutions helping to impart a general social stability.

Institutional strength extending to company level

All the cases considered so far give us examples of rather centralized interventions designed to patch up difficult situations. There are also, however, examples of systems still operating considerably further along the diagonal implying both heavily institutionalized yet market-sensitive solutions. These imply a non-central, company-level component in the institutional mix. A transitional case in terms of the central/local dimension, though one of exceptional stability overall, is Austria (Guger and Polt, chapter 7 in this volume). Looking over a longer historical perspective, it is interesting to see how the government's participation in the central incomes policy institution, the Paritätische Kommission, has declined as the system has stabilized and the social partners have won both each other's and the government's trust (Marin, 1982). In the 1950s, when the mechanism started, government initiatives were central to it. It is now bipartite, with the government retaining the obvious capacity to intervene informally if it is not content with likely outcomes.

Despite the economic problems of recent years, especially in Austria's state industries and difficulties disrupting the country's important trading partners in Eastern Europe, the system remains stable. The schilling's link to the German mark has imposed a tough discipline guaranteeing market conformity, and the economy has maintained its strength as well as relatively low unemployment despite this constraint. At company level market sensitivity is reinforced by works councils which, while closely related to trade unions, are formally independent of them and have a responsibility to work for the good of the employing company.

Although the works councils are an important institution, the centre of gravity of the Austrian system remains rather centralized. The role of works councils in binding together the system-consciousness (or awareness of macro-level externalities) of national and branch-level actors with the day-to-day reality of companies' product markets is, as was noted above, seen at its most complex in the German (formerly West German) dual system, especially in the metal and chemical industries. Observers of incomes policy considering Germany usually look at the role of the multipartite Concerted Action programme; conclude rightly that its very first years in the late 1960s were its heyday, and that it has subsequently been in long-term decline; they therefore rank Germany among the countries without an incomes policy.

It is, however, hardly a country without economic institutions in the sense that term is being used here, as Streeck's contribution to this volume makes clear. From the role of the Bundesbank, through the activities of chambers of trade and industry and of employers' associations in binding together concerted action among employers, to the relations between these bodies and trade unions, and finally on to the role of works councils both in bargaining with regard to company interests and in engaging in mutual interaction and influence with trade unions, the whole system binds together organizational capacity with market sensitivity in a way that usually obviates any need for incomes policy as such. The system does not work 'perfectly'. There has occasionally been a tendency for the Bundesbank to *under*-estimate unions' capacity to cooperate, leading to excessive recessionary shocks (Scharpf, 1991). And the labour market is by no means free of conflict. But its adaptive capacity has been remarkably good.

Moving still further towards decentralization, the most stable economy in Europe has long been Switzerland. Here we see a combination of a voluntaristic works council structure with rather weak unions that have nevertheless long benefited from a social promotion that both locks them into a cooperative system and involves them in extensive participation in the administration of the complex *Selbstverwaltung* that constitutes Switzerland's alternative to an elaborated state structure. Here too one is highly unlikely to encounter anything resembling incomes policy; but one does encounter considerable market-compatible, richly institutionalized action.

All these European cases, even the Swiss, achieve company-level action through unions and through works councils having some relationship to unions. Employers too are likely to be organized. Perhaps the most important instance of company-level institutions is however Japan, where semi-autonomous company unions play their important part – alongside the giant companies, the powerful industry associations and the lifetime employment system – in maintaining an economy that is exceptionally rich in institutions and also highly competitive in market terms. Even then, the system guarantees its behaviour by such institutions as concentrated bargaining dates. It would stand top right in our diagram as a market-sensitive, institutionalized economy. It therefore stands at the furthest extreme from state incomes policy; but to exclude it therefore from discussions of such policy would be entirely to mistake the point.

The vertical route to market

Although elements of what have become known since the 1980s as a 'British' approach to the labour market have been widely imitated, the United Kingdom itself is the only instance, at least within Western Europe, where the move towards market forces has been entirely unaccompanied by any offsetting development of institutions. Instead, institutions, such as branch-level collective bargaining or tripartite consultative mechanisms, have been stripped down and abolished (Brown, this volume; see also Millward *et al.*, 1992; Purcell, 1993). The aim has been to drive straight to market, with intermediary institutions treated solely as impediments to market forces. The price of this has been:

1. Excessive reliance on holding down pay (perhaps by reducing numbers of employees) in the public sector. Not only does this weaken morale among public employees, but as more and more of the public sector is privatized it leaves a rather small tail trying to wag the dog, especially as most privatized corporations remain monopolies or oligopolies.
2. Heavy dependence on 'pure labour market' (that is level of employment) means for containing inflation, which may, following Castles' and others' evidence cited earlier, imply continuing sub-optimal employment levels. It is interesting that, so strong is the hostility in government and some employer circles to institutional as opposed to market communication, there is little concern in Britain to encourage institutions at national level that play a role similar to that of the Bundesbank. Indeed, the British government is strongly opposed to the idea of a central bank autonomous from political control. There is however far more interest in company-level mechanisms that will provide similar incentives to workers and their representatives.

3. Erosion of the institutional base of the economy, which diminishes its capacity to make more general use of institutions in the way described for several countries at the outset of this paper. This occurs, for example, because, as supra-company bargaining declines, so employers' associations decline, and so (in the absence of any significant *Kammer* institutions) does the capacity of business interests to engage in any collective-goods provision, apart from lobbying for their own interests. This diminishes performance in occupational training, research and development, joint export promotion, and other 'industrial district' behaviour.

Future prospects

The spread of the British model?

But one cannot entirely set the British case aside as eccentric. Many elements of the British model are to be found in *nearly all* other countries, even if it never appears in such extreme form elsewhere. The political right and many employers in Scandinavia from time to time want very much to move in the same direction. Behind the apparatus of social pacts several governments in southern and Eastern Europe are seeking flexible, deinstitutionalized labour markets *alla inglese*. Small and medium-sized firms in Germany complain of the constraints on flexibility imposed by the legal and institutional base of the collective bargaining system.

Of course, it is possible that in many of these cases employers and others would like to see a little loosening of institutional rigidities rather than a full-scale imitation of British thoroughgoing deinstitutionalization. It remains to be seen whether that option is always available; the process of deinstitutionalization is something of a 'slippery slope' case. If the scope of institutions is weakened, they in turn become less capable of doing their remaining work. This can lead to further movements away from institutions in order to substitute them with pure market solutions (diagonal or horizontal movement towards the top left in terms of Figure 9.1), which in turn further weaken the capacity of institutions, and so on.

Something of this kind seems to have happened in Britain itself. In the early 1980s the Confederation of British Industry wanted to see a shift of power towards employers in industrial relations, but basically envisaged a continuing model of employers' associations bargaining with trade unions. However, the shift to company-level bargaining that then took place weakened several associations to the point where they either collapsed or lost large numbers of member firms. This in turn produced a further shift to the company level. Not only would any future attempt to generate coordinated bargaining in Britain now be impossible, but organized employers have become incapable of contributing to such institutions as vocational training schemes, which therefore have to be managed on a deinstitutionalized basis. Against this the Danish evidence suggests that where tightly organized employer confederations 'permit' decentralization to branch or company level as a temporary bargaining tactic, they can reclaim the territory if they want to in a subsequent year.

The strength of the appeal of the British model is that, for all its risks, it permits employers to respond to many of the major changes in the labour market that have occurred since the 1970s. First, as already noted in discussion of Scandinavia, modern workforces are very heterogeneous. Widespread solidarity across a broad front is difficult for unions to achieve, irrespective of whether they want to use that solidarity for cooperation in incomes restraint or for militancy.

Second, competition from low-wage producers in the Far East is causing problems for many firms in the advanced industrial economies. Although many have taken the route of moving up-market to higher value-added products, there are still many others who feel they have little option but to seek lower unit wage costs and greater numerical flexibility as part of their response. While such an approach might be negotiated as part of a restraint package, it will often seem easier, and indeed more logical, to achieve this goal by breaking down institutional impediments.

Finally, the recent and current stress on 'whole-company' managerial strategies, while, as the German case shows, not necessarily requiring deinstitutionalization, may in many situations seem to be most easily achieved by doing so.

Whether or not there are conscious 'British' imitations, there are several strong pressures towards a loosening of institutional structures. It is therefore likely that attempts to sustain various forms of coordinated bargaining will in future need more or less 'artificial', that is state-generated rather than institutional, support. One example are the attempts seen from time to time in the Nordic countries of requiring the major groups who otherwise prefer to negotiate separately (manual employees, non-manual employees, public services, private services) to bargain at the same table. This necessitates, at least in early stages, government intervention; though as the Austrian case shows, it might then become institutionalized with a diminishing state role.

New institutional devices

The concentration of bargaining at certain times of the year, as often noted in Japan, serves a similar function (Dore *et al.*, 1991). It forces groups to be aware of what others are doing. It improves the chances that actors will be able to overcome the collective action problem, because the bargaining about individuals' or individual firms' pay rises takes place in the context of a national debate about the collective outcomes of average pay rises.

Where institutional capacity across a broad range has thoroughly failed, attempts at securing cooperative behaviour may require artificial substitutes for, rather than artificial inducements to, institutions. Most important among these in recent discussions have been tax-based incomes policies (Colander, 1986; Layard and Nickell, 1990; Hirst and Zeitlin, 1993). Under these schemes income increases above an agreed incomes policy ceiling would be subject to very high rates of income taxation, perhaps extending to 100 per cent.

Clearly such policies would be highly unpopular and very complex and difficult to implement, though much work has been done on making them practicable. As a long-term solution they would probably become so unpopular and riddled with anomalies that they would break down; and they are unlikely to be flexible enough to be market-sensitive. They might however be used as temporary devices to stimulate cooperative institution-building among social partners. The permanent threat of introduction or continuation of a tax-based incomes policy could become an important catalyst in persuading employers' associations and trade unions to improve their organizational capacity.

While temporal bargaining concentration is explicitly designed to reinforce institutions' existing tendencies to encourage cooperative action, tax-based policies can in theory operate in an institutional vacuum. They might however work best where they encourage institutional coordination. The central point is that technical devices of various kinds are likely to be required to stimulate such coordination in future. The successful achievement of coordination and solidarity in several economies in the past was largely the accidental by-product of the structure of 'Fordist' industry: large-scale manufacturing firms in private industry employing mass manual work forces. The late twentieth-century structures that are rapidly replacing these are far more fragmented, while the gains that might be achieved from coordinated behaviour have not diminished in any way. Unless governments and employers wish to resolve incomes problems solely through free-market means, we are likely to see considerable intervention by governments to try to stimulate coordination – not by long-term direct government measures as such, but by mechanisms to induce co-operative, close-to-firm, close-to-market behaviour by reluctant, fragmenting social partners themselves.

Internationalization

Against this, the new openness of economies provides an incentive to governments of most colours and to unions, though less so to employers, to develop national restraint packages. We noted vulnerability to external markets as an important factor inducing coordinated approaches to incomes in small open economies, provided the organizational structure was appropriate. The rise of the new industrialized countries in the Far East, the growth of 'footloose' multinationals belonging to no one economy in particular and making strategic alliances with other multinationals from various national bases, and the elaboration of the European Single Market, all increase exposure to international competition and inhibit recourse to protective cartels. All European economies are now subordinate to international markets in a way that has long been the case for the Belgians and Danes.

This has paradoxical consequences. On the one hand it makes national coordination, especially that involving an employer side, increasingly dominated by multinationals. On the other however it reinforces the need to coordinate and the rewards to be gained from coordination. However international markets become, electorates and union memberships remain almost entirely indigenous. Governments and unions still depend on satisfying the economic aspirations of populations whose lives are more or less bounded by national economies. If tariffs and non-tariff barriers to trade are no longer available to protect these economies, organizational resources can still be sources of national competitive advantage, while the growing openness of economies provides growing sources of discipline.

It may well be, therefore, that economic openness and global competition will have these consequences: those economies that already have encompassing interest organizations will be able to learn anticipatorily and effectively from competition, and will then be able to turn their organizational specificity into a source of comparative advantage; while those that lack such devices will be forced down the Calmfors–Driffill U-curve into sub-optimal performance unless and until they achieve 'pure' labour markets, should such be available.

References

Albert, M. (1991), *Capitalisme contre capitalisme*, Seuil, Paris.
Bagnasco, A. (1977), *Tre Italie*, Il Mulino, Bologna.
Calmfors, L. and Driffill, D. J. (1988), 'Bargaining Structure, Corporatism and Macro-Economic Performance', *Economic Policy*, 6.
Castles, F. G. (1987), 'Neo-corporatism and the Happiness Index', *European Journal of Political Research*, 15, pp. 381–93.
Colander, D. (ed.) (1986), *Incentive-Based Incomes Policies*, Ballinger, Cambridge, MA.
Crouch, C. (1985), 'Conditions for Trade Union Wage Restraint', in L. N. Lindberg and C. S. Maier (eds.), *The Politics of Inflation and Economic Stagnation*, Brookings Institution, Washington, DC.
—— (1990), 'Trade Unions in the Exposed Sector: Their Influence on Neo-corporatist Behaviour', in R. Brunetta and C. Dell'Aringa (eds.) *Labour Relations and Economic Performance*, Macmillan and International Economics Association, London.
—— (1993), *Industrial Relations and European State Traditions*, Clarendon Press, Oxford.
Dell'Aringa, C. and Lodovici, M. S. (1992), 'Industrial Relations and Economic Performance', in T. Treu (ed.) *Participation in Public Policy-Making: The Role of Trade Unions and Employers' Associations*, de Gruyter, Berlin.
Dore, R, Inagami, T. and Sako, M. (1991), *Japan's Annual Economic Assessment*, Campaign for Work, London.
Due, J., Madsen, J. S., Jensen, C. S. and Petersen, L. K. (1994), *The Survival of the Danish model: A Historical Sociological Analysis of the Danish System of Collective Bargaining*, Jurist-og Økonomforbundets Forlag, Copenhagen.
Foss, P. (1992), 'Problems of Centralized Collective Wage Bargaining and Incomes Policy in Norway', University of Oxford: doctoral thesis.
Hemerijck, A. (1993), 'Origins, Establishment and Fragmentation of Dutch Corporatism', University of Oxford: doctoral thesis.
Hirst, P. and Zeitlin, J. (1993), 'An Incomes Policy For Sustained Recovery', *Political Quarterly*, 64(1), pp. 60–83.
Katzenstein, P. (1984), *Corporatism and Change: Austria, Switzerland and the Politics of Industry*, Cornell University Press, Ithaca, NY.
—— (1985), *Small States and World Markets*, Cornell University Press, Ithaca, NY.
Lash, S. (1985), 'The End of Neo-corporatism? – The Breakdown of Centralized Bargaining in Sweden', *British Journal of Industrial Relations*, 23(3), pp. 215–39.
Layard, R. and Nickell, S. (1990), 'An Incomes Policy to Help the Unemployed', in J. Shields (ed.), *Making the Economy Work*, Macmillan, London.
Marin, B. (1982), *Die paritätische Kommission: Aufgeklärter Technocorporatismus in Österreich*, Internationale Publikationen, Vienna.
Matzner, E. and Streeck, W. (1991), *Beyond Keynesianism: The Socio-Economics of Production and Full Employment*, Edward Elgar, Aldershot.
Maurice, M., Sellier, F. and Silvestre, J.-J. (1982), *Politique d'Éducation et organisation industrielle en France et en Allemande*, Presses Universitaires de France, Paris.

Millward, N., Stevens, M., Smart, D. and Haweds, W. R. (1992), *Workplace Industrial Relations in Transition*, Dartmouth, Aldershot.

Olson, M. (1982), *The Rise and Decline of Nations: Economic Growth, Stagflation and Social Rigidities*, Yale University Press, New Haven, CT.

Pestoff, V. (1991), 'The Demise of the Swedish Model and the Resurgence of Organised Business as a Major Political Actor', University of Stockholm, Department of Business Administration, PP1991:2.

Purcell, J. (1993), 'The End of Institutional Industrial Relations', *Political Quarterly*, 64(1), pp. 6–23.

Scharpf, F. (1991), *Crisis and Choice in European Social Democracy*, Cornell University Press, Ithaca, NY.

Shonfield, A. (1965), *Modern Capitalism*, Oxford University Press, Oxford.

Soskice, D. (1990), 'Wage Determination: The Changing Role of Institutions in Advanced Industrialized Countries', *Oxford Review of Economic Policy*, 6(4), pp. 1–23.

Streeck, W. (1992), *Social Institutions and Economic Performance: Studies of Industrial Relations in Advanced Capitalist Economies*, Sage, London.

APPENDIX:

SOURCES AND METHODS FOR COUNTRY STATISTICS

Union membership

Calculated as the total number of unions' members minus (where possible) those retired members as a percentage of total dependent employment, e.g., excluding the self-employed. The inclusion of retired members in union membership statistics leads density figures to be overstated; thus for 1980 figures are given with and without retired members based on Visser (1989). More recent figures do not exclude retired members. Where new calculations were made, the number of dependent employees was taken from either OECD *Labour Force Statistics 1970–1990* or OECD *Quarterly Labour Force Statistics* No. 1.

Austria: Visser (1989), Blanchflower and Freeman (1992), and Mitgliederstatistik der Österreichischen Gewerkschaftsbundes (Membership Statistics of the Austrian Trade Union Federation), Vienna, relevant years.
Denmark: Visser (1989) and calculated from Denmark: *Statistik Arbos*, 1991.
France: Visser (1989).
Germany: Visser (1989) and calculations from *Statistisches Bundesamt, Statistisches Jahrbuch der Bundesrepublik Deutschland*, SB, Wiesbaden, 1992.
Italy: Visser (1989) and Blanchflower and Freeman (1992).
Sweden: Visser (1989) and *Statistik Arsbok för Sverige*, 1992.
UK: Visser (1989) and Employment Department, *Employment Gazette*, 101, 5 (May 1993).

References:

Blanchflower, David G. and Freeman, Richard (1992), 'Unionism in the United States and Other Advanced OECD Countries', *Industrial Relations*, 31(1).

Visser, Jelle (1989), *European Trade Unions in Figures*, Kluwer Law and Taxation Publishers, Deventer.

Public sector employment

OECD (1992), *Historical Statistics 1960–1990*, OECD, Paris.

Labour force participation rates

OECD (1992), *Labour Force Statistics 1970–1990*, OECD, Paris.
OECD (1993), *Quarterly Labour Force Statistics*, 1, OECD, Paris.

AUSTRIA AND GERMANY (1990 AND 1991)
OECD (1992), *Employment Outlook* (July), OECD, Paris.

DENMARK (1980 AND 1990)
OECD (1992), *Historical Statistics 1960–1990*, OECD, Paris.
OECD (1992), *Employment Outlook* (July), OECD, Paris.

GDP per capita

OECD (1982), *Economic Surveys: Sweden*, OECD, Paris.

1991 data is calculated from:
IMF (1992), *International Financial Statistics Yearbook*, IMF, Washington, DC.

Italy and the UK: Population references statistics are from:
United Nations (1992), *Population and Vital Statistics Report*, New York, Series A, Vol. XLIV, No. 4.

GDP per capita (PPP)

Ward, Michael (1985), *Purchasing Power Parities and Real Expenditures in the OECD*, OECD, Paris.
OECD (1992), *Economic Surveys: Japan*, OECD, Paris.
OECD (1993), *National Accounts, 1960–1991*, OECD, Paris.